Immigrants
in Courts

Immigrants in Courts

Joanne I. Moore, Editor

Margaret E. Fisher, Associate Editor

University of Washington Press

Seattle and London

This book was developed by the Washington State Office of the Administrator for the Courts. The viewpoints expressed by the authors do not necessarily represent the official position or policies of the Washington State Office of the Administrator for the Courts.

This book was developed under grant number SJI-93-268 from the State Justice Institute. The points of view expressed are those of the authors and do not necessarily represent the official position or policies of the State Justice Institute.

SJI

Library of Congress Cataloging-in-Publication Data

Immigrants in Courts / Joanne I. Moore, editor; Margaret E. Fisher, associate editor.
    p. cm.
    Includes bibliographical references and index.
    ISBN 0-295-97780-9 (alk. paper)
    1. Conduct of court proceedings—United States. 2. Immigrants —United States.
3. Criminal justice, Administration of—Cross-cultural studies. 4. Court interpreting and translating—United States. I. Moore, Joanne I., 1951– . II. Fisher, Margaret E.
    KF8725.I47 1999
    345.73'05—dc21   98-45387

The paper used in this publication is acid-free and recycled from 10 percent post-consumer and at least 50 percent pre-consumer waste. It meets the minimum requirements of American National Standard for Information Sciences— Permanence of Paper for Printed Library Materials, ANSI Z39.48-1984. ♲ ∞

Contents

Foreword

Proceedings in American courts are anything but simple. Coming from countries in which the legal systems are completely different, and cultures where peoples' attitudes toward the law and authorities may be the opposite of here, immigrants have almost no comprehension of the proceedings.
—Vietnamese court interpreter

This book was inspired by the observations of court interpreters who brought their concerns about non-English-speaking parties to the Washington State Court Interpreter Administrative Committee, which I chair. Many interpreters recognize that in court proceedings, non-English-speaking parties' comprehension problems can go far deeper than language difficulty alone. *Immigrants in Courts* was designed to discover primary impediments experienced by immigrants involved in court proceedings, examine the native legal systems of many immigrants, and put forth both proven and new suggestions for remedying problems they encounter in courts.

The initial step in developing this book was an examination of the types of cases involving immigrants that are filed in state courts. Because recent immigrants often do not speak English well and usually require court interpreters, state interpreter programs and laws were consulted regarding the use of language interpreters in courts. National court interpreter patterns establish that a substantial majority of immigrant parties appear in court cases initiated by the government, such as criminal cases, juvenile court cases, domestic violence proceedings (which may also be initiated by victims), child support enforcement hearings, and so forth. Language interpreters are appointed for standard civil cases much less frequently. In consequence, while problems common to all types of legal proceedings are examined in this book, the dilemmas arising in criminal cases are particularly emphasized. This emphasis is in response to today's reality in our courts and the emergent situation of many immigrant defendants who are criminally charged.

Five legal systems are explored, representing countries from which many people immigrate to the United States: China, Mexico, Russia, Vietnam, and the Muslim world. These were selected based on census reports on recent immigration patterns and reports from state interpreter programs about the volume of assorted languages required by courts. Though each country's legal system is unique, the legal systems profiled here show some common characteristics, including their sharp contrast to the U.S. legal system in the area of court procedure. The problem areas discussed in the other general chapters apply to the cases of a large number of immigrant parties, including parties from many other countries in addition to the five discussed here.

The book's advisory review committee, which I was also chair, was made up of outstanding legal professionals who have worked in the legal systems of both the examined countries and the United States, generously contributed detailed feedback about the project and the contents of the chapters. Mosabi Hamed, a Detroit attorney, has lived and worked in the law in Jordan. James Mei practiced law in China and is now a Portland attorney. Ruth Monroy, a Mexican attorney, is also a federally and California State certified interpreter. Lam Pham, who previously was an attorney in Vietnam, now practices law in Seattle. Larissa Raskonova, who formerly was an attorney in Russia, currently practices law in Portland. The book was also reviewed by thirty-five judges, attorneys, and directors of immigrant and refugee agencies, many of whom provided comments and suggestions, and whose written and oral comments were instrumental.

Contributions to this book from all over the United States indicate that the crisis of misunderstanding in cases involving immigrant parties is widespread. Addressing this fundamental problem requires ongoing efforts by judges, attorneys, and court officials to secure the rights of persons who, because of their linguistic and cultural backgrounds, are unable to participate fully in their own court proceedings.

Justice James M. Dolliver
Washington Supreme Court

Preface

A threefold approach was followed for this book. First, legal experts were asked to write chapters summarizing important criminal, procedural, and civil features of the legal systems of several different countries. In addition to the individual reports on official laws and procedures, each population's generally shared perceptions about how its legal institutions function are covered. This information profiles the general expectations of many immigrants regarding their native legal systems. Other chapters discuss important additional factors which influence the court experiences of immigrants, such as cultural impacts, working with interpreters in court, and immigration issues that result from state court criminal and domestic violence case decisions.

Second, a focus group of 8 to 10 recent immigrants was convened for the purpose of discussing each of the five profiled legal systems. The Vietnamese focus group was held in Seattle, the Russian focus group in Portland, the Middle Eastern focus group in Detroit, the Mexican focus group in Seattle, and the Chinese focus group in Olympia. Their discussions concentrated on criminal, law enforcement, and civil issues, and their common beliefs about their native legal systems and about the beliefs of many immigrants regarding the U.S. legal system. The focus groups, which were not furnished with any materials before or during their discussions, served to verify information in the country legal system chapters and to contribute experiential beliefs and illustrative statements, which appear in boxes in the country chapters.

Third, surveys and interviews of forty judges, attorneys, and court interpreters were conducted in order to obtain information about how immigrants fare in U.S. courts when confronted with procedures and concepts unlike those of their native legal systems. The results of the surveys and interviews and suggestions for intervention at problem points are reported in the application chapter.

The Washington State Office of the Administrator for the Courts developed *Immigrants in Courts* as one of its innovative approaches to systemic problems in the judiciary. Mary McQueen, Washington State Court Administrator, provided inspiration and sustained support for the book from the beginning. Janet McLane, Judicial Services Director, contributed her farsighted vision and indispensable guidance at many points during the preparation period. The project was funded by the State Justice Institute, without whose financial assistance the book could not have been realized.

More than one hundred people contributed their valuable time and thoughts to this book. Special acknowledgment is due to Cheryl Reynolds of the State Justice Institute for her apt ideas and assistance during preparation of the manuscript; Yvonne Pettus for her perceptive encouragement of professional writing standards; Bob Henderson for his contribution of a multitude of creative approaches; Frank Edmondson for his forbearance in drafting numerous contracts; Sherry Iverson for her faithful rendition of endless revisions; Judge Paul DeMuniz for his invaluable discussion and review contribution; Judge Ron Mamiya for his thoughtful insight throughout the process; Judge Heather Van Nuys for her energizing suggestions and encouragement; Judge Lynn Davis for his detailed and helpful comments,; and Edgar Winans, Kathleen Sullivan, and Evelyn Neaman for kindly sharing their expertise and worthwhile suggestions. Thanks also are due to James Mei for generously providing accurate translations and to Larisa Raskonova for creating precise educational scripts of court proceedings.

Grateful acknowledgment is made to the Washington State District and Municipal Court Judges Association Diversity Committee, particularly Chair Monica Benton, former Chair Ruth Reukaff, and the committee's accomplished staff person, Gloria Hemmen, as well as members Judge Judith Hightower, Judge Jim Rhiel, Judge James Cayce, and Judge Victoria Meadows, for their inventiveness and diligence in presenting training for judges on these issues; to District and Municipal Judges Association Chair Clifford Stilz for his continuously enthusiastic support; and to Liem Do, Marina Brown, and Ruth Monroy for sharing their acute awareness and insights while addressing judges about these topics.

Deep appreciation and thanks are also given to focus group leaders Minghui Yang, Rosemary Nguyen, Glenna White, Mosabi Hamed, and Marina Braun, and to the focus group members who generously shared their views of both their old and their new legal systems, eloquently describing the powerful effects of each upon them. Lastly, thanks go to the judges, attorneys, and court interpreters who gave their time, experience, and innovative suggestions during interviews and reviews. The courts are indeed fortunate that there is a wealth of caring individuals who are aware of these barriers and are working to provide fairness and due process to all persons, including newcomers, who become involved in our legal system.

Joanne I. Moore
September 1998

Immigrants
in Courts

Introduction

by Judge Paul J. DeMuniz

Eighteen-year-old Santiago Ventura Morales screamed, "No es posible! No es posible!" as the jury pronounced him guilty of the murder of another migrant.[1] However, Ventura's anguished cry as he was led from the courtroom was not the end but the beginning of a case that would publicize in Oregon and nationally the difficulties experienced by many immigrants in the American justice system due to their lack of understanding of the American justice system, as well as their cultural and linguistic differences.[2]

Four years after the jury's verdict put Ventura in an Oregon prison to serve a life sentence, his murder conviction was overturned and he was set free. Reinvestigation of the *Ventura* case revealed numerous examples of the manner in which his misunderstanding of the legal system and his cultural and linguistic differences disadvantaged him at various stages of his prosecution. For instance, at the time of his arrest Ventura did not speak English. As a Mixtec from a remote village in the Sierra Madre del Sur in the province of Oaxaca, Mexico, Ventura's native language was Mixtec, an indigenous Indian language, not Spanish as was assumed by the police and later by court personnel. Prior to his initial interrogation, Ventura was not advised of his constitutional rights in his native language, but in an almost incoherent form of Spanish. Nevertheless, the trial court ruled that he had voluntarily waived his right against self-incrimination. The officer who initially questioned Ventura later dismissed the distinction between the Mixtec and Spanish languages, saying, "They go hand-in-hand in Mexican country down there."[3] He was, of course, terribly mistaken.

The erroneous assumption by the authorities about Ventura's native language continued throughout every stage of the prosecution. John Haviland, a linguistic anthropologist at Reed College, later charged that, at the time of his trial, Ventura could conduct only simple conversations in Spanish. Murder trials rarely involve simple ideas, yet the state provided only Spanish interpreters.[4]

A number of witnesses at Ventura's trial were also Mixtecs who, like Ventura, had a great deal of trouble with the English-to-Spanish translations of questions asked them in front of the jury. Often they seemed bewildered by the questions and gave answers seemingly inappropriate and nonsensical or simply not understood by the court interpreter. The following exchange from the trial transcript illustrates vividly the ongoing linguistic difficulties of the Mixtec witnesses.

COURT: Would you translate what he said, please?

INTERPRETER: That was Mestican, I don't understand.

COURT: You have to tell us what he says.

INTERPRETER: It was Mestica words.

COURT: Very well.

DISTRICT ATTORNEY: I would ask Mrs. Roche [interpreter] to tell us whether she knows what those Mestica words are?

INTERPRETER: No, I don't.[5]

In spite of the interpreter's repeated complaints that the witnesses were not answering in Spanish, the trial continued. The judge and the advocates either dismissed the fact that the so-called Mestica words (a mispronunciation of Mixtec) were not Spanish or thought that the words uttered by the witnesses were just a variety of Spanish.[6]

Cultural differences combined with the linguistic difficulties of the Mixtecs often created perceptions that the Anglo trial participants misinterpreted. Misinterpretation of the Mixtecs' behavior and demeanor may have played a significant role in the jury's decision to find Ventura guilty. For example, the officer who initially questioned Ventura insisted that Ventura's lowered eyes during questioning were an obvious guilt reflex. The Mixtec witnesses displayed a similar inability to look into the eyes of the deputy district attorney or judge when questioned. Jurors interpreted that characteristic and the witnesses' linguistic problems as some sort of combined effort by Ventura and the other Mixtecs to thwart the trial process.[7] At least one juror perceived the

Mixtecs' demeanor and linguistic problems as demonstrating that "some sort of cover-up was going on. 'They all acted kind of guilty.'"[8]

Fortunately for Ventura, reinvestigation of his case demonstrated the shoddiness of the state's forensic evidence and established convincingly that another man from the migrant camp was the actual killer. Following his release from prison, Ventura attended the University of Portland on a full scholarship. In May 1996, he graduated with a degree in social work. Ventura has since returned to Mexico where he is fulfilling a village tradition that requires three years of community service.

Ventura's life was returned to him—eventually the system worked in his favor. However, his case demonstrates that linguistic and cultural differences can unfairly penalize immigrants thrust into the cauldron of the American justice system. With increasing frequency, immigrants from a multitude of countries and cultures are now caught up in the American justice system.[9] The problems that Ventura and the Mixtec witnesses encountered in the justice system will continue to plague immigrants if those in control of the system lack the communication skills, education, training, and sensitivity to identify the special needs of some immigrants who cannot readily grasp the basic concepts, privileges, and requirements of the American justice system.

One purpose of this book is to provide judges, court staff, and advocates with easy access to information about the legal and cultural systems of immigrants from Mexico, China, Russia, Vietnam, and the Muslim world. Each country chapter contains a general description that includes information about predominant ethnic groups, religious groups, languages, and important cultural norms. For example, the chapter on Mexico confirms that the Spanish language is not always the native language of an immigrant from Mexico. Instead, indigenous Mexicans such as Mixtec and Zapotec Indians may not speak Spanish fluently. Had the authorities involved in the *Ventura* case understood that language issue early on in the proceedings, many of the linguistic problems that prejudiced the trial could have been avoided. Similarly, had the jurors in the *Ventura* case known that young Mixtecs never look directly at an elder or person of authority, and that avoiding eye contact with an elder or person of authority is a gesture of respect in the Mixtec culture, their evaluation of the Mixtecs testimony and demeanor might not have been so negative.

Each country chapter also discusses the country's justice system and police practices and the roles of judges and attorneys. More importantly, however, these chapters discuss how the country's justice system and its various actors are understood or perceived by the people of that country and how that understanding or perception often contributes to an immigrant's profound misunderstanding of the American justice system. For example, many immigrants may have a great deal of difficulty understanding the American defense attorney's overriding duties of loyalty and confidentiality or the American judge's silence, apparent distance from, and seeming non-participation in the proceedings. Judges and attorneys armed with the knowledge that an immigrant is from a country where the defense attorney works cooperatively with the state or where the judiciary is not impartial, but often acts as an arm of an oppressive government, can take special steps to make sure that the immigrant fully understands the nature of the attorney-client relationship or judicial impartiality before problems detrimental to the immigrant develop. These and many other legal-cultural issues that may negatively impact immigrants in the American justice system are discussed in various chapters throughout the book.

Additionally, it appears that with some frequency immigrants have committed acts that are deemed criminal under U.S. laws but may be considered acceptable behavior within the predominant culture of the immigrant's country of origin. The use by courts of evidence to support a so-called "cultural defense" to mitigate charges and sentencing has been decidedly inconsistent.[10] However, information contained in all the chapters about the cultural systems of the various countries of origin can provide background information to assist attorneys in identifying cultural issues that may be intertwined in the alleged criminal act, and assist judges in determining the proper use of such evidence.[11]

A culturally responsive justice system does not mean that immigrants are not obligated to meet the same requirements and standards of accountability that the system imposes on all Americans. Rather a culturally responsive justice system is one in which the key players have the education, training, and sensitivity necessary to identify the linguistic needs of a diverse population of immigrants and to have some understanding of the legal and cultural forces that may have contributed to the immigrants' behavior. This book is an attempt to help those administering and working in the justice system to understand the basic needs of many immigrants in a continued effort to assure that the American justice system operates fairly for every individual.

Speaking of Culture
Immigrants in the American Legal System

by Dr. Janet Bauer

A community's culture introduces its children to their world. It influences their impressions of themselves, of other countries, and of where they belong. Culture consists of learned, shared ways of thinking and behaving that are passed down from generation to generation. This is aided by symbolic devices like language, signs such as flags, gestures like the wave of a hand, and ritual performances, as well as food, music, and clothing.[1]

When immigrants experience cultural change, they are asked in effect to change who they are. No wonder people may seek to minimize the anxieties of doing this by preserving a sense of the home culture as part of any new identity.[2] It is perhaps the greatest paradox that immigrants can adapt and mold the materials of their culture to their changed environment, while at the same time they are irretrievably shaped and molded by their early cultural experiences.

THE FUNDAMENTAL NATURE OF CULTURE

Anthropologists view culture as not only distinctive behaviors or ways of thinking about the world but also the total lifeways of a group of people, which connect them intimately to specific places and people. People connect through their religious events, political practices, social relationships, and economies. Early socialization to a first or "home" culture includes learning not only behaviors, meanings, and values but also certain frames or expectations. These expectations provide contexts in which to associate meanings and feelings and to know how to react to others. For example, in many parts of the United States, acquaintances expect to exchange certain ritualized greetings upon meeting, such as shaking hands and asking, "How are you?" However, a newcomer to the United States may be misled by both the friendliness of these exchanges and the apparent curiosity of the speaker, who, in reality, is not seeking a detailed accounting of the respondent's health. People learn to view the world and interact with, or respond to, certain situations with specific emotions or verbal responses. When people move to a new culture, these complex responses toward the world and certain events or contexts must be relearned and reexperienced.

Culturally acquired behavior and the way people learn it are both arbitrary and subtle. For example, there is no necessary connection between nodding the head from side to side and "no," although it's accepted as such in North American culture. In fact, in many Middle Eastern cultures, a nod to the side means "yes." Likewise, in some cultures outside North America, it is commonplace for individuals to show respect for authority by adopting whatever facts authorities assert as the accepted truth, even if the individual has contradictory personal knowledge of the facts. For example, immigrants[3] who endure nonsensical interpretations from unqualified court-appointed interpreters may be carrying out a cultural value of stoic acceptance.

This is not to say one can easily predict behavior from a few simple cultural "rules." Due to situational contexts and other factors in cultural learning, there are many variations of both ideals and actual practices within any one society, across different regions, and among different social classes or between genders. For example, though in urban areas of most Muslim countries upper-middle-class women once observed traditional dress and interactional restrictions, these restrictions were not commonly observed in rural areas, where women participated in agriculture and where most people were acquainted or related. Other examples can be found within languages. In most Spanish-speaking countries, familiar second-person pronouns rather than the more formal ones are generally used with children, close friends, and family. However, Hondurans almost always use formal pronouns, even among intimates like husband and wife.

Because culture is learned meaning, parts of it may be shared across an entire country, but it can also vary within societies. While they share some assumptions among themselves, not all Americans, Iranians, or Mexicans can be expected to react in the same manner. For example, within a language such as Spanish, regional differences in meaning and nuance exist that can lead careless interpreters to misconvey the accounts of immigrants through unfamiliarity with jargon.[4] Additional cultural variation occurs when individuals cannot realize their ideals or must implement them differently than they would prefer, due to personal circumstances or practical exigencies. This results in a paradox of culture: while people often treat a "culture" as a unified category of behaviors and traditions, in reality it is a process involving variation and change.

IMPACT OF CULTURAL CHANGE

Culture provides people with a sense of self and place necessary to situate themselves meaningfully in the world. Acculturation, the process of adapting to a different culture, requires an individual to change habits of thinking and interacting. It is a lengthy undertaking, especially when new practices conflict with long-established ones. In fact, early-learned habits of thinking and interacting are often so deeply held that during the process of learning new views, people routinely select those elements that reinforce their existing convictions.[5]

Thus, when cultural differences in communication style or implied meanings are presented, the result can be misplaced judgments on the part of both the newcomers trying to understand American ways and on the part of Americans responding to newcomers' behavior. This meeting of cultures becomes more complicated as immigrants find themselves entangled in two or more somewhat contradictory sets of cultural expectations, a situation that often causes considerable anxiety. A young Laotian woman reports about her first day of school in Texas, "The teacher looked me in the eyes—the eyes! I was frightened. She looked at me in my eyes! Well, you only look at people when you are angry, when they do something wrong. Even after some American explained this to me, I could not believe it. No one had ever done that to me before, except my parents, before I was going to be punished."[6]

The Acculturation Process

Historically, the "melting pot" approach to acculturation was the predominant model for becoming American. Newcomers were expected to leave behind their old language and ways for the new. More recently, a recognition of the lasting importance of home culture to successful adaptation has resulted in models of biculturalism. These models recognize that immigrants tend to incorporate aspects of their multiple cultural heritages and present more realistic expectations for immigrant resettlement.

Most models of acculturation measure the extent to which immigrants are involved in the host society's institutions or adopt host country behaviors and practices, suggesting general patterns of adaptation over time. The terms "separation," "liminality," and "integration" have been employed to describe the adjustment processes through which refugees, undocumented workers, and other immigrants proceed.[7] A second model predicts immigrant adjustment by time periods after arriving in the host country.[8]

Separation Stage. The stage of separation begins when immigrants leave their homeland and encompasses the initial traumas of leaving. These include late-night passages with smugglers across difficult terrain into the United States or the much-reported cases of Southeast Asians leaving home on rafts. One African student recounted his own stress in an autobiographical narrative: "When I arrived at JFK International Airport … I was hysterical…. My fear of what to say and how to say it to the immigration authority was enormous. Everybody spoke English but me."[9] The separation stage can last up to one and a half years after arrival and is described as a period when immigrants are immersed in what they have lost of their culture and identity. The African student described above recounts his state of mind during his first months in the United States as a depressed preoccupation with the political situation back home where several of his relatives had been murdered by the government, mixed with his concern over his lack of income and his uncertainty as to the wisdom of looking for work on a student visa.

Liminality Stage. In the liminality stage (typically one and a half to five years from arrival), immigrants are living between two cultures. They are not fully at home in either but still working to establish new identities and sense of place. During the liminality stage, refugees may begin energetically to rebuild their lives but remain insecure and unsure.

One refugee[10] describes his feelings: "You go on with your life. For me, perhaps the escape and the initial first week of shock made me feel like a refugee, but after that I began to feel something different. It was sort of an in-between state." Termeh Rassi, cofounder of *Second Generation* (an Internet magazine for Iranians), wrote of her parents' generation in the United States, not yet fully integrated into their new country, "They spent their days fantasizing about what they would do when they went back ... who they would be ... how important they would be."[11]

Adaptation Stage. During the third stage (five to ten years), refugees are described as making adjustments but remaining discouraged about the possibilities of achieving their ultimate aspirations in the new society.[12] At this point immigrants often transfer their ambitions for success to their children, for whom they are willing to sacrifice a great deal. The elderly generally have a much harder time adjusting to their new country. S. P. Bip, from Cambodia, reports that "I was the director of a small machine factory outside Phnom Penh.... I arrived in the U.S. when I was 67 in 1979. For me that is very old. I think I was too old to come here.... [My children] talk to me about things I do not understand, and I talk to them about things they have little interest in. I went with my wife to study English, but it was too difficult for me. The teacher talks too fast and I cannot understand her."[13]

Integration Stage. After ten years or so, the last stage, described as the integration stage, is often reached. In this stage, refugees have achieved a kind of stability and have generally come to terms with what their life has become. In many cases, though, they have had to settle for lower status than they had back home. This is true even for the poorest immigrants in the United States, since most who were able to leave their countries in the first place were relatively better off.

For some, the feeling of finally becoming a part of the American community may be marked by obtaining formal citizenship or only after the birth of grandchildren, when it becomes clear their family destiny lies in their new country. However, sometimes integration is never achieved. Dr. Ngo Minh

Son, a Vietnamese refugee, reflects this sentiment: "I became a citizen only because I want to bring [my brother] here.... I will always be a refugee at heart and in spirit."[14]

Immigrants remain a product of both their cultures in differing degrees. Those individuals who are able to integrate their past and present lives do better than those who idealize the past or who completely immerse themselves in their new culture. Developing relationships and identities both inside and outside their own ethnic or cultural communities enhances their opportunities to effectively learn and practice American "ways," while retaining practices that are meaningful to their previous sense of self. However, altering long-established ways of valuing certain behaviors is difficult, and some immigrants are unable or unwilling to change customs in their new country. This is especially true if they are involved in communities that support these choices. Examples include the recent case of Iraqi men marrying 13- and 14-year-old sisters, whose parents approved of the marriages.[15]

These acculturation models of the general stages of immigrant adaptation do not convey immigrants' daily struggles to understand their new culture. A Lao man notes, "I think everyone here has problems in adjusting at first; it is only natural. I know I did. It is just a degree of pain, ... you say, how can I be depressed when everything is so clean and beautiful and there is peace? But you are depressed and you cannot forget any of that."[16]

Dual Cultural Behavior

Alterations in external, observable behaviors do not provide much insight into the way immigrants internally respond to different situations. Some immigrants consciously change their behavior, mannerisms, or dress to mimic those of their new culture without actually changing their ways of viewing the world or without completely understanding the logic or thinking behind these customs. Some individuals may retain their home rituals or other indications of their first culture, while understanding or even preferring American ways of doing things. Some practice and even embellish home customs because of the hostility and rejection they have encountered in American society, while others wholeheartedly embrace American customs because of difficulties within their home communities.

Other individuals adopt "American" behaviors in some settings, using their "home" cultural behaviors in others. Retaining one's native language at home or belonging to an immigrant religious community rather than a non-immigrant one can indicate an immigrant's creative retention of the home culture.[17] Social relationships may also indicate dual cultural choices. For example, Middle Eastern and Asian men may take up American "dating" customs with American women, while rejecting this very kind of social interaction for respectable women in their own community whom they prefer to marry.

The ability to adapt and the choices immigrants make are at least partly affected by whether they are accepted or rejected by their United States communities and whether they yearn to return home or are content to build new lives, as well as by the support of their home communities available to them in the United States. A network of friends and family they can count on helps immigrants to see that many of their problems are commonly shared. Without a network of family and friends to count on, immigrants and refugees may develop a sense that their problems "have gradually changed from being shared ones to being private."[18]

Making Sense of Immigrant Adaptation

Americans expect immigrants to accommodate their style and cultural expectations. Figuring out how to conduct themselves as Americans can be a perplexing process for newcomers, whatever their backgrounds.

Newcomers' Expectations. Studies of diverse groups of newcomers over time indicate that immigrants generally come to the United States with both optimism and a determination to work hard.[19] In fact most immigrants arrive here with such high expectations that the hard realities of life can be a source of immense disappointment. The reception immigrants face and the difficulties they encounter in understanding and interacting with the institutions of their new culture and society can be daunting. The following sections detail more specifically how elements of culture can lead to misunderstanding and confusion among those interacting across or between cultures.

Selective Adaptation. Learning to use stoves, baths, and so on may be the least of immigrants' worries. Although the Hmong hill people portrayed in *Becoming American*[20] are initially perplexed by American appliances, they quickly learn to utilize these devices. However, they cannot easily abandon their cultural value of pleasing authority figures in their new land. This value leads them to be passive in the face of public assaults against them, because they fear that public authorities will be displeased if they complain and will cause them to be sent home to Southeast Asia.

An immigrant teenager may find it natural to adopt an American style of dress but support her family's traditional behavioral expectations.[21] Various aspects of one Hmong rape case are useful in illustrating several apparently conflicting cultural elements in the judicial context. In this case, a young Hmong girl who dressed like an American was raped by a Hmong boy after she accepted a ride with him. Hmong tradition did not allow her to be alone with a Hmong male to whom she was not related. To those outside her community, she looked like a typical American teenager. Her appearance and body language led lawyers and social service personnel to erroneously conclude that her sexual attitudes and values were those of a typical American girl her age. In fact, as the case progressed, the victim grew to feel that the rape should be resolved through community negotiations rather than through the American legal system. However, the legal system continued to prosecute the case despite her and her family's desires. Caught between her community and the legal system, the victim began to lose self-esteem and confidence and became anxious about whether her family would accept a court decision.[22] The young defendant was also confused. From what he'd heard, he assumed that sexual aggressiveness was appropriate for "liberated" American high school males and initially thought he would be treated leniently by the system.

Language Miscues. Language differences often create misunderstanding, misrecognition, or miscommunication across cultures. There is no doubt that the overwhelming majority of immigrants want to learn English, but insurmountable obstacles sometimes get in the way. One new arrival, Mr. P., who has been in the United States for five months, says he knows learning English is important, but he works odd shifts in a factory with other immigrants who do not speak English among themselves and cannot find time to attend free English classes offered by his sponsoring agency.[23] Such obstacles may function to continue an immigrant's almost exclusive use of the native language, especially if the immigrant lives in a large immigrant community.

Immigrants who do not speak English well are often not respected or treated as adults. For example, Reza describes his job interview at a large retail store. "I asked the interviewer to repeat what he said but he just said it louder using different words. I'm not deaf; if he had just said it to me more slowly I would have understood."[24] Many immigrants speak reasonably correct, but heavily accented, English. In the legal context, whether they are able to pursue small claims cases or pay fines may depend on the willingness of court clerks to be patient.

However important learning English is to unraveling the mysteries of American culture and being perceived as a competent human being, verbal language alone does not always provide the context in which to interpret these cultural meanings. Translating, explaining, or learning the "vocabulary" of culture involves more than mastering dictionary translations. Immigrants must learn the shifts and nuances, the slang and special sayings and uses that are constantly changing and that natives seem to always know and be comfortable with. In a 1992 case that elicited international shock, an exchange student from Japan wandered onto the wrong property in Baton Rouge, Louisiana, looking for a Halloween party. The homeowner, who suspected a burglar, shouted, "Freeze!" The student, who did not understand the idiomatic order, kept moving, and the homeowner shot him to death.[25]

Nonverbal Communications Across Cultures. One difficulty facing the newcomer is that the rules of culture are not generally made explicit. Natives themselves may not be conscious of them until some conflict arises or they are asked to explain some custom. The "language" of culture includes an array of not only verbal but also nonverbal signals. These include contexts, relations, emotions, and gestures that convey norms, values, schemas, meanings, intentions, and credibility. The conventions of nonverbal "language," the stylized, routinized cues to meaning, vary across different cultures. These are body and facial movement, eye contact, and use of time and space.

American speakers are expected to maintain eye contact with one another; in other cultures this may be considered threatening behavior. In some cultures, the friendly, smiling facial maneuvers of Americans are seen as naive and childlike. Middle Eastern businessmen may wonder how their American colleagues can be taken seriously, while in American culture this might be seen as a basis for establishing trustworthiness. Likewise when American listeners break gaze periodically, Middle Easterners consider this "shifty" behavior. However, they would consider a woman's constant gaze to be flirtatious.[26]

These differences were highlighted in a rape case involving a Vietnamese victim. When she was questioned in court, the victim would look at the defendants and smile, then look at the judge and smile, "a big smile, almost a laugh." According to her Vietnamese lawyer, this nonverbal communication was her way of saying in public to the defendants, "You have harmed me, my spirit, but I will survive." Without a Vietnamese lawyer to represent her, these smiles could easily have been misread.[27]

Time, Space, and Context Differences. When Americans interact with immigrants, they may experience differences in punctuality and use of personal space. The context in which certain behaviors occur provides cultural signals about intentions. For example, immigrants from rural areas of Mexico, which lack streets or street addresses, may not place importance on memorizing their addresses but be able to provide a set of directions to their residences.[28] A young Laotian woman reports that "Laotians never touch, and for us a kiss on the face or slap on the back is very rude. I also had to learn to wave my hand. In Laos, waving to call a person is a sign of contempt, and to wave to someone waving palm outward is rude.... Texans do not understand this."[29]

Narrative Styles. In legal proceedings, differences in narrative styles can affect the credibility of immigrants. Across cultures, patterns of storytelling, preference for the importance of different attributes, sequencing order, and ways of connecting events or features differ.[30] Most Americans favor linear plots in storytelling or construction of narratives. In many other cultures, the main points may be obscured or arrived at in a more circular fashion after connecting what appear to be inconsistent or unrelated elements.

Refugees' asylum applications are often challenged because they do not relay their stories sequentially or they fail to emphasize the elements that judges consider important. "Cultural differences in the values placed on time, date, and name specificity caused judges to perceive applicants as vague and unresponsive...."[31] In one case, observed in Deborah Anker's asylum claims study, when an applicant testified that he had been married in a Catholic church, the judge asked for the name of the church. When the applicant explained that it had no name, the judge dismissed this answer, asserting that all Catholic churches have names. In fact, the judge was wrong; many institutions in small Central American towns do not have proper names.[32]

When immigrants relate their explanations to judges, jurors, or law enforcement, the differences in styles of conveying meaning and in perceptions of the importance of events or plausibility of actions can lead to misunderstanding. Judges or jurors looking for inconsistencies may be relying on cues, verbal and nonverbal, which are biased toward American cultural expectations. According to the Anker study, refugees' credibility in the observed immigration hearings often revolved around whether, in the judge's experience or perception, refugees conducted themselves and spoke in a familiar manner and/or provided the right details.[33]

The Importance of Social Relationships. In the native cultures of many immigrants, individual testimony and specific contexts of social relationships may carry more weight than written or other evidentiary material. This is especially true if the immigrant's experiences have been in a repressive state, which controls such materials. For many immigrants, maneuvering through personal relations or networks with both strangers and family can be an important part of presenting oneself or the veracity of one's story. Relationships are essential to assessing the position of, as well as pleasing, those in authority, including government representatives, elders, and parents. For this reason, immigrants often refrain from contradicting government representatives' statements, even if they know them to be untrue.

Sometimes an immigrant's hesitation and lengthy process of evaluating the interviewer's status and relationships lead law enforcement or legal advisors to conclude that the immigrant is holding back. They may conclude that many immigrants simply say what they think the interviewer wants to hear.[34]

Experienced interviewers come to understand that it is in the immigrant's own best interests to assess what the interviewer expects to hear and how the interviewer can affect them before providing answers.

Social Relationships and Behavior. One's position in relationships can also dictate the types of behaviors one expects of individuals. In Iran, for example, superiors and inferiors are expected to behave toward each other in specific ways that maintain and indicate mutual respect and deference. This may involve using the appropriate ritualized language or providing material indications of respect. Mistrust is created when individuals fail to act as expected, with some exceptions made in close, personal relationships.[35]

Immigrants are constantly faced with being unsure of what is expected of them in their new country. In one case, several Iranian refugees sent flowers to housing authorities who, as part of their ordinary job duties, had been helpful in facilitating permission to secure private housing and business permits.[36] While appropriate in their native country, in America such a display of gratitude could be seen as inappropriate or even carry legal consequences.

Immigrants continue to use their social relationships, and their position or status in them, to provide guidance about how they should behave toward others of contrasting status and position and about the reasonableness of certain behaviors. The support of community and family remains important to them while they adapt. For immigrants who identify partly with the United States and partly with their home culture, there is potential confusion surrounding their home community's expectations on moral issues and its claim or role in negotiating disputes. In the rape case of the young Hmong girl, tradition demanded a reconciliation of the families involved, and this was in many ways deemed more important than counseling or attention to the trauma of the individual victim.

A Vietnamese lawyer who often seeks protective orders for abused wives describes the hate letters she gets from the Vietnamese community. "You see, we [lawyers] are supposed to defend our clients' rights, but so often this defense is not understood by the community and I offend the community's mores. I am accused of promoting divorce, of urging separation, of destroying the family unit."[37]

Immigrant Encounters with American Institutions

Just as it is prudent for newcomers to try to understand American culture and the legal consequences it implies, it is helpful for those who encounter newcomers in American institutions to be aware of the role of home culture and the difficulties of acculturation. The various facets of culture discussed above can be important in understanding the reasoning immigrants use in interacting with American institutions. Distinguishing appropriate and inappropriate behavior is guided by world views, situational cues, and personal experiences.

Communicating Credibility. Most immigrants perceive a need to adjust their perceptions and manner of presenting themselves to American authorities but may have difficulty assessing what to do. For example, most refugees with whom the author conducted research wanted guidance on how best to present their cases to immigration judges. They wondered whether it would be more credible to remember all the dates or to remember some of them imperfectly and whether their stories would be more believable in conversational and simple English or in stylized, legal, and highly literate English. They believed stylized English conveyed status and credibility, while the author felt simpler English, more consistent with their own English language abilities, would seem more believable. In reality, the amount of detail presented can influence decisions. Refugees interviewed in Germany have revealed that too much specificity led judges there to suspect a memorization of details that individuals would not necessarily recall.[38] But in other cases, the Anker study found too little specificity can hurt the claims of someone seeking asylum in the United States.[39]

Applicant credibility is one of the most important factors cited in determining refugees' asylum cases. As in all types of cases, judges, attorneys, jurors, and law enforcement officers need to be aware that cultural factors can affect perceptions of what is a reasonable course of action in a particular situation. For example, refugees' attempts to explain why they were fearful in certain situations have been disbelieved by judges who believed their actions belied their words. In the Anker study, one judge rejected refugees' testimony that they exited from their houses during the day because they feared the military would capture them at home, but returned at night after the military left. He believed this lacked credibility because there was a possibility that the military would return, and "it just doesn't make sense to me that somebody would feel safe to come back at night…," indicating that the refugees' claimed fear was not genuine.[40] Anker concludes that the immigration judges studied generally imposed their own cultural and political assumptions in assessing applicants' credibility. Both judges and attorneys also used an American frame of reference in questioning, especially when it came to assuming the benevolent nature of government. Anker's study also showed that judges were most responsive to applicants with a political and class background similar to their own, and "tended to project their own political and cultural experiences onto the applicant."[41]

Presumptions about cultural differences are important but they can also be misleading. Not only do immigrants' background experiences vary by education, urban residence, and class, but their mastery of English and American cultural forms and manners will also vary by class, gender, generation, region, and personal experience. Assumptions also cannot be made about how immigrants' previous cultural experiences will affect the way they adapt to their practical circumstances in the United States. As one study of Mexican immigrants demonstrates, family dynamics and gender roles may develop differently depending upon the date of migration.[42]

Further, wrong generalizations can backfire. When the director of an innovative immigrant training program failed to take background differences into account, she inculcated her assumption that their clients had simple rural backgrounds during staff training. She should have known from her agency's records that most of the women came from towns or cities and had some high school education. As a result, the women trainees were constantly frustrated by the treatment they received at the agency, which was based on the erroneous assumption that they had little education or urban experience.[43]

Generational and Gender Conflicts. Both generational and gender conflicts often arise in immigrant families, where elders and particularly male elders struggle to maintain authority. It is common for immigrants to romanticize and idealize life back home after they have experienced difficulties in the

United States. Many men are unable to resume their former occupations due to different occupational requirements, lack of language skills, or limited household resources. Disappointments and frustrations may turn into nostalgia for cultural practices or hyper-exaggeration of the ideals of the home culture. Men who have enjoyed some status simply being males, and who cannot recreate that same status in the United States, often place pressures on women to conform to the ideals of the home culture. This may be done irrespective of whether they could or did expect that at home. In many immigrant groups in North America, including Vietnamese, Iranian, and Korean, the women become the emblems of the group's culture. The women's behavior and social roles become a focus of immigrant community concern in the absence of other routes to status and success.[44]

Given the circumstances of newcomer households, women often need to work and engage in nontraditional behaviors outside the home. At the same time, they are expected to take on traditional roles within the family and community. In some cases, women have more opportunities to be employed sooner, to make contacts outside the home, and to learn English more quickly than their husbands. One Cambodian refugee recounts her experiences: "For me there was no question of whether I should work or stay at home. One of the first things you learn in America is that you need money.... So we needed two incomes and I went to work. I know my husband did not like it, but it could not be helped.... I could work easier than he could and I began to do well and I supported the family. I became the breadwinner. He had bad feelings about this...."[45]

Along with the pressures of impoverishment or changing circumstances, changes in gender roles may increase tensions between spouses and family members. Male family members or the community may inflict more pressure on women to support idealized norms of the community or the male's position, especially in public. A few years ago, Soheila, an Iranian refugee woman in North America, was asked to testify against a male conational charged with assaulting another Iranian woman. The defendant had claimed a cultural defense, saying of assault against women, "It's appropriate in my culture and I forgot I was in a different country." Though Soheila shared the cultural background of the defendant, she took a different view, challenging his cultural defense by testifying that while it was said to be traditional for Iranian men to use physical force against female relatives, such behavior was not necessarily accepted in Iran, especially by women. Many members of her immigrant community subsequently shunned her, considering her testimony a betrayal of another community member who found himself in legal trouble.[46]

It is also important to remember that while the circumstances of immigration may have altered gender relations within the family, many women also derive satisfaction from supporting the home culture's ideals. They usually receive the respect and support given to elders and parents in those cultures. Women may uphold the patriarchal order of family traditions in public, while privately enjoying more influence within these circles.

Children. Generally children are very eager and motivated to learn new cultures when surrounded by majority American peers. Immigrant children usually learn English quickly, are relatively free from stress or concern with family members, and spend time in formal educational institutions. These conditions set up the circumstances for a developing generation gap in expectations, particularly as concerns gender roles and family life. Children growing up in a society that emphasizes egalitarian relations between individuals in the family are dissatisfied with parental expectations to adhere to restricted contact between boys and girls, with the infliction of more severe and physical discipline, and with expectations to marry within the cultural community.

Many immigrant children perform better in school than native-born children of the same ethnic groups.[47] However, it is not unusual for immigrant children to face hostility from others and sometimes lose interest in pursuing education as a source of social mobility, join gangs, or participate in other activities that lead to family conflicts. Likewise when immigrant parents come from segments of cultures where physical punishment or ridicule is commonly used to discipline or socialize children, they may find that their children will alert authorities to their "repressive" treatment. This further exacerbates the generational gap between children and parents.

A Vietnamese woman writes: "My children forget that I am head of home in America as I was in Vietnam. My children do not obey my requests and think I am without the new wisdom they have learned in America. I have the old wisdom.... They tell me, always, I am in America. My children change and I do not change. My children forget me."[48]

Social Networks. When newcomers participate in a community of people from their home culture, they have access to important sources of information, support, and advice for surviving and adapting in a new culture. Those who have more experience will be sought out for financial support as well as for counsel on a wide range of issues. They may be consulted about employment opportunities, child-rearing techniques, sources for medical treatment, interaction with schools, or legal matters. Immigrants rely more heavily on their own community networks or connections through community members than on "experts" outside those networks. Personal connections with other immigrants who share language, assumptions, and schemas for interaction provide a predictable basis for trust and support. An immigrant community can also be the source of opinions about the American legal system. For example, after a Russian defendant was convicted of murdering a Russian teenage girl in Vancouver, Washington, rumors regarding the courts and the way the trial was conducted rocked the Russian community.[49]

As time goes on, immigrants increasingly turn to host country institutions like the police to solve family disagreements or other disputes that would otherwise be resolved among themselves at home. In the Hmong rape case, because outsiders had intervened to resolve the case, the Hmong defendant's family felt no need to proceed with community-sanctioned marriage negotiations. Increasing reliance on police intervention in community disputes can indicate not only a breakdown of confidence in the home community but also generational differences in adaptation.

In matters of family law, members of immigrant communities may expect to resolve disputes through interpersonal mediation. Traditionally, communities with less formal legal systems rely more heavily on social negotiation and pressure to conform within the community or among groups of families. In this respect the power of elders, family, neighbors, and cultural mores in determining right and wrong are important for understanding immigrant expectations for conflict resolution in this society.

Prior Legal Experiences. While immigrants come primarily from countries with formal legal systems, immigrants and even refugees have usually had minimal contact with their own country's criminal or civil legal systems. It is still the case that extended families and networks enjoy enormous influence in settling disputes or disagreements. Reports establish that some immigrants expect that matters of child custody and divorce will be settled within family networks.[50] Many times, individuals, who claim that as a matter of honor they will do the right thing by their children, are resentful of court interference in what would be personal matters.

Fear and aversion toward the legal system are widespread in some countries, as described in some of the country chapters included in this book. This was demonstrated in the case of a Ukrainian immigrant who refused to accept a court-appointed lawyer to help defend himself against charges of bear trapping, implying that a court-appointed attorney was part of the KGB. His refusal was based on his distrust of anyone who might have an association with the government.[51] Immigrants may continue to act on the basis of cultural assumptions about expected behavior even if they have lived in the United States for years.

It is common for domestic violence victims to hesitate to seek needed protection because they fear the legal system will make their problems even worse and, in some cases, fear deportation. Batterers often use these fears against victims in order to coerce them into withdrawing protection order petitions.[52] Immigrant victims of crime often do not report to law enforcement or other governmental authorities for the same reasons.[53]

Public Versus Private Matters. Cultural values can dictate what is open for public discussion. Especially common is a reluctance to relate details of sexual assaults or violence, so that women may be unwilling to relate this information even to those assisting them. In recognition of this fact, many courts strive to appoint same-gender interpreters for these types of court proceedings.

Some other topics are to be avoided as well. For example, in Iran, years of political repression have resulted in a general avoidance of identifying family names or discussing prison experiences, even with close relatives. As a result, asylum applicants may be reluctant to relay this information. It is not so much the topic itself but the social context and the presence of certain third persons that indicate whether it can safely be discussed. Many refugees fear revealing information that, although it may be helpful to their case, might result in retaliation against relatives back home. The presence of interpreters or individuals tied in even some tenuous way to an immigrant's community may also prompt reluctance to describe matters an immigrant does not want spread to his or her acquaintances.

INTERPRETING CULTURE

There are a number of factors that those rendering judgment on or assistance to immigrants should keep in mind. The first factor is that first-generation newcomers and their children will demonstrate different attachments to first-culture habits and different degrees of familiarity with American culture and language. (Class, age, gender, and educational and personal differences will account for the variation.) Second, their differing experiences and circumstances in the United States will help determine how they "combine" their cultures. For the first generation of immigrants, maintaining the support of their home culture community here is extremely important. Third, those who interact with immigrants must be aware of and guard against the tendency to rely on American cultural perspectives or biases.

Those who work with immigrants can productively adopt one successful strategy for communicating with immigrants. This is to actively listen and be aware of cultural differences and sources of conflict, to look for effective ways to convey the expectations of American culture, and to make explicit necessary information. In this way, immigrants can understand and respond more effectively to expectations of American cultural institutions. Ethnography, the observations and descriptions of cultures, and the collection of narratives are effective tools in understanding cultural differences, making clear what is expected and helping individuals to understand and respond to this. This kind of information may be available from immigrant organizations or from churches with large immigrant memberships.

Judges and attorneys must be cognizant of the importance of social relations in both immigrant adaptation and adjudication. This is in contrast to the focus of the American legal system on individual's rights. For example, it may be important, even culturally appropriate, for immigrants to seek counsel from an immigrant community representative or mediator. One must also keep in mind that the status of such a person to other individuals in the community may affect an immigrant's testimony or willingness to participate in the legal process.

When should something be considered simply variation across cultures and when should it be judged as morally or legally wrong? How easily can immigrants be expected to adjust their choices and judgments on such issues and when must they be expected to do so? Obviously, what is custom in one culture, supported and expected by the community, may be considered immoral, abusive, or unlawful elsewhere. An example is the practice of giving gifts to authorities.

Too much attention to cultural explanations for differences in behavior or world views can also be a dangerous thing, as pointed out in a recent *Connecticut Magazine* article on Chinese restaurant businesses in America.[54] In a case against a Chinese employer, despite an abundance of evidence collected on illegal and unethical treatment of employees, the judge decided that this was simply the way the Chinese did business. Clearly, from interviews in the article, there are Chinese workers who object to these abusive so-called cultural practices. Moreover, most immigrants are aware, from their own cultural experiences, of the importance of situational contexts in making moral judgments. That is, the ways in which different behaviors are considered appropriate vary under different circumstances.

When judges are presiding over cases involving immigrant witnesses, an effective way to get the whole story is to listen closely, with an "ethnographic ear," and to lay the groundwork for mutual respect and trust in the process.[55] This may involve reserving judgment until getting the whole story and perhaps deliberately assessing the impact of nonverbal cues on one's first impressions. As Anker's study concludes, "applicants should be encouraged to tell their stories in their own way; considerable leeway should be given to applicants giving narrative answers." Anker's study further found that the observed judges were so intent on using their own cultural criteria for finding inconsistencies, by which to determine the applicant's character and reliability, that applicants often were not allowed to tell their full stories to the judges.[56]

CONCLUSION

The challenge of understanding immigrant behavior is indeed complex. On the one hand, judges, lawyers, and interpreters must be careful not to make judgments of others based simply on their own ways of viewing the world. On the other hand, they should only generalize so much about the extent to which "cultural background" determines immigrant behaviors. Culture is not a static or easily isolated set of values or behaviors and may vary by education or class background. To accurately assess an immigrant party's participation in court, judges, attorneys, and others involved in the process must appreciate that all immigrants are affected by their backgrounds and most are affected by their lack of knowledge of the United States legal system.

Interpreters in Court Proceedings

by Joanne I. Moore and Judge Ron A. Mamiya

Since the late 1980s when Santiago Ventura Morales was erroneously convicted of murder, in part due to interpreter miscommunications, court interpreting has come to the forefront of American jurisprudence. A growing number of courts recognize that an untrained, uncertified interpreter can completely change material testimony, direct the non-English-speaking party's behavior, and distort the judge's statements.

A court interpreter's primary mission is to accurately and completely interpret every statement made into and from English and the target language. The court interpreters' importance during a non-English-speaking immigrant's case is illustrated in the following interpretation:

ATTORNEY: Now at that time, or shortly thereafter, did anything unusual occur?

INTERPRETER'S RENDITION: *During that time, more or less, later, some other thing happened?*

WITNESS: Yep. Someone began to push me with a black tow truck. Later, he began to move me.

INTERPRETER'S RENDITION: *Yep. Someone began to honk at me, and I moved.*

ATTORNEY: Do you mean that the tow truck actually had contact with your vehicle?

INTERPRETER'S RENDITION: *Are you saying [pause] that the car [pause] that the automobile that lifts cars is in contact with you?*

WITNESS: Yes, it hit my bumper and it moved me forward.

INTERPRETER'S RENDITION: *Yes, it hit me and it moved me forward.*

ATTORNEY: What happened next?

INTERPRETER'S RENDITION: *What was that happened in a second?*

WITNESS: When I was crossing the street, a yellow Mustang was coming from there to here.

INTERPRETER'S RENDITION: *When I was crossing the street, a Mustang was coming from here to there.*

The above colloquy is the literal translation into English of a candidate's performance on an introductory consecutive interpreting section of the Washington State court interpreter certification exam. Needless to say, the candidate failed, because the candidate's rendition was inaccurate and inarticulate. What is distressing is that before failing the test, this candidate had interpreted for hundreds of misdemeanor and felony cases.

Good interpreters are hard to find because the job is very difficult. This chapter will profile the state court interpreter certification movement and explore methods of determining whether an interpreter is needed, selecting an interpreter, and working with interpreters.[1]

THE STATE COURT INTERPRETER CERTIFICATION MOVEMENT

In 1988, almost all jurisdictions relied on untrained, untested court interpreters; only the federal courts and the courts of California, Massachusetts, and New Mexico regulated the quality of court interpreting by requiring the testing and certification of court interpreters. New Jersey and Washington developed court interpreter programs soon after, and during the past ten years, another 14 states have instituted certification programs, largely by means of the State Court Interpreter Certification Consortium,[2] a cooperative test bank organized by the National Center for State Courts in 1995, which presently includes Colorado, Delaware, Florida, Hawaii, Idaho, Illinois, Maryland, Minnesota, New Mexico, New Jersey, Oregon, Utah, Virginia, Washington, and Wisconsin. The expansion of testing and certification is a result of the growing awareness of the crucial role of accurate interpretation in access to justice for non-English-speaking parties. Interpreter education, strangely lacking in most states' higher education systems, is generally regarded as the next step needed to improve the level of interpreting skills within a state.[3]

While 17 states have at least begun testing the qualifications of interpreters, 33 have not. Poor interpreting still remains a stumbling block in courts, even those with certification laws. Every interpreter law includes an "escape clause," which allows uncertified interpreters to be appointed at the judge's discretion, often on the ground that there is no certified interpreter available.[4] Due to economic factors and the lack of interpreter education, no certified court interpreters reside in many rural and some urban areas. Thus, a huge quantity of cases are still interpreted by untrained, uncertified interpreters. Through adoption of certification requirements by more states and the institution of effective education programs, court interpreting quality should improve dramatically during the next decade.

WHEN INTERPRETERS ARE NECESSARY

Nearly one out of every seven Americans over the age of five does not use English as a primary language. Of those 32 million persons, 43.9 percent speak English "less than 'very well.'" On any given day, over 150 different languages are spoken in the United States.[5]

In cases involving an immigrant party, there is often no question whether an interpreter is necessary. A majority of immigrants are not fluent in English when they arrive in the United States.[6] If the party speaks little English, the need for an interpreter is apparent. Non-English-speaking parties may be recent immigrants or migrant workers who have come to the U.S. only temporarily or, less commonly, they may be highly educated professionals.

Questions sometimes arise whether an immigrant party who speaks some English can proceed without an interpreter, especially if the party has resided in the United States for a number of years. Most immigrants are very eager to learn English and equally eager to use their English skills whenever possible. English as a Second Language (ESL) classes are filled to capacity,[7] and waiting lists are long in some communities. Even if an immigrant is able to get into an English class, there may be limits as to how well he or she can learn English. In some countries, children study English from an early age and are often quite proficient by the time they become teenagers. A good example is foreign exchange students who come to the U.S. with strong bilingual skills because they have formally studied English for most of their school years. On the other hand, adult immigrants who have never before studied English have an especially difficult time learning a new language. Studies have shown that the ability to acquire a new language drops sharply after puberty for most people. During adulthood, it is very difficult to absorb new syntax and grammar rules and master a foreign language's vocabulary and pronunciation.[8] Like American adults who study a foreign language for the first time, immigrants who take ESL courses may remain a long way from speaking the new language well no matter how hard they try.[9] In addition, ESL classes are often limited in duration, and many students do not have the opportunity to practice English due to the circumstances of their employment.[10]

Limited-English Speakers

As a result of language acquisition barriers, many immigrants, especially those who moved to the United States as adults, have mastered their second languages at a conversational level rather than at a "fully bilingual" level. For example, many immigrants are able to master conversational English, with or without grammar problems or heavy accents, so as to be able to talk with employers about job duties, go to the store, or converse with co-workers.[11] Their conversational ability in their *native* tongues is often much greater and may range up to much more complex linguistic levels.

Court language is much more difficult than conversational language. Several independent studies of the linguistic level of court language have concluded that it is at or beyond high school level, and legal terminology drives up the difficulty level even further.[12] For an immigrant party to be considered bilingual in a legal proceeding, the party's language level should be at least at the 12th-grade level in both languages. In addition, to possess sufficient English skills to understand as much of the proceeding as an English speaker would, the immigrant party must possess the same familiarity with English legal terms as a native English speaker (for example, most U.S.-born people know the meaning of words like "jury," "defendant," "bail," "judgment," "prosecutor," and so forth). If limited-English-speaking parties do not understand English to this degree, they will miss a large percentage of what is being said unless interpreters are appointed.

There is no doubt that if a party is truly bilingual, appointing an interpreter is an unnecessary expense to the court, and hearing every question and statement twice may be considered an unfair advantage to the party. Though a request for an interpreter should be presumed to be bona fide,[13] when there is a question whether the party's English ability is adequate, voir dire of the limited-English-speaking party should be undertaken. Open-ended questions are recommended, calling for explanatory sentences rather than monosyllables. Watch for repeated vocabulary, grammar, and syntax errors in the party's answers. Those factors indicate a faulty grasp of English and an inability to fully participate in the proceeding without an interpreter.

Suggested questions for assessing bilingualism:

1. Please describe when and how you learned English.

2. What is your educational history, in the U.S. and in your original country?

3. Do you read and write English? Please tell us the last book, magazine, and/or newspaper you read in English.

4. Where do you speak English, and where do you speak your other language?

5. Please define these legal terms: bail, arrest, prosecutor, charge, evidence, etc. (and/or other relevant legal terms).

The court interpreter is the critical link in enabling full and meaningful participation of the non-English-speaking person in the proceedings. Failure to appoint an interpreter may have a profound effect not only on the non-English-speaking person but upon all participants and such impact may be of a constitutional magnitude.[14] Although appointment of an interpreter rests within the sound discretion of the court, application of a rebuttable presumption that an interpreter should be appointed for a non-English-speaking immigrant who requests one will assist the court in making its determination and will weigh in favor of appointment.[15]

Appointment of Interpreters

Appointing a skilled interpreter is the most important step in ensuring accurate interpretation. If an interpreter with appropriate credentials and experience is appointed, the interpreting process will probably go smoothly with minimal supervision by the judge. If an unskilled interpreter is appointed, the interpreting process cannot be adequate regardless of judicial supervision. Unfortunately, by the time a proposed interpreter is evaluated by the judge immediately before a hearing or trial, rejection of a proposed interpreter may be difficult. For this reason, the method of *obtaining* an interpreter is a determinative step in the appointment of a skilled interpreter. Judges and court administrators should closely supervise processes used to contact court interpreters.

First, in order to contact skilled interpreters, the process for alerting the court that an interpreter is necessary must be timely. In criminal cases, the court is often advised of the need for an interpreter by law enforcement or counsel. In civil cases, usually the non-English-speaking parties or their attorneys advise the court that interpreters should be appointed. However, in many court systems, notification of the need for a court interpreter for criminal or civil cases may not be given to the appropriate court employee until soon before the hearing. This can result in a scramble to find an immediately available interpreter rather than a certified or highly qualified interpreter. Implementing an early notification process allows court personnel more time to find the best interpreter for the hearing.

In court systems in which bail determinations are based on information verified and prepared by court or law enforcement personnel, it is important that interpreters be available during the pretrial interview and verification process. A recent study concluded that one factor contributing to racial and ethnic disparities in felony case pretrial release is that "cultural differences bring problems of language and communication that make verification of employment or residence, or other evidence of ties to the local community problematic. Yet ties to the community are critical in judicial determinations of pretrial release and the setting of bail."[16]

Though some court interpreters are full-time employees, in most states many interpreters are independent contractors who are hired by courts to interpret for one or a handful of cases. Courts obtain these independent contractor interpreters in various ways.

Court Employees Obtain Interpreters. In many jurisdictions, court employees obtain interpreters by calling them directly from a list of certified or previously employed interpreters. This system avoids bias because it is clear that the court is hiring the interpreter and results in high-quality interpreting if the court insists on certified or highly qualified interpreters. However, this system depends on the commitment of the court employee to search out, often on short notice, the best interpreters available. Employees who are provided training on language issues and are aware of the critical importance of the interpreter's role are more readily able to obtain high-quality interpreters efficiently and effectively.

Courts can substantially improve their interpreter lists through active recruitment of interpreters. Potential court interpreters may be available through the local community college or through inquiry at immigrant organizations regarding excellent speakers of the native language who are bilingual. Telephone interpreting can also result in high-quality court interpreting for non-evidentiary hearings; however, proposed telephone interpreters should be closely questioned regarding their qualifications.[17]

Attorneys Obtain Interpreters. In some jurisdictions, counsel for the non-English-speaking party obtains the interpreter, who is then appointed by the court at the hearing. The obvious danger in this arrangement is the interpreter's real or apparent bias in favor of the party who arranged the interpreter's employment. If counsel directly pays the interpreter, the appearance of bias is even stronger. Judges should scrupulously voir dire and formally appoint interpreters in these situations to make it clear that the interpreter is working for the court, not the party.

Agencies Obtain Interpreters. In some jurisdictions, nonprofit or profit-making interpreting agencies are called by the courts to supply court interpreters. Agency-supplied interpreters may cost more per hour than free-lance interpreters. Because a percentage of the hourly rate the court pays usually goes to the agency, the hourly rate the agency interpreter earns may be lower than the amount a free-lance interpreter earns, which can impact the agency's ability to obtain certified or qualified interpreters. Some agencies interview and screen interpreters, others require no experience or credentials of their interpreters, and the quality of agency interpreters ranges from substandard to excellent. Like all other interpreters, it is critical that interpreters who have been obtained through an agency have their qualifications established in court.

Before appointing any interpreter, the judge should establish the interpreter's qualifications "on the record." At a minimum, the following questions are suggested as voir dire of the proposed interpreter:

1. Are you a certified court interpreter? Please show your official certified court interpreter identification. (The remaining questions are optional if the interpreter is certified.)

2. What languages do you speak?

3. When and how did you learn English and _____?

4. Describe your educational background in both languages, and your speaking, reading, and writing skills in each.[18]

5. Describe your court interpreting experience. When and where have you interpreted?

6. Describe any special court interpreter training you have attended.

7. Describe the simultaneous and consecutive methods of court interpreting.[19]

8. Please define in English a few legal terms, which will be used in this case, such as "negligence," "plaintiff," "defendant." What is the translation for these terms?

9. Do you know any of the parties or witnesses?

10. Are you a potential witness in this case?

11. Have you read and do you understand the ethics code? Briefly describe the main points.

12. Do you have any problems communicating with the party? If you haven't actually talked to the party, do you need a few minutes?

The proposed interpreter's answers should demonstrate, at a minimum, education or training in both languages, a knowledge of basic interpreting requirements, no apparent conflict of interest, a familiarity with legal terms, and previous interpreting experience. Once the proposed interpreter has been accepted, an oath should be administered.[20]

Working with Interpreters during Proceedings

After the interpreter is sworn, it is helpful to advise the non-English-speaking party of the interpreter's role. Suggested explanations are that the interpreter works for the judge, that the interpreter's job is to interpret everything the party says into English and everything else said in court into the party's language, that the interpreter cannot give any explanations or legal advice, and that if the party doesn't understand the interpreter the party should tell the judge.[21] This provides important information to the non-English-speaking party, who most likely has no conception of the interpreter's role. As many judges and interpreters are aware, a large percentage of non-English-speaking parties mistakenly assume that the interpreter's role is to assist them in a multitude of ways. When parties are unrepresented, they are even more likely to treat interpreters as advocates.

Juries should also be told at the outset about the interpreter's role. One Seattle interpreter who was not introduced to a jury reports that a juror approached her after the trial to tell her the jury was glad that she, who they assumed to be the defendant's mother, had been able to sit next to him and give him encouragement throughout the trial!

During the trial, the judge should frequently check whether the interpreter is constantly talking, using simultaneous interpreting to convey the entire proceeding to the non-English-speaking party and consecutive interpreting for witnesses. Observing the interpreter's posturing during the hearing is also important. Unskilled interpreters sometimes suggest answers with body language, such as slight nods or eye expressions. Interpreters should be carefully observed and directed to interpret everything if they are not doing so, which is evidence of poor interpreting skills.

Another indication of inadequate interpreting is confusing answers by witnesses or the necessity to keep repeating questions. As pointed out in the Introduction, if there are a number of unresponsive answers, the interpreter likely is having problems communicating with the party. If a non-English-speaking party seems to have communication problems, one approach is to explain through the interpreter that the party has the right to hear everything being said and then ask how well the party understands what is being said.

If the party's answers are unsatisfactory, another interpreter should be called to interpret.

Attorneys may need reminders during interpreted hearings. If an attorney speaks very quickly, especially when using technical language, the interpreter may request the judge to have the attorney slow down. This is especially likely to happen if a relatively inexperienced interpreter has been appointed. On the other hand, it is important not to slow down the hearing too much, which may cause witnesses and attorneys to change their phraseology to the detriment of the process. Interpreter tests require candidates to demonstrate their ability to handle upwards of 40-word sentences when interpreting testimony—one gauge of a competent interpreter.

Judges need to be aware of the interpreter's human limitations. One common problem occurs when two speakers talk at once. The judge should announce that the interpreter can only interpret one voice at a time. Judges should allow for recesses for interpreters to keep their minds fresh and to keep them from talking nonstop for hours, and not allow interpreters to be pressed into service by counsel during every regular break. The United Nations and the federal courts have determined that interpreters who perform simultaneous interpreting start losing efficiency after about 30 minutes.[22]

INTERPRETER ETHICS

Usually, no one else in the courtroom is able to speak both languages, and court interpreters are put in the position of constantly choosing between upholding the standards of ethics or undermining them, knowing that no one will be the wiser. It is for this reason that court interpreters are in a special position of trust.

An ethics code is usually one of the first steps taken by a jurisdiction to regulate court interpreting. In the absence of such guidelines, untrained and unskilled interpreters are unable to appreciate their responsibilities and role as officers of the court. Additionally, ethics codes provide the judiciary and counsel with standards of performance by which to hold interpreters accountable. Although enforcement procedures have not generally been adopted, individual courts have addressed ethics violations on a case-by-case basis through common law and statutory contempt proceedings.

The Model Code of Professional Responsibility for Interpreters in the Judiciary, drafted in 1993 by a group of judges, lawyers, certified court interpreters, and court administrators, reflects common provisions found in various state codes and has been adopted by several states. It is reprinted in its entirety in Appendix 3. The following is a discussion of each ethics canon and a description of selected typical problems that frequently arise in courts.

Canon I: Accuracy and Completeness

Interpreters shall render a complete and accurate interpretation or sight translation, without altering, omitting, or adding anything to what is stated or written, and without explanation.

Usage: Uncertified interpreters' undetected alteration of material is one of the most frequent complaints of judges, non-English-speaking parties, newspaper reporters, and auditors examining court interpreters. Every known court and news audit has found similar interpreting distortions in legal proceedings where uncertified, untrained court interpreters are used. For example, the Grand Rapids Press audited Michigan courts in a six-month investigation in 1992 and 1993, finding cases in which the word "shoot" was elevated to "kill," or a "car" became a "couch," and routinely found interpreters leaving out phrases and changing key words, even in murder trials.[23] In 1989, the *San Jose Mercury News* conducted an audit of interpreting in many California courts. Omissions and inaccuracies abounded throughout the interpreted proceedings, such as "no" for "as for the Vietnamese, I never associate with them," and "I say" for "oh God!" Soon after the newspaper audit, California revamped its certification laws.

A 1988 Washington State Court Interpreter Task Force audit found that many untrained, uncertified interpreters in the state courts regularly left out large portions of what was said in court and inaccurately interpreted testimony; for example, "I will aim at you" was interpreted as "I will kill you" in a murder trial.[24] Following the audit, the Washington legislature passed its certification law.

Since interpreters' statements are almost never recorded, appeal on the basis of distorted testimony or the defendant's inability to hear what was said in the proceeding is often difficult, if not impossible.[25] A few appeals have been based on defendants' assertions of what they heard in the court proceeding due to the absence of a record. Non-English-speaking parties have successfully shown that guilty pleas may be invalid if the interpreter did not accurately interpret all the required elements of the case,[26] and that the defendant's conviction should be overturned on grounds of ineffectiveness of counsel if the interpreter fails to interpret the entire proceedings to the defendant.[27]

The best way to avoid inaccurate interpreting is to appoint a certified interpreter, if possible. If none is available, establishing the interpreter's qualifications on the record before appointment and emphasizing the interpreter's obligation to follow ethical precepts is very important.

Whether or not the appointed interpreter is certified, it is recommended that courts consider making a record of the interpretation. Recording the interpreter's words will establish accountability, which may otherwise be missing since no one other than the interpreter usually understands both languages. In addition, the recording can provide a record for appeal that is much more reliable than the statements of the interested parties and the interpreter.

Canon II: Representation of Qualifications

Interpreters shall accurately and completely represent their certifications, training, and pertinent experience.

Usage: Interpreters should produce an official card or other proof of certification when they are appointed. Unfortunately, states with certification programs have found that it is easy for uncertified interpreters to produce business cards or resumes asserting that they are certified. This happened with enough frequency in California that legislation was introduced in 1997 to make certification misrepresentation a misdemeanor.[28] Since the interpreter is largely unsupervised, an interpreter who makes a misrepresentation to the court should never be approved.

Canon III: Impartiality and Avoidance of Conflict of Interest

Interpreters shall be impartial and unbiased and shall refrain from conduct that may give an appearance of bias. Interpreters shall disclose any real or perceived conflict of interest.

Usage: Interpreters should never interpret in a case involving a friend, relative, or associate. Interpreter ethics codes recognize that bias can subconsciously affect interpreters' word choices and language use even if the interpreters insist in good faith that they can overcome it. A narrow exception may apply if the party, due to the rarity of a dialect or other barriers, cannot communicate with anyone other than the associate. In such cases, the proposed interpreter should be oriented to ethics standards and the court interpreter role. Orientation videos can be used for this purpose (see note 37).

Most commonly in civil cases and cases where no interpreter has been called, friends or relatives are sometimes appointed by courts in order to save time or money. When this happens, the court will invariably hear not what the party is saying but what the friend thinks the facts should be. Moreover, when the interpreter is selected and paid by one of the parties, rather than the court, judges should be very careful in appointing them.[29]

Appearance of fairness requires that, beyond actual bias, the interpreter not appear to favor one side. For example, law enforcement officers serving as court interpreters are commonly perceived not to be impartial. The appearance of bias can also be subtly created by an interpreter's behavior inside the courtroom. Court interpreters can create the impression that they are associated with one side when they carry out favors for attorneys (such as delivering papers or messages),[30] converse with parties or attorneys, or try to "help" non-English-speaking parties by providing transportation or making appointments. Interpreters are frequently asked by judges and attorneys to perform such tasks.

In addition to following protocol established by the court, interpreters should refrain from conduct outside the court that makes them appear biased. The integrity of the justice system can be jeopardized, for example, when interpreters associate socially with persons for whom they interpret or with counsel,[31] because an interpreter's neutral attitude toward each side must be and appear to be unquestionable.

Canon IV: Professional Demeanor

Interpreters shall conduct themselves in a manner consistent with the dignity of the court and shall be as unobtrusive as possible.

Usage: The focus of attention should be on the non-English-speaking party or witness, not the interpreter. For example, juries are less able to assess a party's credibility if court interpreters block the jury's view of the non-English-speaking party. Judges should make sure the jury is looking at the witness, not the interpreter, so they don't miss the witness's expression.[32] Many certified interpreters use electronic equipment during simultaneous interpreting, which allows them to sit a few feet away, underscoring their status as unobtrusive court officers.

Canon V: Confidentiality

Interpreters shall protect the confidentiality of all privileged and other confidential information.

Usage: This canon protects interpreters from counsel or others who seek to obtain information or testimony from them. Court interpreters commonly complain that opposing counsel asks them for inside information about attorney interviews with the non-English-speaking party, either informally or by calling them as witnesses. Interpreters are required to assert the attorney-client privilege in either instance. Unless subpoenaed as a witness and ordered by the court to testify, they must refuse to reveal privileged information. The attorney-client privilege requires interpreters not to comment on their observations, such as the party's ability to understand English or other factors that the interpreter noticed during attorney-client interviews, as well as the content of the interview.[33] In addition to the obvious need to preserve attorney-client privilege, interpreters are probably not as good a source of case information as they might seem. Experienced interpreters maintain that interpreters are a poor source of information, since during the many hours of interpreting they perform during the week, the facts they hear go "in one ear and out the other," making the accuracy of their recollections problematic.[34]

Canon VI: Restriction of Public Comment

Interpreters shall not publicly discuss, report, or offer an opinion concerning a matter in which they are or have been engaged, even when that information is not privileged or required by law to be confidential.

Usage: Untrained or irresponsible court interpreters can do damage to the integrity of the judicial system by publicly commenting on court cases. For example, after a recent Washington murder case, an uncertified court interpreter who served in the trial was reported in the newspaper to have concluded that the defendant's conviction was unjustified; he also put forth his own opinion of the case, based on his assessment of the evidence.[35] In addition to the harm caused by comments to the media, an indiscreet court interpreter who appears to be an expert on the U.S. legal system and on a particular trial can present a skewed view of cases and courts to an immigrant community.

Canon VII: Scope of Practice

Interpreters shall limit themselves to interpreting or translating, and shall not give legal advice, express personal opinions to individuals for whom they are interpreting, or engage in any other activities which may be construed to constitute a service other than interpreting or translating while serving as an interpreter.

Usage: Giving legal advice, explaining the proceedings to the non-English-speaking party, and acting as a "cultural ambassador" to patch up misunderstandings are frequent practices among uncertified, untrained interpreters.[36] Judges and counsel may err themselves by asking interpreters to provide such services. For example, attorneys may ask interpreters to explain the defendant's rights, fill out (and explain) forms with the defendant, or advise the defendant of appeal rights. Non-English-speaking defendants often ask interpreters whether they should plead guilty, ask for an attorney, waive a jury trial, and so forth. Interpreters' legal advice and explanations are frequently incorrect.[37] It is not uncommon for untrained, uncertified interpreters to use their position to pressure parties to plead guilty, even in the presence of the judge.[38]

The prohibition against interfering with the court process applies even if the interpreter knows something about the parties or case due to cultural, linguistic, or other factors. If an interpreter smells alcohol on a party's breath, for example, it is impermissible for the interpreter to advise the court;[39] if the interpreter is aware that a non-English-speaking defendant does not understand English-language court terms routinely used by the judge, it is improper for the interpreter to explain them to the party.

Canon VIII: Assessing and Reporting Impediments to Practice

Interpreters shall assess at all times their ability to deliver their services. When interpreters have any reservation about their ability to satisfy an assignment competently, they shall immediately convey that reservation to the appropriate judicial authority.

Usage: Many communication problems can be avoided if interpreters are permitted to engage in casual conversation unrelated to the case before the proceeding begins, with the understanding that they will report communication difficulties to the judge. Santiago Ventura Morales's murder trial might have had a different result if his two Spanish interpreters had reported to the judge that they couldn't understand many of his statements. In addition, interpreters alone are able to evaluate their ability to communicate with non-English speaking parties. This canon requires interpreters to advise the court if they do not understand a word or phrase, rather than just skip over it. At interpreter orientation workshops, interpreters are encouraged to always bring dictionaries to court and to request permission to look up unfamiliar words.

Canon IX. Ethical Violations

Interpreters shall report to the proper judicial authority any effort to impede their compliance with any law, any provision of this code, or any other official policy governing court interpreting and legal translating.

Usage: As discussed above, many interpreters tell stories about attorneys' attempts to persuade them to violate ethics codes by providing legal advice or explanations to their clients, or about occasional pressure to reveal privileged information by overly zealous opposing counsel. This section states the interpreter's duty to report such attempts to the judge. Most often used by interpreters as a "shield," it underscores the judge's supervisory role over court interpretation.

Canon X. Professional Development

Interpreters shall continually improve their skills and knowledge and advance the profession through activities such as professional training and education, and interaction with colleagues and specialists in related fields.

Usage: Several states have initiated mandatory continuing education requirements for certified interpreters. California requires continuing education of uncertified as well as certified interpreters, and California and Washington require certified interpreters to report a minimum number of interpreting hours spent in court each year. Professional interpreting organizations exist in many states as well as on the federal level. Through such means, the court interpreting field is metamorphosing from its ad hoc status of 25 years ago into a highly respected profession.

CONCLUSION

When a non-English-speaking immigrant is a party to a legal proceeding, the interpreter's role is pivotal. Selecting a certified interpreter if possible, and if not, a truly qualified interpreter, is a prerequisite to the party's access to justice. The fairness of proceedings often depends on knowledgeable judicial supervision of the interpreter. With quality interpreting, accurate communication with the non-English-speaking party can become a reality.

Immigration Information for Criminal Cases in State Courts

by Norton Tooby

High on the list of problems faced by immigrants in United States courts is the danger of suffering unforeseen adverse immigration consequences resulting from a criminal conviction, even if the conviction is a very minor one. Often, the defendant is unaware until after the sentence has been served and an INS hold is placed that deportation proceedings have been started on the basis of the conviction.

The validity of the criminal conviction cannot be contested in immigration court.[1] Frequently, no action can be taken to avoid deportation, so long as the conviction remains intact. As a result, the immigrant may face mandatory loss of lawful permanent resident status, mandatory deportation, and permanent exclusion from readmission to the United States as a result of the criminal conviction.

For example, federal immigration law classifies the second conviction of simple possession of 40 grams of marijuana as an "Aggravated Felony," even if the state conviction may be no more than a state misdemeanor, because it would be a felony under one of the federal statutes.[2] Aggravated felony convictions, no matter how minor they may be in fact, invariably trigger mandatory deportation.

Similarly, a domestic violence misdemeanor may trigger mandatory deportation for an immigrant, regardless of the wishes of the spouse and family. A civil or criminal court finding that an immigrant has violated a domestic violence protective order likewise will cause deportation.[3]

Federal immigration laws are a patchwork of mostly mandatory laws, which, generally, are applied to criminal aliens without consideration of how long they have lived in the United States, whether they have lawful status or family members who are citizens, and the like. This chapter will offer suggestions for ensuring that immigrants and their families are aware of the immigration consequences of a criminal conviction before they make decisions about their cases. It will also provide an overview of immigration information for parties, judges, prosecutors, and defense counsel, for the purpose of learning in advance the immigration consequences of minor and not-so-minor criminal convictions.

COURTS CAN ALERT IMMIGRANT DEFENDANTS

There are two approaches to alerting the defendant of immigration consequences. First, statutes in many states require the court routinely to advise immigrant defendants of the potential immigration consequences of pleading guilty. Second, in a number of states, judicial decisions have established a standard of competent representation for defense attorneys requiring them to investigate and inform their clients of the immigration consequences before a plea.

At least 15 states have adopted statutes or court rules requiring the court to warn criminal defendants before accepting a plea that a conviction may affect their immigration status or result in deportation, exclusion from admission to the United States, or denial of naturalization.[4] Many statutes require the court to vacate a guilty plea if the court failed to give the defendant the required warning. Several also require the court to continue the case to give the defendant time to consult with counsel after hearing the statutory warning. Even in the absence of a statute requiring a warning, many courts administer one, since "justice to alien defendants can only be enhanced if the trial courts make sure such defendants know the [laws] ... under which they plead."[5]

With its large immigrant population, California has adopted a comprehensive statute to govern these issues:

> The Legislature finds and declares that in many instances involving an individual who is not a citizen of the United States charged with an offense punishable as a crime under state law, a plea of guilty or nolo contendere is entered without the defendant knowing that a conviction of such offense is grounds for deportation, exclusion from admission to the United States,

or denial of naturalization pursuant to the laws of the United States. Therefore, it is the intent of the Legislature in enacting this section to promote fairness to such accused individuals by requiring in such cases that acceptance of a guilty plea or plea of nolo contendere be preceded by an appropriate warning of the special consequences for such a defendant which may result from the plea. It is also the intent of the Legislature that the court in such cases shall grant the defendant a reasonable amount of time to negotiate with the prosecuting agency in the event the defendant or the defendant's counsel was unaware of the possibility of deportation, exclusion from admission to the United States, or denial of naturalization as a result of conviction. It is further the intent of the Legislature that at the time of the plea no defendant shall be required to disclose his or her legal status to the court. —California Penal Code § 1016.5(d)

This statute recognizes the defendant's need to understand the consequences of the plea by requiring the court to warn the defendant of the potential immigration consequences and allowing for a continuance to permit negotiations with the prosecutor. If the warning is not given, it requires that the plea be vacated to allow the defendant to renegotiate the case, this time with full knowledge of the immigration consequences. These provisions are similar to those of Hawaii and Ohio statutes.

Even without such a statute, a criminal judge may ensure that criminal defendants are warned of the potential immigration consequences prior to acceptance of a plea by telling the defendant about the possibility of adverse immigration effects and granting time for the defendant to check out the exact consequences with counsel. Many courts take these steps, in recognition of the fact that "deportation is a drastic measure and at times the equivalent of banishment or exile."[6]

EFFECTIVE REPRESENTATION OF IMMIGRANT DEFENDANTS

Case law in many states holds that defense counsel representing an immigrant criminal defendant has the duty to advise the defendant of the immigration consequences the defendant faces if convicted.[7] The effective assistance of counsel issue can come before the court in two ways in cases involving noncitizens. First, new counsel may file a petition for post-conviction relief from a conviction on the grounds original counsel rendered ineffective assistance of counsel.[8] Second, an increasing number of judges are exercising vigilance to prevent invalid convictions from occurring in the first place by monitoring counsel's performance to some extent during the proceedings.[9]

In other states, courts have stated that counsel's failure to investigate or advise the defendant of immigration consequences before the defendant pleads guilty is not ineffective assistance of counsel.[10] These cases are often based on the collateral consequences doctrine, holding that immigration proceedings are civil proceedings and therefore of a collateral nature.

Despite the lack of consensus among state courts, courts have noted that even in the absence of ineffective counsel precedent, "it is highly desirable that both state and federal counsel develop the practice of advising defendants of the collateral [immigration] consequences of pleading guilty"[11] as a matter of fairness.

Because ineffective assistance of counsel for failure to prevent serious immigration damage from minor convictions is an increasing ground for vacating criminal convictions in many states, courts may wish to review the steps counsel should take to accurately advise an alien defendant of immigration consequences. For a summary, see Appendix 6.

IMMIGRATION CONSEQUENCES OF ADULT CONVICTIONS

During the 1990s, Congress rewrote immigration laws a number of times, including two major pieces of legislation in 1996, to expand both the kinds of criminal behavior that trigger immigration penalties and the severity of those penalties.[12] This section will give a brief overview of current law governing the immigration consequences of crimes. More detail on this subject can be found in Appendix 6.

The immigration consequences of adult convictions depend heavily on the immigration status of the defendant. Most immigrants fall into one of two categories: (a) lawful permanent residents, or (b) undocumented immigrants.

For lawful permanent residents, the top priority is to avoid becoming deportable. Under 1996 immigration laws, the new term is "removable." Other immigration consequences, such as becoming "inadmissible" (the old term was "excludable"), may be of less or no real importance to them, although many lawful immigrants who have held permanent resident status for five years are rightly concerned to avoid forfeiting eligibility for naturalized citizenship, which may happen if they become inadmissible.

In addition, lawful residents who are inadmissible (even if not deportable) may not be able to visit relatives in their native countries, since the Border Patrol could refuse to "admit" them into the United States when they return.

Immigrants who are presently undocumented may still place importance on the immigration consequences of criminal cases. It is true they are deportable already because of the lack of documents, regardless of the outcome of the criminal cases. But they may have lived here for many years, have families who are U.S. citizens or lawful immigrants, and care very deeply about obtaining lawful immigration status, which they can obtain only if they avoid becoming "inadmissible."

There are a dozen other immigration statuses, or forms of immigration relief or benefits, each with its own crime-related requirements.[13] That is why it is necessary for defendants to check with counsel to determine the specific risks and opportunities for their particular situations.

Most adverse immigration consequences flow from criminal convictions. A juvenile court finding is not considered a conviction, and a case that is on appeal is not considered a final conviction until the appeal has been completed. Only at that point may the Immigration and Naturalization Service begin deportation proceedings based on that conviction. Obviously, acquittals and dismissals do not constitute convictions. If a conviction occurs, and the case is later given a technical dismissal for successful completion of probation, for example, the situation is more complicated. The INS may or may not continue to regard the conviction as a conviction, as more fully described in Appendix 6.

Several categories of criminal convictions can trigger adverse immigration consequences. They are described here and are examined in more detail in Appendix 6.

Aggravated Felonies: Mandatory Loss of Status

"Aggravated felonies" trigger mandatory loss of lawful status, mandatory deportation (with no hope of any discretionary relief in immigration court), and permanent inadmissibility. Moreover, if the immigrant returns illegally following deportation after such a conviction, the aggravated penalties for the federal offense of illegal re-entry rise to a maximum of 20 years and a minimum of six or seven (depending on criminal history). When the immigrant is transferred from criminal custody into INS custody, the law prohibits release on immigration bond.

Despite the name of this category, the offense does not necessarily need to be either aggravated or a felony. A second offense misdemeanor such as simple possession of any amount of any controlled substance, for example, qualifies as an "aggravated felony." The most common aggravated felonies include:

1. Virtually any drug offense except first-offense simple possession.

A conviction of accessory after the fact to the sale of drugs would not be considered a drug offense so long as the defendant was not ordered to serve one year or more in custody.[14] See section "Other Drug Offenses," below.

2. The following offenses, *but only if custody of one year or more was ordered:*

- A "crime of violence" as defined in 18 USC § 16 (the definition of a "crime of violence" is quite broad)[15]
- Driving under the influence[16]
- A theft offense (including receipt of stolen property)
- Burglary
- Offenses relating to commercial bribery, counterfeiting, forgery, or trafficking in vehicles with altered identification numbers
- An offense relating to obstruction of justice, perjury or subornation of perjury, or bribery of a witness
- Using fraudulent documents to obtain an immigration benefit (except for a first offense to help an immediate family member)[17]

These offenses will not be considered aggravated felonies if no specific state prison (or one year county jail) sentence is imposed, and the defendant does not receive more than 364 days in custody as a condition of probation, even if several of these are "stacked" with consecutive sentences of 364 days or less for each.

3. Murder, rape, or sexual abuse of a minor.[18] Statutory rape probably will be held to constitute sexual abuse of a minor.

These are only the most common. Another 20 or 30 offenses are also listed; see Appendix 6 for a more complete list. It is important to note that misdemeanors can be aggravated felonies if other requirements are met.[19]

If there is no aggravated felony conviction, discretionary relief may be available in immigration court for other deportable convictions.

Other Drug Offenses

Any offense involving a federally controlled substance will trigger deportability. A conviction of first-offense simple possession, while not an aggravated felony, is in most cases still a basis for deportation (except simple possession for personal use of 30 grams or less of marijuana).[20] In many cases, expungement (i.e., a technical dismissal for satisfactory performance on probation under circumstances in which an expungement would be available in federal court under 18 USC § 3607) will eliminate a single conviction for first-offense simple possession.[21] (Any drug conviction will render the immigrant inadmissible, except first offense simple possession of 30 grams or less of marijuana for which a hardship waiver may be available.)

Crimes of Moral Turpitude

Crimes of Moral Turpitude (CMT), such as theft involving intent to defraud or inflict serious injury, etc., can trigger deportation as well. One CMT within five years of the immigrants' receipt of lawful resident status, or two CMTs at any time, will trigger deportability, but the long-term lawful immigrant would be eligible to apply in immigration court for a waiver of this ground of deportation. (Any CMT renders an immigrant inadmissible and ineligible to naturalize if it occurred within the five-year period before the naturalization application is filed.)

Firearms Conviction

Any firearms conviction will trigger deportation, but not inadmissibility. But the immigrant with seven years' lawful residence can apply for a waiver in immigration court. (A conviction for felon in possession of a firearm, however, constitutes an aggravated felony, for which no relief is available in immigration court.)

Domestic Violence Conviction

Any domestic violence conviction, or civil court finding of violation of a domestic violence order, will trigger deportation, but not inadmissibility. The immigrant with seven years' lawful residence can apply for a waiver in immigration court.

Finally, there are some grounds of deportation, and quite a few grounds of inadmissibility, that depend on conduct rather than a conviction. Since these do not depend on a conviction, they are described in Appendix 6.

POST-CONVICTION RELIEF

When immigrants plead guilty without being informed of the immigration effect of the conviction, the availability of post-conviction relief may be critical. Vacating or expunging unlawful prior convictions can sometimes prevent immigration consequences from being triggered. When an immigrant seeks to vacate a conviction, original defense counsel may be faced with claims of ineffective assistance of counsel, and the prosecutor may be required to exercise prosecutorial discretion. Hopefully, all participants can cooperate in cases where post-conviction relief is appropriate.

Vacating the conviction in its entirety, by direct appeal, habeas corpus, coram nobis, motion to withdraw the plea or vacate the conviction, or the like, will eliminate any adverse immigration consequences (along with all other consequences) flowing from the conviction.[22] When a judgment is vacated, the conviction is eliminated *ab initio,* as having been illegal from the time it was imposed.[23]

Vacating the judgment will also eliminate the effect of any sentence or imprisonment resulting from the conviction. Moreover, a petition for extraordinary writ may be brought simply for purposes of vacating the original sentence and obtaining a fresh sentencing hearing. The new sentence will be the one evaluated by the immigration authorities, even if the defendant has already completed the original sentence.[24]

Expunging a conviction has the effect of eliminating convictions of crimes of moral turpitude for immigration purposes. An expungement also eliminates a first-offense conviction for simple possession of drugs, even if it is a felony.[25] It is also sometimes possible for a court to grant appropriate punishment, but only a short period of probation for the current offense, to allow quick expungement to eliminate its immigration effects. At present, the effect of an expungement on a firearms conviction or an aggravated felony is uncertain.

CONCLUSION

Noncitizen defendants should know the immigration consequences they face. As established by the Supreme Court, deportation is a drastic measure, at times equivalent to banishment or exile. When deportation is imminent, it is too late for the defendant to address the situation. This quandary is preventable if judges and attorneys take a few key steps to ensure that the defendant is adequately advised of potential immigration consequences of the charge before a plea is entered.

Law and Legal Culture in China

by Pitman B. Potter

Many legal concepts used in China today derive from traditional Chinese law.[1] For example, a traditional Chinese view retained by the People's Republic of China (PRC) holds that law should be used by government as an instrument of rule, rather than a source of citizens' rights. As a result, law in the PRC is influenced strongly by current government priorities. Modern Chinese law also incorporates the traditional view that law should be concerned more with regulating public relationships between individuals or groups and the government than with governing private relationships between and among individuals or groups themselves. Thus, economic and business relationships tend to be governed mainly by public rules issued by administrative agencies, rather than by laws. This approach is similar to that of the former Soviet Union, but very different from the "private law" tradition of Europe and North America.

The legal system of the PRC also has been somewhat influenced by the laws of the Republic of China (founded in 1911 and removed to Taiwan in 1949). This is evident in the organization of modern PRC judicial institutions. Courts in the PRC are components of the administrative bureaucracy of government. This structure, influenced by the European civilian tradition, lacks the principle of separation of powers. Judicial institutions have committees of the Communist Party of China (CPC) attached to them, in much the same way that courts under the Republic of China had Nationalist Party Committees attached to them. As well, PRC law tends to emphasize codification rather than common law and *stare decisis.*

Ed. note: The boxed quotations in the margins have been added by the editors and represent the opinions of focus group members or other quoted individuals and do not necessarily represent the views of the authors, editors, or publisher.

DEVELOPMENT OF PRC LAW

The history of Chinese law[2] after 1949 can be divided into four broad time periods: the period of state-building (1949–57); the period of economic and political crisis (1957–66); the Cultural Revolution period (1966–76); and the post-Mao reform period (1976–present).

Period of State-Building (1949–57)

Chinese law during the period of state-building incorporated two main components: consolidation of power and establishment of government. The Chinese communists came to power in China with a revolutionary program. This meant the elimination of all opponents of communism and the establishment of a revolutionary socialist system in which private property was gradually eliminated. Laws were introduced to achieve these goals. Regulations were issued redistributing land to the peasantry while also restricting the business activities of the old merchant classes. The central government asserted tighter control over the economy. A marriage law was enacted that recognized greater rights for women. Regulations were enacted that punished "counter-revolutionaries." Through these and other methods, the new communist government used the legal system to strengthen its power and eliminate the last vestiges of the previous regime.

During the period of state-building, the new government also focused on establishing a formal legal system. A state constitution was enacted in 1954 that set forth the basic structure of government. Administrative regulations were passed on criminal law questions and on the organization of the courts and other government bodies. Codes of criminal procedure and civil law were debated. Law schools were established and the training of judges and lawyers was formalized. By 1956, a basis had been laid for a national legal system.

Period of Crisis (1957–66) and
the Cultural Revolution Period (1966–76)

The next two periods of Chinese law were characterized by crisis and the undermining of law and legal institutions. In 1957, the government launched the Hundred Flowers campaign in which Chinese intellectuals were encouraged to criticize the government. Unfortunately, many lawyers and judges who did criticize the government during this time were arrested and imprisoned during the "Anti-Rightist" campaign of 1958. The law schools were disciplined, as were the courts and the People's Procuracy, an organ whose function was to ensure that criminal prosecutions were being handled according to law. Legislative activity was sharply curtailed, and the rule of law generally was replaced by politics. Between 1966 and 1976, during the period of the Cultural Revolution, the decline in influence of law and legal institutions was accelerated. Legal institutions were actually closed and legal scholars and professionals suffered direct persecution.

Post-Mao Reform Period (1976-present)

After the death of Mao Zedong and the end of the Cultural Revolution, and particularly following the Third Plenum of the 11th CPC Central Committee during 1978, an effort was begun to revitalize the Chinese legal system. This was part of a larger effort to bring about economic and political reform. A host of legislation was enacted, governing such diverse areas as economic and business activities, social life, political procedures, criminal law, and foreign trade and investment. The courts were re-established, along with the People's Procuracy. The law schools began admitting students again, and persecution of judicial personnel eased. Many legal intellectuals who had been imprisoned in the Anti-Rightist campaign were released and their records cleared. This period of reform continues today, although political crises like the Tiananmen massacre of June 1989 continue to intrude periodically.

Basic Chinese Legal Institutions

China does not have a federal system of government,[3] but rather is organized as a unitary state where higher-level legislative as well as administrative organs have direct authority over their counterpart institutions at lower levels in the hierarchy. As well, the CPC, through its network of committees and Party Secretaries, has significant control over personnel and policy decisions at all levels. In this context, the Chinese legal system encompasses several major institutions, most notably the National People's Congress, the People's Courts,

> **"The Party can destroy laws made by magistrates or by government."**
> — *Chinese focus group*

the Public Security Bureau, the People's Procuracy, and the Ministry of Justice, each of which has different functions and responsibilities.

The National People's Congress. The National People's Congress (NPC), the supreme legislative body, enacts all laws that have national application, while the local people's congresses enact local legislation subject to the parameters of national law. Many committees debate and draft specific types of laws, but most legislative work is coordinated by the NPC's Legal Affairs Committee. While the NPC is theoretically an independent body, it is heavily influenced by the Chinese Communist Party, which often initiates legislation, decides most major issues of policy, and in effect has veto power over enactments of the NPC and local people's congresses. Delegates to the NPC are elected from lower-level people's congresses, although many deputies are appointed. Deputies to local people's congresses are generally selected through a relatively competitive election system, although many are also appointed.

People's Courts. There are several different types of courts in China, including the People's Courts, the Maritime Courts, and the Railroad Courts. Of these, the People's Courts are most important. The People's Courts are not courts of general jurisdiction, but rather have different specialized chambers that handle cases in distinct subject areas, such as criminal law, civil law, economic law, foreign business law, intellectual property law, and administrative law. The People's Courts are divided into four levels: Supreme People's Court, Higher Level People's Courts, Intermediate Level People's Courts, and Basic Level People's Courts.

Public Security Bureau. The Public Security Bureau (PSB) is charged with investigating crimes and arresting criminal suspects. As China's criminal law covers a wide array of possible offenses, and because state surveillance remains an integral part of the social control apparatus, the PSB is active in virtually all aspects of Chinese life. The PSB is also responsible for approving foreign travel by Chinese citizens and granting permission in foreigners' visa extension matters.

People's Procuracy. The Procuracy is charged with handling criminal prosecutions. Thus, after the Public Security Bureau has made an arrest, the Procuracy examines the evidence and determines whether the defendant should be brought to trial or released. The Procuracy is also responsible for supervising the work of the People's Courts, in civil and economic cases. Procuracy offices exist at the central, provincial, prefecture, and in some cases, district/county level.

Ministry of Justice. The Ministry of Justice is responsible for all aspects of judicial administration and education. This includes handling legal education and supervising the work of courts, procuracies, notaries, and lawyers. While in theory the Ministry's responsibilities involve most aspects of the legal system in China, in practice it is mainly involved in supervising lawyers and notaries.

CHINESE LEGAL SYSTEM

The process of enacting laws and regulations in China continues in response to the policy goals of the Chinese Communist Party and the government.

Constitutional Principles

The fourth and most recent Chinese constitution, enacted in 1982 and revised in 1993, describes the basic rights and duties of citizens. In contrast to the constitutions of most Western industrialized democracies, constitutional rights in China are not inherent, but rather are granted by the government subject to limiting conditions. Citizens must uphold various duties to support the Communist Party of China and socialism as a pre-

> **Basically the Chinese are as law-abiding as Americans, but because the Chinese are governed by social norms, these are more adhered to than laws.**
>
> — *Chinese focus group*

condition to enjoying their constitutionally mandated rights concerning speech, assembly, religion, and so on.

The Chinese Constitution provides that all are equal before the law, thus expressing the ideal that even high officials must obey the law, although this provision does not prohibit the government from enacting legislation or regulations that treat different classes of people differently. The Constitution also prescribes the basic organization of the Chinese government, including the National People's Congress, the State Council, the People's Courts, and the People's Procuracy.

Corruption and Reform

Although empirical data is difficult to come by, it has frequently been reported that corruption exists in significant proportions throughout the Chinese legal system. The frequency with which private parties seek *ex-parte* contacts with judges is high. It is also common for litigants to provide presents and other inducements to judges. Although efforts are being made in China to resolve the corruption problem, it is widespread throughout the society, and the courts are not immune.

The past 15 years of legal and judicial reform in China have seen the enactment of many laws and regulations covering virtually every area of Chinese life. In an effort to build legitimacy and in order to lend greater predictability and certainty to the state's management of the society and economy, the Chinese government and the CPC have expressed a limited commitment to subjecting their political and administrative rule to a modicum of legal restraint. However, significant problems remain with the enforcement of the laws and regulations that have been enacted. These problems derive in part from imperfect drafting as well as from the uncertain willingness of officials to enforce rules that may ultimately undermine their own power and authority. Nonetheless, Chinese legisla-

> **There's lots of corruption, which exists from the judge down to the police. Once a person is in trouble, there are creative ways [officials can] ... get money.**
>
> *— Chinese focus group*

tive efforts during the post-Mao era represent a significant accomplishment.

Criminal Law and Procedure

The Criminal Law enacted in 1979 and amended in 1997 contains a list of offenses that are punishable as crimes in China. Punishments including fixed-term imprisonment, life imprisonment, and the death penalty are imposed for crimes such as murder, theft, rape, and kidnapping. In addition, various economic crimes such as profiteering,

> Ordinary people obey the criminal laws ... sentences can be harsh. Vandalism—if you return the money—it's not serious. Stealing—you pay a fine. For big property crimes, rape, murder, you get a death sentence.
>
> — *Chinese focus group*

bribery, and corruption are subject to severe punishment. The 1979 Criminal Law provided for punishment of acts of counter-revolution, although this was amended in 1996 to provide for punishment of acts endangering state security.

Process of Criminal Cases. The Code of Criminal Procedure[4] was enacted in 1979 and revised in early 1996, effective 1997. It specifies the process to be followed when a suspect is arrested, prosecuted, and tried. The 1996 amendments include provisions that criminal guilt must be established based on sufficient evidence and grant defense counsel greater authority to present a defense. However, the extent to which these revisions will operate effectively to protect the rights of criminal defendants remains uncertain. As with many provisions in PRC law, the statutory enactments represent ideals rather than practical guides for behavior. While the discussion below is drawn largely from the record of practice over the past nearly 20 years of the Chinese criminal punishment system, the potential for gradual improvements as a result of changes in the criminal law and the criminal procedure law should not be disregarded altogether.

Police Practices. Police in China are generally considered to be corrupt and oppressive. There are very few meaningful restraints on police activity, although efforts have been made recently to bring the police under greater control. Nonetheless, the popular view of the police is one of distrust mingled

> **A lot of new immigrants are afraid of cops ... the police role [in China] has been to suppress people and control them—not to serve them.**
>
> *— Chinese focus group*

with fear. When confronted by a police officer, the typical popular reaction is to tell the police officer whatever might induce the officer to go away.

Arrest. The process for arrest set forth in Chinese criminal procedure rules calls for the Public Security Bureau to obtain an arrest warrant with the approval of the People's Procuracy. In "special circumstances," approval for an arrest can be obtained after the arrest itself has been made. Typical practice in the PRC has been that the Public Security Bureau makes arrests without the benefit of warrants and without prior approval of the Procuracy. In theory, notice must be given within 24 hours to the family and/or work unit of the individual arrested. In practice, however, individuals are often held for much longer periods without proper notice being given to the family and/or work unit. Often, arrest or the threat of arrest is used to intimidate, even when the Public Security Bureau and/or the Procuracy have no plans to proceed with a criminal trial.

Jail Conditions. Jail conditions in China are generally considered to be poor. Often, incarcerated prisoners are subject to "reform through labor" and "re-education through labor," which result in confinement in what often are little more than slave labor camps. Although there have been efforts by Chinese prisoners and by human rights activists to seek legal recourse for poor jail conditions, these have almost universally been unsuccessful. Poor food, poor sanitary conditions, beatings by jailers, and beatings by other inmates have been reported.

> **"Everyone knows China's jails have really bad conditions."**
>
> *— Chinese focus group*

Bail/Release Before Trial. The Chinese criminal procedure law does provide for the possibility that an individual defendant may be released to the custody of family or work unit pending a trial. However, in practice this seldom occurs. As suggested elsewhere, the trial is not considered a fact-finding exercise, but rather operates in the nature of a sentencing hearing. As a result, there is often little time between the arrest and the trial and sentencing of an individual during which the defendant might be released on bail.

Trial Procedures. While recent reforms in the Chinese criminal procedure code may herald the beginning of a new era in which defense counsel have a meaningful opportunity to conduct an effective defense; heretofore, criminal trials in the PRC have not been fact-finding exercises. Rather, the guilt of the accused is presumed and the purpose of the trial is to serve as a formalistic ritual by which the accused admits guilt and the court pronounces a sentence that both rectifies the breakdown of social order signified by the defendant's actions and serves a warning to potential wrongdoers. Trials are generally extremely brief, sometimes lasting less than an hour. Often the defendant has not had an opportunity to review the evidence for more than a few days, if at all.

Attorneys' Roles. Although the new Criminal Procedure Code attempts to rectify this, attorneys in criminal cases in China generally have not been afforded an opportunity to conduct an effective defense. Access to prosecuting evidence has been partial and has often been delayed until just before the trial. Criminal defense lawyers are under significant political pressure not to wage a vigorous defense on issues of guilt, but rather to confine their efforts to pleas for leniency for defendants whose guilt is not questioned.

In traditional China, lawyers were considered to be very low on the social scale. Indeed, a common Chinese term for lawyers was "litigation tricksters." However, in the past ten years or so, respect for lawyers has climbed a bit. Law faculties at Chinese universities are among the most popular and often attract the best students. This is gradually having an impact on public perceptions, as lawyers are slowly garnering slightly more prestige than they enjoyed previously. However, the general Chinese traditional view that

> **Since 1988, the government has spent a lot of money to publicize the law ... since then administrative laws have improved. Good lawyers have fought with people in higher positions.**
>
> *– Chinese focus group*

lawyers are untrustworthy still remains strong. This undermines the effectiveness of criminal defense counsel.

Judge's Role. The tribunal that presides over criminal trials generally consists of a judge and two "lay assessors," although trials are often heard by a single judge. The trial judge may have some minimal level of training, although most judges in China are retired military or PSB officers with no post-secondary education of any kind. The selection of judges in China reflects the fact that the position of judge in the PRC is an administrative career position, rather than a prestige position. Law school graduates who apply for jobs in the courts do so in much the same way as they would apply for jobs in other government agencies. Selection is intended to be based on the quality of the applicant, although membership in the Chinese Communist Party and expressions of political loyalty are essential. Lay assessors have little or no higher education, and they are often selected from the local community based on CPC membership and other indicia of political reliability.

Trial tribunals do little more than receive evidence and prepare the record of proceedings. Decisions in Chinese criminal cases are generally made by the court "adjudication committee," which is made up of the chief judge and senior judges, at least one of whom is the Communist Party secretary of the court. The decision-making influence of the trial tribunal is minimal, and in many cases the tribunal members are not on the adjudication committee that approves the final sentence. As well, in many instances the sentence to be imposed has been decided before the trial even occurs (this is the so-called practice of *Xianpan houshen*—"sentence first, investigate afterwards").

Evidence Rules. Under the Chinese criminal procedure code, a wide range of evidence is admissible. Oral testimony, expert testimony, physical exhibits, and documents are all admissible. The Chinese rules require that items of documentary and physical evidence be verified by the court through an administrative proceeding before being admitted. Often, however, this proceeding does not protect individual defendants from being sentenced on the basis of

> **"In China, you're assumed guilty until proven innocent..."**
> — *Chinese focus group*

faulty evidence, as the "verification" accepted by the court may be little more than the unsworn testimony of police or Procuracy officers that the evidence provided is what it purports to be.

"If you confess, you get a lighter sentence... People confess more in China [than here], if they're guilty."

— Chinese focus group

Witnesses. As discussed above, people in China generally try to have as little contact with public institutions and the legal system as possible. As a result, people are generally reluctant to be witnesses in court actions. It is often difficult to locate witnesses because many people will go to great lengths to avoid being called, even to the extent of leaving the jurisdiction. Court orders directing witnesses to appear can be obtained, but are often difficult to enforce.

Confession. The criminal justice system mirrors many aspects of the traditional Chinese legal system with regard to the importance of law in preserving social harmony. It is seen as important that defendants recognize their guilt (this is seen as facilitating the reconciliation of criminal defendants to the social order). As a result, confessions are not only acceptable but are strongly favored. Indeed, there are numerous reported incidences where confessions by torture have been accepted in criminal cases. This parallels patterns from traditional China. Recent revisions to the Chinese criminal procedure code and prior administrative notices from the Ministry of Justice have asserted that torture would no longer be acceptable as a basis for extracting confessions. However, repeated reports of ongoing use of torture to extract confessions in China suggest that the practice continues.

Range of Sentences. Chinese criminal law provides for five basic sentences and three supplementary penalties. The basic sentences are: (1) control, (2) criminal detention, (3) fixed-term imprisonment, (4) life imprisonment, and (5) death penalty. In addition there are three supplementary punishments that can be imposed in addition to the basic sentences, namely: (1) fine, (2) deprivation of political rights, and (3) confiscation of property. Community service is not part of the sentencing scheme. Although the administrative penalties of re-education through labor and reform through labor are sometimes described by Chinese officials as forms of community service, most foreign observers do not consider the comparison to be apt. The general pattern of sentencing in criminal trials tends to be harsh, with the emphasis placed on lengthy fixed-term imprisonment to be followed by administrative detention for unspecified terms. The death penalty is widely used in China, even for what some consider to be minor offenses such as robbery and fraud.

Goal of Criminal Punishment. The criminal punishment system in the People's Republic of China is not generally concerned with the rights of individual defendants. Rather, it is a major mechanism of state-directed social order. Procedures are brief, opportunities for defense are minimal, and sentences are harsh. As a result, individuals in China try very hard to avoid any contact with the legal system. Individual defendants in both misdemeanor criminal cases and major criminal cases would expect significantly harsher penalties and significantly less attention to the rights of the accused than they would in the United States. This affects not only the attitude of the defendants toward their dealings with the court and defense counsel, but it also affects the conduct of potential witnesses.

Administrative Punishment

While the criminal punishment system affords defendants some modicum of procedural order, the administrative punishment system in China is not subject to meaningful legal restrictions.[5] Administrative detention often includes so-called shelter for investigation, which entails detention without trial for indefinite periods. "Coercive measures" are also used, which involve the transfer of offenders to labor camps for reform through labor and re-education. Once in the labor system, the offender may be detained virtually indefinitely. Despite many calls from inside and outside China for reform in the administrative punishment system, it remains an integral part of the mechanisms of social control in China today.

> **Law isn't absolute—
> it's forever changing,
> [especially] enforcement
> and punishment..."**
> *– Chinese focus group*

Civil Law and Civil Procedure

The General Principles of Civil Law, enacted in 1986, set forth the basic framework for civil acts and civil liabilities, as well as civil rights. As is the case with many European civil codes, the civil law covers property, personal injuries, and contracts of natural and legal persons.

The Civil Procedure Law governs lawsuits brought in the People's Courts on contract, divorce, inheritance, and other civil matters. The Civil Procedure Law specifies the location of the court where a suit may be brought, and the court procedure to be followed in hearing and deciding a case. Although technical differences exist, the Civil Procedure Law is broadly similar in structure and content to the civil procedure rules of Europe.

Marriage. Marriage law in China permits every person to choose and to divorce his or her spouse and, at the same time, grants equal status to both husband and wife.

Contracts. Presently, Chinese law distinguishes between domestic and foreign contracts. The domestic contracts law was a major component of the post-Mao economic reform policies and represents a compromise between the Western concept of "freedom of contract" and the policies of central economic planning espoused by the Maoist model. The law governs ten different types of contracts, including sales contracts, construction contracts, lease contracts, and contracts for storage of goods. The law provides that the rights of the contracting parties are equal, regardless of the parties' size or political position.

All foreign-related contracts, whether they involve foreign trade, foreign investment, or technology transfer,[6] are governed by a separate law; this distinction between domestic and foreign contracts is gradually disappearing. A unified contract statute is currently being drafted.

Administrative Law. An important aspect of legal reform in China concerns administrative reform. The conventional Chinese approach to administrative law emphasized the structure and power of bureaucratic organs and the allocation of authority among them. This focus emphasized substantive administrative authority rather than procedural protection for the persons subject to that authority.

The enactment of the Administrative Litigation Law signalled an effort to make administrative agencies more accountable.[7] Through this reform, individuals and enterprises may challenge in court the legality of decisions by Chinese administrative organs. While only the administrative organizations themselves may be defendants,[8] the cause of action may arise as a result of an individual official's act.[9] However, the legislation does not authorize the courts to review decisions by Communist Party organs, but it does authorize judicial review of administrative decisions of virtually all Chinese state agencies. In addition, the law may permit challenges against administrative agencies to be filed as a result of individual officials eliciting graft from business enterprises.

Civil Cases. Although China is rapidly building a private civil law system to deal with contract disputes and other private law matters, the attitude of the public as well as government officials is still driven largely by the perspective that law is a public and punitive institution. Thus, breaches of contract, violations of intellectual property, even questions of property settlement in divorce are often accompanied by references to criminal sanctions. As the Chinese economic reforms progress and the number and variety of private actors in the economy increase, there has begun to emerge an attitude toward civil law that is distinct from the attitudes about criminal law that currently prevail.

Civil trials in China are handled in ways that would be quite familiar to a European civilian lawyer. Bills of complaint and response are prepared and delivered to the court. The court reviews these for veracity and compliance with the mandated forms. If all is in order, the court may permit the trial to proceed. Parties in the trial process present evidence, make oral argument, and often undergo mediation aimed at a voluntary settlement. Evidence rules permit a broad array of material and testimony evidence, although verification of documents and physical evidence is still required. As with the criminal system, the individual chairing the civil trial tribunal is not generally the person making the decision in the case. This is done by the court adjudication committee. One particularly difficult factor in civil cases in China is the generally low level of legal education among judges. Another issue involves the difficulties in enforcing civil judgments. Despite the problems with the private law system in China, however, there is evidence that an increased number of people are willing to make use of this system.

Informal Dispute Resolution. The dispute resolution system in China places primary emphasis on what in the West are referred to as alternative dispute resolution (ADR) systems. In the past, the primary mechanism for dispute resolution involved mediation by a party member or neighborhood committee. With the beginning of economic reform, increased attention was given to more formal mechanisms, including arbitration of commercial disputes, although mediation remains important in family and other civil matters. In the past, these alternative dispute resolution mechanisms were often applied by the courts as a precursor to formal adjudication, although this practice has faded somewhat. While informal dispute resolution remains generally popular in China, several reports suggest that many Chinese believe the absence of procedural rigor in these proceedings permits the politically powerful and/or well-connected disputants to prevail consistently. Thus there has been an emerging note of support for more formal mechanisms such as arbitration and even litigation.

CULTURAL NORMS AFFECTING PERCEPTION OF LAW

To a very large extent, Chinese society is one in which personal relationships and social harmony are considered to be the most important priorities.[10] There are many consequences stemming from these norms. First, there is a general tendency to disregard the interests or viewpoints of those with whom one does not have an established personal/social relationship. Relationships *(guanxi)* are the glue that holds society together. Individuals with established guanxi are under an informal moral obligation to assist others in the same network of relations, but are under no such obligation to assist or even deal with individuals outside the network. This tends to contribute to phenomena that have been identified in China as "unitism" *(benwei zhuyi)*, when individuals within particular work units *(danwei)* work hard to further the interests of others within the unit but disregard almost totally the interests of those outside the unit. This parochial view is sometimes compounded by a focus on individual family and kinship ties, to the disregard of the non-familial relations.

The emphasis on social/personal relations affects virtually all aspects of Chinese behavior and perceptions of reality. Indeed, the very description of a seemingly simple event may often be affected by the individual witness's relationship to one of the participants, by the lack of such a relationship, or by perceptions about likely relationships among the participants.[11] While the influence of Western liberal culture over the past 15 years has been substantial and has eroded many traditional Chinese values, particularly among young, educated intellectuals, the traditional emphasis on relationships as the core of social organization behavior remains powerful.

Relationships with Authority

A second aspect of Chinese culture involves relationships with authority. Until the recent Taiwan elections, no Chinese state in the world has had a democratically elected government. In conventional Chinese perceptions, political authority has generally been seen as corrupt, self-serving, and oppressive. The popular attitude toward officialdom in general and the courts in particular has been to minimize contact and conflict. Many Chinese traditional sayings concern avoiding any interaction with political or legal institutions, and the sentiments underlying these phrases retain their influence in China today. As a result of these attitudes, many Chinese individuals, when confronted with the authority of political or legal institutions, will do or say whatever they believe will please their interrogators. Often, this motivates individuals to vary their description of events in order to present to their interrogators a version of the "truth" that the interrogators will accept. In this dynamic, pleasing the interrogator is more important then relaying an objective version of "truth."

A major factor contributing to Chinese social perceptions of political and legal authority involves the goals of those authorities themselves. In the traditional Confucian ethic, highest priority is placed on the need to maintain social harmony. A breach of the social harmony was considered to reflect a failing of the ruler, and conversely political rule was considered effective when social harmony was enforced. One result of this has been a rather formalistic approach to fact finding and the resolution of conflict. In the traditional Chinese law system, the guiding imperative for legal and political officials faced with breaches of social order was often to find a person who could be held responsible. Punishment is imposed both to redress the breakdown in social order and to serve as a warning to others.

> **"The law says very clearly what is legal. But if you do something the authorities don't like, like have more than one child, the government can punish you."**
> *— Chinese focus group*

Crime and the Social Order

In the legal order in traditional China, and often in China today, the question of whether the accused might actually be guilty often has taken on less importance than whether the legal authorities are rectifying a breach of the social order. Examples of this in traditional and contemporary Chinese law prior to the 1997 Criminal Procedure Law amendments lie in the "rule of analogy," by which a judge who cannot find a provision in law on which to base punishment of an accused wrongdoer is authorized to mete out punishment based on the next most applicable provision. As well, the traditional Chinese criminal code included so-called catchall statutes, which provided punishments for such wrongs as "doing what ought not to be done" and "not doing what ought to be done." Many similar ideas are incorporated into PRC criminal law, particularly under the provisions for violation of social and economic order, and counterrevolutionary crimes. As a result of this institutional culture, popular attitudes reflect norms urging avoidance of entanglement with law and legal institutions at all costs.

SUMMARY

The Chinese legal system involves a complex structure of laws, institutions, and practices. While the system reflects the purposes of the Chinese communist government, it also has features derived from previous regimes. Legislative and judicial institutions in the PRC have more organizational similarities with the European systems of civil law and government than with the Anglo-American system. The role of the Communist Party in legislative and judicial affairs is perhaps the most significant point of distinction between China's legal institutions and those of Western industrialized democracies. As well, education and staffing, and the enforcement of law and judicial decisions remain a problem. However, legislative accomplishments and gradually changing attitudes during the post-Mao reform period about the role of law suggest that the Chinese legal system is continuing to develop in the context of China's changing conditions.

Mexican Immigrants in Courts

by Juan-Vicente Palerm, Bobby R. Vincent, and Kathryn Vincent

Mexicans are among the immigrant populations most frequently encountered in U.S. courts because Mexico has been the foremost source—12 to 15 percent—of all legal immigration to the United States in the last two decades.[1] According to the 1990 census, 13.7 million persons of Mexican origin live in the United States; of these, 6.7 million, or nearly half, were born in Mexico.[2]

Undocumented immigrants also contribute to the growth of the Mexican-origin and Mexican-immigrant population, but it is uncertain by how much. A recent Immigration and Naturalization Service (INS) study[3] reports 5 million undocumented immigrants in the United States, 54 percent (or 2.7 million) of these from Mexico. The INS claims an annual undocumented flow of 275,000, including approximately 140,000 from Mexico. While many of the undocumented are members of a transnational labor force that moves fluidly between Mexican-sending communities and U.S. job sites, some permanently settle in the United States.

Compared to other immigrant groups, Mexican immigrants are distinguished by being young and having low educational levels, high labor participation, low family and per-capita income, and large (the largest) household sizes. Mexican male immigrants are on average 17 years old, and Mexican females, 23 years old. One 1992[4] report determined that 57.2 percent of all Mexican-origin adults are under 34 years of age. More than 60 percent of the adult Mexican-immigrant population have no more than an elementary education, 69.8 percent work (mostly in blue-collar and service occupations),

---

Ed. note: The boxed quotations in the margins have been added by the editors and represent the opinions of focus group members or other quoted individuals and do not necessarily represent the views of the authors, editors, or publisher.

30.9 percent of all households earn less than $12,999 per year, and 52.6 percent live in households of five or more persons.

The circumstances in both countries that fuel Mexican immigration to the United States are expected to continue into the 21st century. Recent reports place the Mexican population at 92 million, with nearly half under the age of 15. Due to the relatively young age of the population, the birth rate will continue to be high despite government programs, improved educational opportunity, and the feminist movement in Mexico—all of which have had some effect on slowing population growth.

Since the mid-1970s, Mexico's economic crises and population growth have prevented the nation from providing sufficient employment. As a result, Mexicans experience high unemployment, chronic underemployment, diminishing real wages, and lack of job security, complicated by government austerity programs and draconian inflation-control measures. Although there has been notable economic improvement in recent years (and Mexico is now ranked among the 13 most industrialized nations in the world), the nation is far from overcoming its problems. Rural towns and communities are overpopulated and very poor; metropolitan areas are teeming with unemployed urbanites and rural immigrants. These factors, in simple terms, fuel a constant flow of immigration from Mexico to its northern neighbor, the United States, where an expanding labor market offers low-wage, low-skilled jobs. In addition to this "push-pull" phenomenon, the established tradition of migration, along with continuing efforts at family reunification, will continue to drive immigration even under improved economic conditions.

North America is changing, and the movement of peoples, ideas, and investments between the United States and Mexico is reciprocal. The sustained encounter of the U.S. and Mexican cultures that takes place every day, not only in the cities and towns of the border region but throughout both nations, constitutes a dynamic cultural exchange that is never resolved. Still, the historical hostility between the two nations—which has contributed to deep-seated prejudices—has combined with Mexicans' experiences with their own and U.S. legal institutions and their representatives to create an atmosphere of distrust and fear among most Mexican immigrants to the United States.

MANY MEXICOS

Mexico, its culture, and its people can be best characterized by highlighting their rich diversity.[5] More than 260 distinct indigenous languages—not dialects, but independent languages—are used in Middle America, the region that spans Mexico's northern and Guatemala's southern borders. Most of the languages are mutually unintelligible. Spanish is the lingua franca of Mexico, but other non-indigenous languages such as Catalan, Yiddish, and English are readily spoken on the streets of Mexico City and other major urban communities.

Mexico's human variation is matched by its environmental richness, which includes steamy tropical lowlands in the south; vast desert regions in the north; long strands of beaches and coastlines on the Pacific, Gulf of California, Gulf of Mexico, and the Caribbean; perpetually ice-capped mountains; and nearly every other imaginable physical characteristic. It is a country rich in biological diversity; for example, in one narrow strip of Mexico's southeastern highlands live more species of birds than can be found in the entire United States.[6] Mexico's rich mineral resources, including oil, have long been its most important exports.

Mexico's cultures exhibit polarized extremes from which are derived genuine schisms: vast differences in wealth, rural-urban contrasts, and indigenous-mestizo-criollo tension.[7] Even before the arrival of the Europeans in 1519, Mexico was extremely varied and populated by competing cultures often in conflict. The Aztecs ruled over an expansive, if not always peaceful, empire. After the conquest, the Spanish established and managed a world-linked economy founded in silver mining, agriculture, and indigenous labor to supply European and Asian markets. With European rule came a civil society and polity based on European models and the Catholic church. Mexico achieved independence from Spain in 1821, but it faced continuous challenges to its territory and sovereignty from European nations and the United States throughout much of the 19th century. From 1876 to 1910, Mexico was governed by a one-man dictatorship that was ended by the Revolution of 1910.

Three hundred years of colonial control transformed the population and culture of Mexico. Wolf elegantly described Mexico as a great meeting ground, where American Indians, Europeans, whites, and African blacks encountered one another and recognized their common humanity.[8] The cultures and peoples melded into a new and unique blend some call "the cosmic race."[9] Indeed, unique to New Spain was the emergence of a true mestizo society, which integrated Indians, Europeans, Africans, and Asians.[10] This combination of influences today is identifiable as uniquely Mexican and characterizes at least two-thirds of the population. Still, there remain in Mexico many original Indian populations that have conserved their unique languages and cultures, and the country is host to a broad array of immigrants and refugees from Europe, Asia, the Middle East, and South America.

Despite the redistributive effects of the 1910 Revolution, Mexico remains a country of people severely divided along class lines. Mexico has a small, very rich, powerful elite and a large, very poor, disenfranchised general population. The relatively small and diminishing middle class has suffered tremendous losses in the country's recurring financial crises. The very poor, with low educational attainment, live in rural hovels and urban slums. Indian communities in the south are among the poorest of the poor and, moreover, suffer almost complete public neglect.

Nearly one-third of Mexico's 87 million people (over 20 million) reside in one giant megalopolis—the Distrito Federal (Mexico City) and its expansive outskirts. Even with massive and rapid industrialization, Mexico continues to maintain a large and growing rural population involved in agricultural production. Another one-fifth to one-third live in small rural towns and communities, where growing populations make increasing demands on land resources, fueling a continuing flow of rural-to-urban migration. Indeed, modern industrialization, booming population growth, and rural-to-urban migration have made Mexico City into what it is today: the largest, most populated, and most contaminated and unhealthful city in the world. It is also one of the most powerful. From Mexico City, a heavily centralized government firmly rules the nation.

Since 1924, Mexico has been governed by a one-party monopoly, the absolute rule of the Partido Revolucionario Institucional, known as PRI. The decade of the '90s has witnessed a rapid and sometimes painful democratic opening in Mexico, however, culminating as this essay is being written with the seating of Mexico's first opposition-controlled congress. Mexico has not experienced the most favorable circumstances from which to develop a tradition or experience of democracy and reliable government institutions. Indeed, Mexico's modern history has united its people in their cynicism and mistrust of government and governmental institutions. This is especially true of Mexicans' perceptions of, and experiences in, the country's legal system.

> **"A lot of Mexicans' approach to government is: you're doomed no matter what. Just make the best of it."**
> — *Mexican focus group*

MEXICO'S LEGAL STRUCTURE

Mexico's Constitution and laws are based in a unique combination of Spanish, French, and indigenous law, expanded by original expressions of Mexico's national character and some concepts borrowed from the United States.[11]

The Constitution of 1917, implemented in 1920, is still in force. Preserved from the pre-Revolution constitution were the principles of liberal, federalist construction; separation of church and state; equality before the law; freedom of speech and of the press; freedom to petition, assemble, and receive an education; and the rights to bail, to carry arms, and to habeas corpus. The 1917 constitution's most notable new provisions were directed at further reducing the influence of the clergy; the restitution and redistribution of land to landless farmworkers in the *ejidal* system; restriction of foreign ownership; and the establishment of protections for workers, including collective bargaining rights.

The Mexican Constitution establishes three branches of federal government (legislative, executive, and judicial). There are 31 states with individual governments, and a federal district, Mexico City, which houses the nation's capital. The power of government is strongly centralized in the capital and the executive.

The federal judiciary, similar to the U.S. system, includes a Supreme Court of final jurisdiction; circuit courts (federal appellate courts); and at the level of first instance, district courts and jury courts (in which a jury may be used but rarely is employed). In addition to standard federal issues and resolution of inter-state disputes, the federal judiciary hears cases of *amparo,* that is, cases invoking constitutional protections. Amparo suits can be invoked as personal rights, to defend against unconstitutional laws, to question the legality of a judicial decision, to establish a case against administrative actions, or to pursue ejidal rights of peasants. Because the Mexican Constitution is a large, complex, and often contradictory document, amparo in practice becomes a way to elude judicial administration.

Through its Spanish lineage, Mexico's judicial system is established in the ancient civil law tradition. The basic elements of English common law, trial by jury and the law of evidence, are generally not employed in civil law courts. In addition, in comparison to common law, civil law minimizes the power of the judiciary, which interprets codified principles rather than establishes judicial precedents. Beyond this, the Mexican political system concentrates political power in the executive branch, minimizing the judiciary's political influence.

Mexican Law in Practice

Mexico's Constitution of 1917 sets forth goals while acknowledging the country's inabilities to reach them. It follows perfectly from this that modern Mexico would ascribe on principle to far-reaching agreements, such as human rights accords and labor rights, that it is unlikely to be able to enforce.

The unrealistic expectations and the general, sweeping terms of many laws as set forth in Mexico's basic legal structure have led to dualism: law in theory and law in practice. Dualism accounts for the sophisticated pyramid of corruption that characterizes the Mexican legal hierarchy, and its practice is the most important factor in the ordinary citizen's perception of justice.

The thorough corruption and ineffectiveness of Mexico's justice system has been acknowledged by virtually every modern president, but few have been as eloquent and specific in this as Ernesto Zedillo Ponce de León. On September 1, 1995, in his first Message to Congress, Zedillo said:

The citizenry is victimized by the distance that exists between the word of the law and its observation, between the regulations and their application, between the structures of justice and their administration.... Society is profoundly and justifiably angry.... They are exasperated to observe that in many cases those in charge of guaranteeing order and justice are the very ones who ride roughshod [over the law]. We justifiably distrust the institutions, the programs, and the individuals responsible for public safety.

With this, President Zedillo called for unification of "efforts to establish an infrastructure and adopt effective measures in different areas of government that can ensure the purification, professionalization and improvement of technical skills of the police departments." Significant amendments to the Constitution in December of 1994 reformed the federal judiciary and set forth some of the institutional framework necessary to begin this daunting task.

Despite the President's efforts and the increasingly open criticism of the justice system, Mexico continues to operate in a complex hierarchy and culture of institutionalized corruption and vigilante activities that intimidate the general population. Indeed, dismantling the structure that now exists and replacing it with one that is open and effective will dramatically alter the way business is conducted at virtually every level of the country. Armed criminal bands—more than 900 of them, of which 50 percent are made up of retired or current members of law enforcement agencies, according to one report[12]—operate throughout the country with police protection.

Even the most honest and diligent citizen cannot escape participation in the scheme of *mordida* (bribery) when attempting to comply with ordinary legal requirements. For example, a person attempting to secure a driver's license must pay additional "user" fees to the clerk in order to move the application along the path. To resolve significant legal

> **"There have been tremendous increases in crime in Mexico— drug wars, bandits, and drug killings are on the uprise."**
> — *Mexican focus group*

"If you have more money, you win the case."

— Mexican focus group

matters, only money and power are effective. First, a relatively large sum of money is necessary to employ a lawyer who navigates a case through a drawn-out series of hearings and questioning of witnesses, as stacks of documents are submitted to the court and finally read by a judge who, months or even years later, renders a verdict based upon them. Movement through this system is accomplished only by surreptitious payment of everyone involved along the way. Each recipient submits a portion of his or her payments up the line to the highest levels. Almost invariably, the prevailing party is the one with greater money and/or power.

Criminal Law and Procedure

As in the United States, petty offenses may be disposed of perfunctorily by a lower jurisdiction court. More serious offenses against the public proceed from a complaint filed with the police with prosecution initiated by the local prosecutor. A victim must file and actively pursue a complaint for a private offense, which includes such acts as rape, kidnapping, and embezzlement.

Under the constitution, accused persons have the right to counsel (and the court must provide a public defender if the accused cannot afford to pay an attorney). Public defenders—of diverse quality and experience—are paid by the government. The accused is entitled access to the court to present, examine, or secure evidence and to confront opposing witnesses. Release on bail is possible in minor cases (those offenses drawing average penalties of less than five years in prison). The amount of the bond is based upon the nature of the offense and the accused's ability to pay. Prompt proceedings are guaranteed: four months for minor offenses and one year for more serious crimes. Persons may not be required to testify against themselves. If an accused is denied any of these rights, the erring agency is sanctioned, but the case is not dismissed.

The entry level into the criminal justice system, as victim or as accused perpetrator of a crime, is extremely risky, because the first line of contact is with a member of the Mexican police. A familiar joke in Mexico is, "Don't yell if you are mugged; the police might come!"[13] Victims of crime in Mexico are routinely further victimized by the police if they are foolish enough to seek protection or redress. The individual who captures and turns in the one who attempts to rob him on the street can expect to be threatened with arrest for making false accusations. An injured person taken from the scene of an accident by ambulance may be visited in the hospital by police attempting arrest—and immediate removal to jail—for leaving the scene. People are routinely stopped, threatened, and robbed at gunpoint by police, but more subtle bribery is a game of complex negotiation between the victim and the officer.

> **"There's a tremendous fear of the police—if you have an accident or anything, you try to get away before the police come. They're just one more group to pay off."**
> *— Mexican focus group*

Police are reported to commit grave violations of human rights; the Mexican Federal Judicial Police (especially its anti-narcotics brigade), the State Judicial Police, and the Mexican Army (which operates at the President's direction within the country) are government agencies that are frequently cited by international and domestic human rights organizations. Extrajudicial executions are not unknown, and incidents of torture are well documented by agencies such as Americas Watch.[14]

Judicial administration is not open to public scrutiny and the ordinary citizen does not participate in it. Juries are not used in Mexican courts except under obscure provisions. Despite a structure painstakingly designed to reflect fairness and objectivity, the system often operates in secrecy behind closed doors. The lower in the pyramid an official of justice is situated, the greater the ambiguity within which the official can operate. Judges and lawyers, who are usually political appointees, are seen not as administrators of the law who ensure that justice is done, rights are protected, and procedures are followed, but rather as ultimate and powerful authorities to be feared.

A simple criminal case can take years to reach final adjudication. A medium-range felony—robbery, for example—will carry no right to bail, and trial may not be held for four years, while the accused remains in pretrial custody. In Mexico's system, confession—obtained in the period of interro-

> **"If you can't bribe your way out before you get stuck in the system, you might as well forget about it— it'll take years."**
> — *Mexican focus group*

gation following arrest and prior to the accused's being brought before a judge—is the norm and may elicit a lesser penalty. Plea bargains are unknown. Increasingly, counseling and substance abuse treatments are ordered, especially for juvenile offenders.

While in theory the Mexican prison system is rehabilitative in nature, in reality prison conditions are extremely harsh. Family members of the convicted criminal are expected to provide basic necessities and to pay the prison guards to deliver them. Conjugal visits are allowed. There is no capital punishment or life imprisonment. Parole is provided under conditions similar to those of U.S. systems. The maximum lengths of sentences are typically shorter than U.S. terms for the same crimes. But in drug-trafficking cases, sentences are typically harsher than in the United States, and parole and probation are not granted for these crimes. As narco-traffic has expanded, the protection of illegal drug-related activity has come to involve increasing numbers of those employed in law enforcement as police and prosecutors.

The Mexican criminal law system is so dangerous and dysfunctional that Mexican citizens with any recourse will do whatever it takes to stay out of, or escape from, that system. Lawyers are viewed as too expensive by all but the upper-middle and wealthy classes. *Pasantes* (law graduates who have not yet been licensed to practice law) act as paralegals to the working poor in criminal matters for a small fee. But many believe that extortion of the weak and vulnerable is, indeed, an expression of the popular culture of the Mexican legal system. The poor and powerless within it simply suffer, especially if they are in jail.

Civil Law and Procedure

The present Mexican civil code was implemented in 1932; it reflects Latin American and European influences along with unique Mexican characteristics. While private law lies within the purview of the state courts, all of the state codes are closely modeled on that established for the Federal District.

Family Law. The traditional teachings of the Roman Catholic Church are the basis for laws governing marriage and children, except for divorce, but the church has no legal authority. Mexican law approves monogamous heterosexual marriage and children born only within marriages, gives parents full authority over their children and obligates each member of a family to support the others with certain conditions, and condemns extramarital sexual relationships and incest. Marriage is a civil ceremony that may be confirmed by a church ceremony. Upon marriage, the couple determines whether marital property will be held separately or in community; prenuptial agreements can be fashioned to suit particular circumstances. The husband of a legal marriage is obligated to support his wife unless he is incapacitated.

Despite laws to the contrary, couples often are married via unofficial means in church and community ceremonies. Children born with illegitimate status may be acknowledged by their parent; children born of "common law marriage" (which is widespread), known as concubinage, acquire rights of legitimacy.

There are 27 grounds for divorce, including mutual consent, which carries no implication of fault for either party. A childless marriage between adults may be ended in 15 days without going to court. The "innocent" wife is entitled to alimony after divorce unless she remarries. The "innocent" husband may receive alimony only if unable to work. All close relatives have standing to make requests of the court on behalf of the children of a divorcing couple.

Divorce, however, is for the most part limited to middle- and upper-class couples and the urban setting. Divorce is virtually unknown in rural areas, where a family may simply be abandoned, sometimes by one who moves north to establish a second home with a separate family. Although polygamy is prohibited, the children of the second home acquire the same rights as those of the first. Polygamy is not an uncommon practice among some Indian groups.

> **"Divorce is not common, due to Catholicism. People just go off and live somewhere else."**
> — *Mexican focus group*

Domestic violence, child protective services, and other family issues are handled by a nonpolitical program known as DIF (Desarrollo Integral de la Familia, or Integral Family Development). Originally established as a family-planning program, DIF has rapidly expanded in response to the economic and social factors that have increasingly affected families in recent years. Through DIF, a spouse may seek protection from an abusive partner, may file charges, and can access counseling and medical resources, shelter, and other basic necessities while the family is disrupted. These services are supported by a massive infrastructure of social workers, mental health workers, and lawyers available throughout Mexico, even in remote rural areas.

Still, many rural Mexicans attempt to resolve disputes informally within their families and communities, avoiding entry into the judicial or patronage system at all costs. This is especially true of marital and other domestic conflicts, which are deemed by rural Mexicans to be the private business of the family and outside the jurisdiction of the state.

Liability. Article 1913 of the code provides an interesting set of rules to govern the use of "dangerous" things, and this has significant import for liability in automobile accidents. In effect, one may be liable for all damages caused by one's use of a dangerous thing, without concern for fault. Most simple driving offenses are handled by a "fine" paid directly to the apprehending officer. Drinking while driving is typically a minor offense, but drunk driving is becoming a crime of serious import in most states, especially for repeat offenders. Because of fear of involvement with police, many will attempt to escape the scene of an accident, although it is illegal to do so.

> **"If there's an accident, you try to agree between yourselves and not get the bureaucracy involved."**
> – *Mexican focus group*

Settling Obligations. The Mexican civil code includes as sources of obligations the standard Anglo-American categories of contracts (including gifts and irrevocable offers), torts (including workers' compensation and breach of fiduciary duty), and restitution. The remedy usually sought and awarded is fulfillment of the obligation rather than money judgments. There are strict limitations on damages, which result in awards typically much smaller than would be expected in U.S. courts.

Property. Mexican law of property is mostly in the Roman tradition, with some exceptions borrowed from U.S. law and particular limits on land ownership. A property owner may dispose of, use, and enjoy the benefits of his or her property. The security interest, created in ways similar to security interests under U.S. law, is recognized as a true right. Other divisions of ownership are familiar within U.S. law, including co-ownership and trust *(fideicomiso)*. Voluntary and involuntary transfers of ownership occur much as in the United States, including through wills and intestate succession.

Notarios Públicos. The public notary is a highly qualified lawyer appointed to a position of considerable importance. Notaries authenticate facts, interpret and draft legal documents, search real estate titles, and serve as the public recorders of transactions. They are paid set fees by their clients and can make an excellent income from this work since the number of notary positions is strictly limited.[15]

Ejidal Law

Finally, there is a unique system of justice in operation in Mexico's rural ejido communities. Created as a result of the post-revolution agrarian reform, these communities are empowered to allocate family plots to eligible land grantees and to resolve conflicts within the community regarding land management and land use. Local officials are locally elected to administer ejido communities.

The majority of Mexican immigrants and migrants to the United States come from rural Mexico. They are knowledgeable about ejidal law and have experienced it directly. Through ejidal organization, rural Mexicans participate in local legal systems that operate on the basis of strong democratic structures but which also are open to abuse via patron-

> **"Many rural people have very small land grants and they participate in the ejidal system."**
> *— Mexican focus group*

client relations and the ancient *caciquismo* practices of local political bosses. Headed by a local VIP known as the *cacique,* the system employs private and public strong-arm men as enforcers and resolvers of feuds, dispensers of favors, and "brokers" who deal with those higher up in the system.

THE MEXICAN-ORIGIN POPULATION IN THE UNITED STATES

The accelerated arrival of Mexican nationals is now recognized as the largest historical mass immigration to the United States from a single country, exceeding even the previous waves from Italy and Ireland. Because employment is the principal engine of migration, Mexican immigrants settle near employment centers: labor-intensive manufacturing and low-skilled services in major metropolitan areas, and labor-intensive agricultural production and food-processing locations in rural areas. Mexican immigrants are adding population to both large industrial cities and small agricultural towns and communities. In them, they establish well-defined neighborhoods and communities.[16]

Diversity

The Mexican-origin population in the United States not only reflects the Mexican ethnic, regional, and class variations described earlier, but also a new diversity shaped in the United States. The United States has sustained a layering of the Mexican-origin population over time. Some are U.S.-born, of families that have been U.S. citizens for generations; others have immigrated and settled in the remote past or only recently; while still others are in the country only temporarily. The experiences of longtime residents versus newcomers are varied, and their attitudes about U.S. institutions and the law—along with their command and knowledge of the English language—vary accordingly.

From early in the century until the 1980s, the vast majority of Mexican immigrants to the United States were drawn from similar points of origin: mestizo rural communities located in the northern part of the Mexican central highlands; the states of Jalisco, Guanajuato, Michoacán, and Zacatecas provided the largest number.[17] The Bracero Program (1942–1964) was primarily responsible for recruiting workers from these states at a time when there was considerable upheaval and population displacement in Mexico due to land reform and agricultural modernization. Since then, these sending communities have established a tradition of migration as well as strong links with family and *paisano* (countrymen) communities in the United States that continue to support the migration flow. That is, migration is not a precipitous response to problems but rather a well-established practice of most rural communities. They rely upon migration and wage remittances to diminish population pressure and to organize a viable economic life.[18]

Since the 1980s, however, other populations from Mexico have been drawn into the migration stream. Among them are large numbers of Mixtec and Zapotec Indians from rural communities in the southern state of Oaxaca,[19] and increasing numbers of urban, unemployed mestizos and criollos from Mexico's major cities—Mexico City, Monterrey, and Guadalajara.[20] Also in the 1980s, a substantial movement of the business and professional class—wealthy, high-income Mexicans—sought refuge from Mexico's failing economy, political climate, and austerity measures, and settled with their wealth in places like San Diego County, California. Finally, the border cities such as Tijuana and Ciudad Juárez, hosts to new, booming manufacturing centers, have become major staging areas for immigration into the United States.[21]

Each immigration group, based on its immigration experience in time and place, shapes attitudes and relationships with legal institutions and the law; while most elude the law, some may seek it. For example, the border industry primarily employs young women who, with newfound economic independence, set out to renegotiate their relationships with husbands, fathers, and families. Failing to find support in Mexican society and institutions, they "escape" to the United States and seek the protection of U.S. laws. Indeed, the cohort of young, single mothers is one of the newest, fastest-growing groups in the migration stream; they find easy employment in hotels, private homes, and in child- and elder-care positions.

Settlers and Sojourners

The authors of a study completed by the recently established Public Policy Institute of California[22] report that less than one-third of all Mexicans who enter the United States remain permanently and that more than one-half of them return to Mexico within two years. They found also that only 9.5 percent of illegal immigrants who were parents had their children with them in the United States. This information reveals that the vast majority of the Mexican immigrant population is in the United States temporarily. They are circular migrants, mostly working at low-skilled, minimum-wage jobs while their families remain in Mexico's small rural communities. While they are here, they ask—and receive—little.

There are, in effect, two distinct Mexican populations in the United States: those who have established permanent homes and settled with their families and those who trek back and forth, seasonally or periodically, in search of jobs and income to support their families in Mexico. There also is much overlapping of the two communities, including workers who keep home bases in the border region and work seasonally from them and workers who keep homes in both Mexican and U.S. communities, efficiently moving family members between the two in order to best manage their resources.[23]

Seasonal migrants are in the United States for the sole purpose of working and accumulating wages. During their circular migration they do not welcome distractions from the primary objectives—finding work, working as much as possible, and returning home. For them, delays are costly, and involvement with the law (as defendants or plaintiffs) is an impediment to their livelihoods and a threat to their families in Mexico. Many believe, therefore, that such encounters must be avoided at all cost.

Legal and Illegal (Undocumented) Immigrants

The legal-illegal (documented or undocumented) status of Mexican immigrants is continuously in flux. Laws and regulations concerning Mexican immigration have revolved several times around the circle of welcome: the mat is extended, and then withdrawn. The vacillating nature and often contradictory content of U.S. immigration laws have not helped immigrants to understand or to comply. Sometimes the need for migrant labor and U.S. immigration laws coincide, but at others they are in contradiction. Few of the provisions of the Immigration Reform and Control Act (IRCA) regarding employer sanctions have been enforced. Regardless of the status of the law, there are always U.S. employers wanting Mexican workers, and ultimately it is the job and the employer and not the laws and regulations that determine the workers' decisions to immigrate, legally or illegally.

When Mexicans enter the United States to work illegally, they are aware that they are breaking the law. They will, as a result, avoid as much as possible contact with the law, a uniformed officer, and anyone who appears to be "official," and with all government offices and agencies as well, even those they perceive to be public such as hospitals, clinics, and schools. Even census takers have found it difficult to access and interview immigrants.

Although a much smaller number of Mexican immigrants remained undocumented after the federal amnesty program of 1986, the numbers have begun to grow again due to continuing immigration. IRCA, moreover, contributed to modifying and increasing the immigration flow. Indeed, many amnestied migrant workers decided to settle permanently in the United States upon regularizing their immigrant status and subsequently began to bring their families from Mexico to their new homes. Previously made up of single workers traveling alone, the immigration flow now began to be defined by families—mostly women and children, and some elderly people. U.S. family reunification preferences greatly assisted this process, but many others also immigrated illegally to join their legal spouses, parents, and siblings, with the aspiration that they also would find opportunity to legalize in the future.

As a result, many formerly undocumented, now legal, immigrants continue to avoid the law and contact with government officials because their households contain undocumented family members who are vulnerable to apprehension and deportation by the Immigration and Naturalization Service.

The immigrant's regional, ethnic, and class group, degree of acculturation or assimilation in U.S. society, depth of understanding of U.S. laws and institutions, permanent or itinerant presence, and his own and his family's legal or illegal immigration status—all affect the immigrant's relationship to the justice system. The picture is further complicated by many regional and cultural factors that also shape attitudes, perceptions, and behavior. Most importantly, living and working conditions and behavior are not always the result of cultural preferences, but rather they are dictated by economic necessity.

The violent youth gangs to which some Mexican-immigrant youth are drawn are a uniquely U.S. phenomenon. Mexican youth can quickly abandon their respectful and obedient behavior toward their parents and communities when exposed to the relative freedom of U.S. youth culture. It is part of the increasingly well-documented breakdown of Mexicans' valuable family, nutritional, and health traditions as they move into U.S. society. They are, after all, displaced populations who have lost, temporarily or permanently, their access to community life, order, regulation, and the social web of established relationships.

Mexican Immigrants in U.S. Courts

Mexico provides the United States with well-educated professionals—indeed, the Mexican government is focusing new resources on regaining its recent losses to foreign job markets of highly trained human resources—and these individuals have little difficulty functioning in the U.S. courts as parties in civil and criminal cases. Middle- and upper-class Mexicans in the United States understand that one can hire a lawyer to press or defend a complaint, that one can expect a hearing, and that bribery is not advised.

But most immigrants from Mexico to the United States are poor and up to 60 percent have not completed an elementary education.[24] The following discussion of the particular challenges faced by Mexican immigrants when they enter the U.S. court system focuses on the working poor, the young and uneducated, and the vulnerable immigrants from Mexico's rural communities and urban barrios. These are by far the largest number of immigrants from Mexico to the United States, and it is these who encounter in the United States a justice system that is bewildering and frightening.

Assuring access and effective interaction for Mexican immigrants in the U.S. court system does not depend simply on informing them of the differences between the two structures. In addition to the problems of language, Mexican immigrants are likely to know nothing about the proceedings: who is in charge, what the roles of the various persons are, and what is happening. They may be confused by the presence of a jury of "peers" who determine the measure of a defendant's guilt or a plaintiff's relief. While it must be re-emphasized that there are no generalized assessments of how all Mexicans manifest their culture in U.S. courts, discussion of poor, uneducated, mostly rural Mexican immigrants—the largest cohort in the United States—can be illuminating.

Rural Community Experiences. Rural Mexicans understand old community systems, based in land tenure and land rights, and communal local controls. In the local community, most contracts are verbal agreements based upon an individual's word and local social relations, including *compadrazgo* (fictive kinships) or patron/client affiliations. When problems such as fault, breach of contract, or other disagreements arise, solutions are found at the local, informal level based on community pressures, gossip, ostracism, or—when all other measures fail—by the wronged individual taking the law into his own hands, which, although punishable by national law, can receive local community sanction. The interference of outsiders in these agreements and sanctions is greatly resented.

Language. It should not be assumed that Mexican immigrants speak Spanish, or that "cultured" Spanish will be easily understood by some rural folk who use diverse idiomatic forms. There are many indigenous languages alive in Mexico, and since immigration paths are well established from some indigenous Mexican communities, those languages are evident in the United States. In addition, monolingual Spanish speakers should not be presumed to be uneducated—a common mistake made by educated monolingual English speakers! Some immigrants may be reluctant to ask for an interpreter or to admit that they need help in understanding the proceedings and expressing themselves to the court. They may understand some English but find that their vocabulary falls short in the unfamiliar language of the courtroom; they may fear that there is a cost associated with the interpreter's use; or they may be embarrassed to admit that they do not speak English. They are unlikely to be represented by a Spanish-speaking attorney. Court personnel must pursue the question of the immigrant's English-language abilities beyond asking a simple yes-or-no question such as, "Do you understand English?" A better question would be, "How well do you understand English?" or "What language do you speak?" Interpreters must be provided, because the language barrier cannot be allowed to prevent people from participating fully in the proceedings that affect them.

Pride. Rural Mexican culture puts great stock in appearances. Mexican immigrants may be reluctant to offer any information to the court that reflects badly upon themselves or their families.

Respect for Authority. If there is a high risk involved in the situation, Mexican immigrants may refuse to divulge information to anyone in authority—attorney, judge, or counselor. Conversation may be an effort by the immigrant to learn what the person in authority wants to hear. Generally, rural Mexicans believe it is rude—or a challenge—to look directly at a person of authority; thus they may avoid eye contact in a respectful gesture that gives the impression of excessive humility or untruthfulness in the context of Anglo culture. Even more important, it is considered extremely impolite (and impolitic) to contradict a person in authority. Thus authority figures should avoid asking questions in forms that imply the answer, such as "Is it not true that…?"

Many immigrants already have had, or know someone who has had, poor and costly experiences with lawyers in the U.S.—especially immigration and personal injury lawyers—or those who represent themselves to be lawyers, such as notarios. These experiences reinforce their poor opinion and mistrust of the legal system developed in Mexico. As a result, Mexican immigrants may not understand and trust legal counsel and thus may elect not to participate actively in their cases. It is important that judges in family and civil courts refrain from reassuring Mexican im-

> **"Hispanic men are less likely to look women judges and jurors in the eye. This is not dealt with in jury instructions; some lawyers may address it in voir dire."**
>
> *— State court judge*

migrants that they or their families will not be reported to the INS; perversely, this is seen as an implied threat to do so.

Names. All Mexicans officially carry two surnames, composed of their father's paternal (first) surname and their mother's paternal surname. Thus the child of José Rodríguez Sánchez and María Barrero Ruiz will receive one or more first, or given, names, such as María del Pilar, along with each parent's first surname, in this case Rodríguez Barrero. If she is to be addressed by only one of her names, it would be her paternal surname, in this case Rodríguez. Hyphenation of the two last names in the United States is a modern effort to keep the two names together in an Anglo world accustomed to recognizing only one surname. When women marry, they keep their own first surname and officially adopt their husbands' first surnames as well. María Barrero Ruiz becomes María Barrero de Rodríguez. The complete Mexican name is intended to provide information about both the mother and father of a child and, in the case of a married woman, about her own and her husband's family. The system of names is not in itself confusing or ambiguous, but it can appear to be so when compatibility with the English system is demanded. For example, because middle names are not commonly given in Mexico, one might attempt to complete a U.S. English form by inserting the second surname in the space provided for the middle name.

Machismo. The complex Latino cultural trait known as machismo is stereotypically seen to be a cruelly dominating attitude toward women. Although Mexican culture incorporates excessive prominence of males based on *pater postestad,* machismo relates also to noble "masculine" traits such as bravery and integrity. Mexican men are expected to provide for their families and keep them safe. The stereotype of machismo contributes to a perception that abusive domestic relationships are a Mexican cultural norm. This is an incomplete assessment, and attributing domestic violence to cultural predisposition will detract from its true causes and inhibit effective intervention strategies. In fact, most Mexican-immigrant families are living in the United States under extremely stressful conditions in overcrowded, substandard housing; in unstable and often brutal working conditions; without access to adequate health care and other basic services; in a climate of discrimination, distrust, and exploitation; and, when members of the household are without legal immigration status, in constant fear of apprehension by the INS. These factors may contribute to incidences or cycles of depression, domestic violence, and substance abuse.

Women. The trait of machismo is apposed to the stereotype of the "submissive" female, especially in public settings. Female submissiveness should not necessarily be interpreted as fear, but rather as appropriate wife and mother behavior. Mexican women, especially mothers, in fact have considerable power within the family. Life in the United States may change them more quickly than it does men, because of the enormous distance between women's economic and social opportunities in rural Mexico and the independence and multitude of options open to them in the United States. Still, Mexican immigrant women lag far behind Anglo women in nearly every measure of well-being except the health of their infants; infant mortality for the two groups is nearly equal in the United States. They are likely to be employed outside the home in low-wage service fields; they also are well represented among agricultural workers. In 1987, 48 percent of Mexican-origin female-headed households had incomes below the poverty level.[25]

In cases of abuse, Mexican women, when undocumented, may conclude that deportation is a worse outcome than tolerating an abusive husband and thus will not cooperate with the courts in seeking their own protection. Indeed, undocumented women often are terrorized by an abusive partner's threats to report them and/or their children to the INS, or by their refusal to sign sponsorship documents for them and their children. In addition, they may fear that if they bring the family's circumstances to the attention of social services, their children may be taken from them.

> **"A battered undocumented woman often ... fear[s] that out of retaliation her husband will 'turn her in.'"**
>
> *— Domestic Violence in Immigrant and Refugee Communities, Jang et al., 1997.*

Family. In rural Mexico, family matters are typically resolved internally; if help is needed, it is sought from within the local community or network of kin. The concept of a public interest in family relationships is alien. Thus, public intervention into family life can be seen as a humiliating and intolerable violation of privacy and loss of control. Mexican women may be reluctant to seek help for an abusive domestic situation because they are concerned about maintaining the family's social respectability. Mexican men may find family court experiences to be especially painful. They may be unresponsive to questions from those in authority about their family relationships. They may abhor the notion of mediation or counseling in matters involving the raising of children or spousal relationships. Restraining orders that separate men from their wives or children, or orders to vacate the home, will be difficult for such men to accept, because they cannot acknowledge the jurisdiction of the court in their private lives.

> **"Many times the victim and batterer don't understand why domestic violence cases can't end upon the victim's say-so. Victims have stated that they don't want a non-contact order because of the need to provide for their family."**
> — *State court judge,*
>   Yakima Herald Republic,
>   *Aug. 30, 1996*

Exercising Their Own Rights. Mexican immigrants may elect to abandon pursuit of their individual labor, housing, or other rights because they fear exposure of their own or family members' illegal status. Especially if they move about the country, or move between Mexico and the United States, they may be not only unwilling but unable to invest time in court or administrative proceedings that will distract them from their work and earnings.

Bail. Mexican immigrants may understand the payment of bail as payment of a fine, or even a bribe, which in their native system concludes all proceedings. It is critical that the process of posting bond be explained to and understood by Mexican immigrants. Migrants may interpret bail as having paid

> **"[I] sometimes worry Spanish-speaking offenders might mistake their bail amount as a bribe demand...."**
> — *State court judge,*
>   Yakima Herald Republic,
>   *Aug. 30, 1996*

for their fault, especially when they are pressed to move on due to the necessity of employment cycles.

Immigration Consequences

Criminal conviction can significantly impact the immigration status of Mexicans both legally (permanent resident, temporary visa holders) and illegally (undocumented) in the United States. In fact, the consequences for current and future immigration status can be more serious than the penalty for the criminal act. Plea bargains, even for "petty" minor crimes, should be structured with full understanding of the implications for immigration consequences. Those charged with representing and sentencing immigrants in criminal matters must be vigilant in ascertaining the likely immediate or future consequences of conviction or plea to a criminal act.

RESOURCES FOR COURT PERSONNEL

The 43 Mexican consulates in the United States are not only prepared but eager to assist Mexican nationals who require representation, protection, or basic resources. In addition, some international agreements obligate judicial systems to notify and keep consulates informed about serious cases involving their nationals. Court personnel can find reassurance and support in the Mexican consulates' active role and their commitment to working cooperatively with responsible individuals in the U.S. legal system.

IN SUMMARY

Mexican immigrants come to the United States to face grossly incorrect perceptions, negative stereotypes, both malignant and benign prejudices, hostility, and antipathy. The history of U.S. aggression, the cycles of welcome and rejection of Mexican labor, the climate of suspicion and fear of immigrants and their children, and incidents of discriminatory behavior combine to reinforce the immigrants' need to exercise extreme caution in their interactions with U.S. institutions and individuals of authority. The sheer numbers of

Mexican immigrants in the United States and their great diversity assure that they will, with increasing frequency, come into contact with the U.S. courts, as plaintiffs, defendants, witnesses, or subjects of actions. It is incumbent upon personnel in the courts—law officers, clerks, attorneys, mediators, arbitrators, and judges—to assure that all have equal access to justice. In the case of Mexican immigrants—especially those from rural Mexico—additional effort probably will be required to assure access and equal protection.

Such efforts go beyond offering interpreters to the non-English-speaking, or public defenders to the poor. Court personnel, starting with judges, need to be trained so as to confront the stereotypical views they may hold; to be alert to those who do not understand proceedings or who need help; to have patience with fearful, embarrassed, or illiterate people; and to follow up on the outcomes of cases in order to better understand—and so improve—the potential effects of court-ordered actions. Once Mexican immigrants have a footing, self-assurance, and confidence, then they will be able to exercise the rights due to them in the United States justice system.

ACKNOWLEDGMENTS

While the opinions expressed in this essay should be attributed only to the authors, we are grateful to the following individuals for sharing their insights, expertise, and experience with us: Robert Alvarenga, Hortencia Arias, and James F. Smith.

The *Shari'a:* Islamic Law
What Muslims in the United States Have in Common

by M. Cherif Bassiouni

In addition to indigenous African-American Muslims, there are an estimated
four million Muslims in the United States. Most of them are first- and
second-generation immigrants who came from Africa, Asia, and the Middle
East. Though bound by the common thread of Islam, they hail from different
cultures whose legal systems are dissimilar except for some common aspects
of *Shari'a,* Islamic law, concerning the regulation of marriage, divorce, children's
custody, and inheritance. But even in these aspects there are differences in the
Shari'a, depending on which Islamic legal school is recognized and applied in
the countries from which Muslims come.

The recognition of these cultural and legal diversities within the over-arch-
ing basic tenets of Islam is necessary to understand what is and what is not
part of the common legal heritage of Muslims in the United States.

MUSLIMS IN THE WORLD

An estimated one billion Muslims live predominantly in some 80 countries,
accounting for anywhere between 2 percent to 100 percent of the population
of these countries.

The geographic distribution of Muslims in the world is as follows: coun-
tries whose population is 90 to 100 percent Muslim are Afghanistan, Algeria,
Bahrain, Comoros, Djibouti, Egypt, Iran, Iraq, Jordan, Kuwait, Libya,
Maldives, Mauritania, Morocco, Niger, Oman, Pakistan, Qatar, Saudi Arabia,
Senegal, Somalia, Syria, Tajikistan, Tunisia, Turkey, United Arab Emirates,

---

Ed. note: The boxed quotations in the margins have been added by the editors and represent
the opinions of focus group members or other quoted individuals and do not necessarily
represent the views of the authors, editors, or publisher.

Western Sahara. Countries of 50 to 90 percent include Albania, Azerbaijan, Bangladesh, Bosnia-Herzegovina, Brunei, Chad, Eritrea, Ethiopia, Gambia, Guinea, Indonesia, Kyrgystan, Lebanon, Malaysia, Mali, Mayotte, Mozambique, Nigeria, Palestine, Sudan, Tanzania. Between 20 and 40 percent: Burkina-Faso, Cameroon, Democratic Republic of Congo, Gabon, Guinea-Bissau, Ivory Coast, Kazakstan, Kenya, Liberia, Malawi, Sierra Leone, Suriname, Uganda, Zambia. Between 2 and 20 percent: Benin, Bulgaria, Cambodia, Canada, Central African Republic, China, Cyprus, France, Georgia, Germany, Ghana, Guyana, India, Madagascar, Mauritius, Mongolia, Mozambique, Netherlands, Philippines, Russian Federation, Singapore, Sir Lanka, Thailand, Trinidad and Tobago, United Kingdom, and United States.

Muslims account for 20 percent of the world's population and that percentage is growing because the rate of conversion to Islam is the fastest-growing rate for all religions.

THE BIRTH AND SPREAD OF ISLAM

Islam developed out of the Middle East, which is the cradle of the three monotheistic faiths: Judaism, Christianity, and Islam. For Muslims, the *Qu'ran* (also spelled Koran), the holy book, is the last of the divine revelations.

Islam does not consider itself a new religion, but the final embodiment of all preceding monotheistic revelations. Muhammad is considered a prophet, as are Abraham, Moses, Jacob, Isaac, and Jesus. None of them is deemed to have divine characteristics.

Abraham, the first Patriarch, was born in the city of Ur in what was called Mesopotamia, now Iraq. He traveled south to the Arabian Peninsula and to Mecca,[1] now Saudi Arabia, where he received the divine message to sacrifice his youngest son, Ishmael. There, Abraham received another divine message, which spared his son and replaced his sacrifice with a ram. From that day on, Muslims have celebrated their high holiday, *Eid,* with a pilgrimage to Mecca, at the end of which each pilgrim, means permitting, slaughters a lamb in commemoration of Abraham's revelation and sacrifice. During these annual pilgrimages, Mecca receives over one million pilgrims from all over the world.

The Muslim state was established when the Prophet Muhammad immigrated from Mecca to Medina in 622 A.D.[2] That year was called the *Hejira* ("immigration" in Arabic), and it is the beginning of the Muslim calendar. During the Prophet's life and thereafter for the first four *Khilafat* (the period of the first four *khalifa*), the Muslim state was a centralized system of government whose seat was in Medina. But this era was followed by several political periods including centralized government, regional fragmentation, and several empire periods, the latest being the Turkish Ottoman Empire, which ended in 1919 with the Turks' defeat in World War I.

Three Fundamental Unities of Islam

Islam is a universal faith predicated on the belief that there is but one god, Allah, the Creator of the universe and of humankind. The word "Islam" means "to surrender": a Muslim is one who surrenders to God.

The three fundamental unities of Islam are God, Humankind, and Religion. Islam requires that its followers have faith and fulfill religious tenets. Islam is a law-oriented religion. It provides the guidelines and principles upon which Islam and all other societal laws can be established.

"Allah" in Arabic means "God," but it implies the one and only deity, the beginning and end of everything. He who is neither born nor gives birth. For Muslims, Allah is He who is beyond human description or understanding. The singularity, centrality, unity, and uniqueness of Allah and the fact that Muhammad is His prophet and messenger are basic tenets of the faith.

Islamic Law—The Shari'a

The Qu'ran is the principal source of Islamic law, the Shari'a. It opens with the words "In the name of Allah, the Merciful, the Compassionate."

The Qu'ran. The Qu'ran covers all aspects of human interactions and relations between man and his Creator. It contains the rules by which Muslims are governed and forms the basis for relations between man and God, man and man, and man and all other creatures and objects that are also part of creation. The Shari'a contains the rules by which a Muslim society is organized and governed, and it provides the means to resolve conflicts among individuals and between the individual and the state.

The Qu'ran is the first source of the Shari'a, the law of Islam applicable to Muslims and to non-Muslims who live in Muslim states (with the exception of certain religious issues to which the confessional laws of non-Muslims apply).

The Sunna. There is no dispute among Muslims that the Qu'ran is the essence of the Shari'a and that its specific provisions are to be scrupulously interpreted and observed. The Sunna is a complementary source to the Qu'ran. It consists of the sayings of the Prophet and accounts of his deeds. Though the Sunna helps to explain the Qu'ran, it is not to be interpreted or applied in any way that is inconsistent with the Qu'ran. All Islamic schools of jurisprudence look at the Sunna as authoritative and above all other sources of interpretation of the Shari'a.

Jurisprudential Schools of Thought. Islamic jurisprudence has developed over 15 centuries during which various schools have emerged, each with its own interpretation and application of the Shari'a. These schools splintered over the course of time and created sub-schools, which developed subtly different interpretive approaches and applications of the Shari'a.

The two major traditions from which all recognized jurisprudential schools stem are the *Sunni* and the *Shi'a* traditions. The Sunni tradition comprises approximately 85 to 90 percent of all Muslims and is based more on a literal and fundamental interpretation of the Qu'ran and the Sunna. The Shi'a have different priorities in the rules of interpretation and other differences.

Sunni Jurisprudence. The different Muslim jurisprudential schools are similar to their counterparts in the positive legal system. That is probably what leads some scholars to say that Islamic jurisprudence, like Roman law, was the product of classical jurists who applied their legal science to interpretation and application of norms and prescriptions. The science of jurisprudence is both a process and a normative methodology for the interpretation of the law and the development of interpretative and applicative legal techniques. The science of jurisprudence is guided by rules and rigid parameters of logic and reasoning.

The political rift between followers of each tradition has generated other differences between Sunni and Shi'a approaches to jurisprudence. For example, the Shi'a view the sayings of Fatima (the daughter of the Prophet Ali), the Prophet's cousin (who was the husband of Fatima), and the fourth khalifa of Islam as confirmational sources of the Sunna. The Sunni, however, do not view these sources as confirmations of the Sunna.[3]

But the most important of all differences between Sunni and Shi'a relates to the interpretation of the Qu'ran. The Sunni use a literal method and therefore look more closely to the letter of the Qu'ran while the Shi'a take a less literal approach and look more toward the spirit of the Shari'a in light of the Sunna.[4]

Modern Legal Systems

Almost every state with a majority Muslim population (listed above) has emerged from colonial occupation in the 20th century, some only in the past 40 years. The principal colonizers were England and France, and they have, with few exceptions, imposed their own legal systems on their colonies. These legal systems, however, have survived colonialism, even though most have evolved while preserving the original common law or French civil matrix. Many of these states now have modern codes and laws inspired by other legal systems or developed out of their own experiences and needs.

Even during colonial occupation, however, the Shari'a was allowed to be applied to Muslims in a variety of legal aspects, such as laws pertaining to personal status (e.g., marriage, divorce, child custody), inheritance, and some property rights. The same was also allowed non-Muslim minorities who followed their confessional laws. Many Muslim states have since continued the same practice and allowed some aspects of the Shari'a to apply alongside secular laws while some of the confessional laws of Christians and Jews apply to persons of these religions, but only with respect to domestic relations laws.

All Muslim states have legal systems with courts, laws, and judges, as elsewhere in the world. There are, however, legal differences among Muslim states. In some countries, such as Algeria, Egypt, Lebanon, Morocco, Syria, and Tunisia, there is a tradition of legal codification and jurisprudence based on the French civil system, except for family law and inheritance law, which follows the Shari'a.

Structures for the administration of justice are also well developed. There are usually tri-level judiciaries comprising trial courts, appellate courts, and a supreme court. The practice of adjudication of claims with representation by counsel is well established. In some countries, such as Saudi Arabia, Kuwait, the United Arab Emirates and other Gulf states, there is less of a tradition of codification and a greater reliance on the Shari'a. But there are also in these countries a number of laws applying to contracts, commercial relations, agency, and the like, in addition to a judicial system and a jurisprudence specific to commercial matters. In the last three decades many countries have enacted civil, commercial, investment, and labor codes modeled on the contemporary laws of Egypt, the United States, France, and England.

Criminal Law and Procedure

There are three categories of crimes in Islam: *hudud, qesas,* and *ta'azir.* Hudud crimes are punishable by a penalty established in accordance with "God's rights" and prescribed by the Qu'ran or by the Sunna.[5] Prosecution and punishment for such crimes are mandatory, as opposed to ta'azir offenses for which prosecution is discretionary. Qesas are a category of crimes that combine what the common law considers crimes against the person and torts of the same type.

There are seven hudud crimes. Not in any order, they are (1) apostasy, (2) transgression, (3) theft, (4) highway robbery, (5) adultery, (6) slander, and (7) drinking alcohol.

Qesas, the second category of crimes, is not given a specific and mandatory criminal definition or penalty in the Qu'ran. Instead, legal doctrine, judicial decisions, and, in recent times, legislation have shaped the meaning and content of such crimes. The qesas crimes include (1) murder, (2) voluntary homicide (manslaughter), (3) involuntary homicide (manslaughter), (4) intentional crimes against the person, and (5) unintentional crimes against the person. The latter two categories are equivalent to the contemporary crimes of assault, battery, mayhem, and other attacks upon the physical integrity of a person. The penalties for qesas start with what is known as "talion law" but an alternative preferred by the Qu'ran is victim compensation.

Ta'azir offenses are those that are not encompassed by either of the above two categories. They comprise conduct that results in tangible or intangible individual or social harm and for which the purpose of the penalty is corrective, and that is exactly the meaning of the word ta'azir. Ta'azir also includes regulatory offenses. Penalties for ta'azir include imprisonment, the infliction of physical punishment, compensatory and punitive damages, and fines. These penalties can also be applied cumulatively. No ta'azir penalty can be greater than the penalty for the hudud crimes. The penal action and penalty for ta'azir crimes are discretionary with the judge. In allowing a ta'azir action to go forward, the judge will consider the following criteria: the social interest in prosecuting the case, rehabilitating the offender, meeting the claims of the aggrieved party (i.e., victim compensation), and correction or retribution for violating a regulatory norm.

Different rules of evidence apply to each category of crimes and, within it, to each separate crime. Each of the four Sunni schools of jurisprudence and their sub-schools, as well as each of the major Shi'a schools of jurisprudence, differs as to the definition, elements, evidentiary requirements, legal defenses, exonerating conditions, and penalties applicable to each of the three categories of crimes and, within each category, to each crime. These differences may or may not be substantial depending upon how specific the Qu'ran and the Sunna are and how much concordance exists in precedents established during the life of the Prophet and the period of the first four khalifa, known as the wise ones *(Al-Khalafa 'a al-Rashidoun)*.[6] But it should also be noted that each school's interpretation of the Qu'ran and the Sunna differs from the others; some on substantive questions, others on lesser ones. Yet all these different schools' interpretations are recognized as equally valid. The application of these crimes and of these rules of criminal responsibility and penalties will therefore differ depending upon what school of jurisprudence is followed in a particular Muslim state, and that makes it very difficult to generalize.[7]

Because of the diversity in the jurisprudence schools of Sunni and Shi'a traditions, the discussion that follows represents generally accepted consensus interpretation, though mostly in the Sunni tradition. It is otherwise an impossible task to describe, in a way that represents all these schools and sub-schools, the definitions of crimes, evidentiary requirements, conditions for responsibility, exonerating conditions, procedures, and penalties. Following is a brief identification of the basic principles of criminal law and some basic rights of the accused protected by the Shari'a.

Basic Principles of Criminal Justice

Regardless of which category of crime is involved, the following principles and rights of the accused apply: (1) no crime without law; (2) no punishment without law; (3) no retroactive application of the criminal law; (4) presumption of innocence; (5) the right of each person to the protection of life, liberty and property; (6) the right to due process of law; (7) the right to a fair and public trial before an impartial judge; (8) confrontation and cross-examination of accusers and witnesses; (9) freedom from compulsory self-incrimination; (10) protection against arbitrary arrest and detention; (11) prompt judicial determination; and, (12) right of appeal. These basic principles and the accused's rights are today found in international and regional human rights conventions and in many national constitutions.

It is also a well-established principle in qesas crimes that such circumstantial evidence that is favorable to the accused is to be relied upon by the judge, while if unfavorable to him, it is to be disregarded.[8]

The Islamic system of criminal justice recognizes the concept of hierarchy of crimes and that of lesser included offenses. Thus, for example, if a hudud crime has not been proven in accordance with the evidentiary requirements of that crime, the judge can still find the accused guilty of a lesser included crime as part of ta'azir offenses, since the latter have less exacting standards of evidence and also carry lesser penalties. The same is true for the crime of qesas; thus, for example, a physical touching or technical battery not resulting in physical injury would not be considered a crime of qesas, and therefore, the talion or victim compensation would not be applicable. Instead, a ta'azir penalty can be applied if the conduct caused fright to the victim or caused a public disturbance.

Truth is the goal of judicial proceedings; thus substance is more important than form. The rule of law does not mean rule by law even though the vast discretionary power of judges enhances the potential for abuse of power. But that is why the selection of judges is deemed so important, and why within it, the personal qualities of judges are deemed paramount.

The Sunna is replete with examples in which personal freedom has been upheld and its violations by those who represent the state are condemned. Imam Khattabbi, a leading scholar, explains that there are only two kinds of detention under Islamic law: (1) detention under the order of the court, and that is mainly when a person has been sentenced by a court; and (2) a detention prior to sentencing during the court's investigation of a criminal violation. He concludes that there can be no other ground for deprivation of a person's freedom.[9]

The Sunna requires that a mere accusation, in the absence of a tangible proof, is insufficient and that an accuser who is an interested party cannot present the sole basis of evidence sufficient to sustain a criminal conviction. The accuser who initiates the criminal action must appear before the judge personally and be accompanied by at least one witness who has the legal capacity to testify[10] to the facts constituting the crime charged and to corroborate some or all of the facts that the accuser asserts.[11] But there are no formal limitations on the admissibility of evidence and the judge decides on what is credible and what is not on the basis of certain general rules.

Civil Law and Procedure

The Shari'a recognizes the right to private property and its legitimate uses save for the right of the community to eminent domain. The use of property in accordance with the best interests and dictates of the owner is safeguarded, provided the rights of others are protected. There is throughout the notion that the utilization of wealth must balance the rights of the owner against the rights and interests of the community, which extends to the preservation of the property itself. Use is permissible; abuse and destruction are forbidden.

The relationship between man and his Creator and the social responsibilities of a Muslim require that property be used not only for one's personal advantage and benefit but also for the advantage and benefit of the community. This does not mean that every commercial, industrial, or agricultural enterprise must ultimately turn into a charitable activity, but there must be human, ethical, and moral factors that relate to the use of property. Thus, if the choice is between an ethical/moral consideration and profit, the former prevails over the latter, other things being equal.

Contracts. Because every Muslim is accountable before both Allah and his community, a great deal of faith is placed in a Muslim's word. Contractual freedom is required and implies the ability to make free choices without undue influence. Islamic economic theory is inherently similar to the notion of free enterprise and socially responsible capitalism. The principles of Islamic economic theory would invalidate transactions in which deceit or undue influence is used by one person against another.

Contracts of various types are regulated by the Shari'a. Contracts are essentially predicated on the free will of the parties and must manifest the true expression of their intent. Economic activities based on implied contracts are also balanced by a variety of what would now be called equitable principles to ensure against undue influence and lack of fairness, which affect questions of competence, validity, recision, and damages.

Individual contracts, implied contracts, and contracts of adhesion are to be regulated in such a way as to enhance fairness, produce equity, protect the weak and the unwary, and promote social interests. The logical extension of these principles is that no one can enrich himself to the detriment of others. In such a case the injured party has a right to compensation for his loss, not to exceed the extent of profit of the one causing the unjust loss.

Legitimacy of Profit. Islam distinguishes between legitimate and illegitimate profit, of which usury is a part. Speculation is prohibited, as an undue profiting from the need or misery of others.

The ethical-moral foundation of all economic relations as set forth in the Shari'a includes subjective considerations, which are usually judged in the context of each given transaction.

Fulfillment of Obligations. In all of his dealings, the Muslim is required to pay his debts as well as due compensation to those who work for him. He is to honor his obligations and stand by his word. Rectitude in business dealings and personal relations is as important to the Muslim as is any other tenet of faith. That is why Muslims frequently do business by means of oral agreement or a handshake as opposed to a written contract. This also explains why there is usually a reluctance to adjudicate claims on an adversarial basis, during which artful arguments may be found to rationalize or justify changing positions. Therefore, in cases of disagreement in business practices, Muslims frequently resort to arbitration.

Women in Islam. As in most of the nomadic tribes of the ancient world, women were deemed unimportant in pre-Islamic Arabia. Indeed, in a society shaped by the rigors of desert life, women were relegated to the margins of community life. But the advent of Islam fundamentally altered the status of women in several ways. First and most importantly, it overturned tradition by according women equal status before Allah. They, like men, were worthy of dignity and respect. As a result of this new status—and the revolution it worked on Arab society—women became pillars of early Muslim society and were counted among its strongest supporters.

As Islam became a world religion and its influence spread, women assumed a more prominent role in society. In early Islam, because men left their flocks and businesses to spread Islam, women assumed larger burdens and responsibilities.

Islam gave women the right to own, manage, and dispose of their property freely, without interference from their husbands or other male relatives. No woman could be married off by her father or anyone else without her express consent.

The Qu'ran, however, differentiates between men and women. Indeed, on these differences is erected an elaborate structure of individual and social rights and obligations. Some appear inequitable on the surface, but on closer examination they reveal a deeper logic. A man, for example, stands to inherit twice as much as a woman, but then he must provide for his own wife and female members of his family should the need arise.

The same holds true of traditional rules of dress and behavior. Women are enjoined to cover their bodies (except for the face and hands) and lower their gaze in the presence of men not related to them. Moreover, although women and men are subject to the same religious obligations—such as prayer, fasting, pilgrimage to Mecca—women pray separately from men. Nonetheless, these rules of dress and behavior—however restrictive they may appear to Western eyes—serve a social function. In societies that by tradition provide few protections outside the family, they ensure a woman's integrity and dignity. For that reason, too, men are enjoined to lower their eyes before women and to be appropriately covered from above the chest to the knees.

In other areas, women enjoy strict parity with men. A woman's right to own property is just as absolute as a man's. Male kin cannot handle a woman's financial interests without her permission. A woman must specifically consent to marriage and cannot be forced to accept a husband she does not approve of. Although a husband has the right to divorce his wife unilaterally— a right not shared by women—a wife can divorce her husband on specific legal grounds by court order.

In education, too, women have the same rights as men. In contemporary Muslim society, in fact, women have attained the same levels of education as men and in many countries occupy positions of power and influence.

Nothing in Islam prevents a woman from attaining her goals. Muslim societies do, however, erect barriers. But in time, these social barriers will disappear—as they are already eroding—because Muslim women with education will expect and demand it. As a result, it can only be expected that women will play an increasingly larger role in Islamic society. But existing social inequities must first disappear. Nothing in the spirit of the Qu'ran subjugates women to men, though some provisions can be interpreted as giving male spouses authority over their wives and fathers over their daughters. Many of the disparities and inequalities that now exist are the product of male-dominated societies. In such societies, Shari'a is interpreted by men, and almost always to the advantage of men over women. That, too, will change in time as Muslim men become more sensitized to women's rights. But women will have to struggle to assert themselves in Muslim societies and gain their rights.

MUSLIMS IN THE UNITED STATES

Muslim immigrants to the United States come from many countries. The number of Muslims in the United States is difficult to establish because the U.S. Census Bureau does not identify persons by religion. But sociologists have put the numbers at between three to four and a half million. States with a high concentration are California, Illinois, Indiana, Iowa, Michigan, New Jersey, New York, and Ohio.

ISSUES FOR MUSLIMS IN THE UNITED STATES

Aside from the overall cultural diversity of Muslim immigrants, the main concern of Muslims in the United States is how to live a Muslim way of life, educate one's children accordingly, and carry out the dictates of the faith in a cultural environment that is not particularly conducive to these purposes. This includes religious practice issues requiring the five daily prayers and going to mosque for the Friday prayer; dietary requirements such as the prohibition of pork and alcohol, and the availability of meat products slaughtered in the *halal* way; dress codes for women and girls over 12; and gender relations. These issues are not only religious but also have legal implications.

Muslims have to overcome prejudice and assert their legal/religious rights. These difficulties are evident in public schools, where Muslims do not have opportunities or dedicated areas in which to pray or conduct Friday services; in employment relations, where employers are more likely to dismiss Muslim workers than to allow them time for their five daily prayers and Friday services; and in public life, where there is no recognition of the three Muslim high holidays (*eid-el-fitr,* end of Ramadan; *eid al-adha,* day of commemoration of Abraham's sacrifice; and the birthday of the Prophet).[12]

For Muslims, however, the legal issues of marriage, divorce, child custody, and inheritance are among the most serious ones they face in U.S. courts where the Shari'a is not recognized as applicable law. This is also true with respect to the recognition by U.S. courts of foreign judgments based on the Shari'a. Such judgments apply to marriages, as Islam tolerates polygamy and marriage between first cousins is permitted; divorce, in which unilateral repudiation by a husband is permitted; and property settlement, since the Shari'a leaves these matters to the parties' contractual agreement at the time of marriage. Each spouse has sole control of his/her assets and the Shari'a recognizes no effects of marriage on property rights. Custody of children, in case of a divorce, is given to the wife until the age of puberty, unless she is determined unfit, and thereafter, custody goes to the father. As for inheritance, the male inherits twice the share of the female in the class of heirs. Clearly, in a secular society such as the United States, these religious-based legal considerations are not given recognition. But when these matters are part of the positive laws of other countries and are embodied in judicial judgments, U.S. courts are faced with the option to recognize these judgments, as they would any other foreign legal judgment, unless it is contrary to the public policy of the state that is asked to enforce such a judgment. An understanding of Islam is necessary in order to assess the significance of those legal/religious issues.

Middle Easterners in American Courts

by Mosabi Hamed and Joanne I. Moore

A Middle Easterner focus group of eight people from Jordan, Yemen, Lebanon, and the West Bank was held in the Detroit area in 1997. In addition to the group report, extended interviews were held to gather information about Middle Eastern immigrants in U.S. courts.

While there are a range of legal systems in Muslim countries, many Middle Eastern immigrants to the United States share some expectations and problems when they are involved in legal proceedings in the United States.

PRETRIAL RELEASE

In U.S. courts, bail can be very confusing to Middle Eastern immigrants. Back home, an option in many criminal cases is to resolve the matter by paying a fine and being released. Once the fine is paid, no follow-up is required of the party

The concept of bail in the home country means having family members come to law enforcement and swear that the defendant will return, sometimes putting up their passports as security. In the United States, many defendants post bail and never return because they think the criminal charges are resolved by their bail payment. When they are apprehended, they have to cope with a bench warrant in addition to the original charges.

ATTORNEYS

In Middle Eastern countries, there is generally no right to a court-appointed attorney. Many immigrant defendants fear that court-appointed attorneys are working for the state, not for them. Once an attorney is appointed, a lack of effective communication is often the real problem. The client wants to explain his or her side of the story to the attorney but often perceives that the attorney just wants to tell the client what the facts are according to police reports and why the client should plead guilty.

PLEA BARGAINING

Middle Eastern defendants are often bewildered by plea bargaining, which doesn't exist under Muslim law or modern Middle Eastern legal systems. To Middle Easterners, it may not make sense that a person can be charged with one crime and then told the charge could be converted to another crime. One attorney relates that in a recent case, a defendant who sold Tylenol IV to an undercover agent was charged not with distribution but with possession, a lesser included offense. His attorney negotiated a plea bargain for attempted possession. During the guilty plea colloquy, the defendant protested the charge, and the judge refused to take the guilty plea. In this situation, the attorney subsequently explained to the client that while he had a prescription, he had no license to sell the prescription medication, and then described how the charges would be reduced if the client pled guilty.

For several years, one Detroit attorney resorted to extreme measures to solve the plea bargaining enigma for his Middle Eastern clients. He allowed his clients to view him pretending to hand a $20 bill to the prosecutor. The clients then felt comfortable bargaining to reduce the charges, because they had seen why the prosecutor wanted to do so. Community education and careful explanations can effectively address the plea-bargain enigma.

INCRIMINATING STATEMENTS AND CONFESSIONS

Accused Middle Easterners frequently wish to explain their side of the story to law enforcement. Because there is no right to remain silent in most Middle Eastern countries, they often are unfamiliar with the concept. The propensity to talk is reinforced by the fact that in some Middle Eastern countries, accused persons may be abused or even tortured until they confess. One focus group member related stories of pretrial detention in Yemen, where shackles with nails embedded in them were put on him while he was detained as a bombing suspect for five days. He never confessed and was finally forced to leave the country. Focus group members agreed that in many Middle Eastern countries, police are known to beat accused persons until they confess.

In the United States, the focus group members thought that accused persons sometimes are socially or religiously abused in order to make them confess or make incriminating statements. Two important examples of this kind of pressure for Muslims are not being allowed to see their families when they come to jail to visit defendants and being deprived of the right to pray. Muslims must wash themselves and pray five times a day, and this is often impossible in jail, which is considered an unclean, unholy place. The focus group felt that in these situations some Middle Easterners will say something just to get out, figuring they can straighten it out later.

COMPREHENSION OF LEGAL PROCEEDINGS

Middle Eastern defendants often have problems understanding the Advice of Rights. For example, there are several concepts that they may not know anything about, such as "waiver" and "jury." Arabic translations of the Advice of Rights would help, but explanations still must be given in translation. However, this alone will not solve the problem of Middle Eastern defendants' unfamiliarity with terms.

Many Middle Eastern defendants find legal proceedings to be uncomfortable and are eager for their cases to end, even if they lose. It is difficult to locate competent Arabic interpreters for cases at all levels. Many are poorly qualified, but parties do not question their competency because they feel that if they do, the judge will hold it against them.

Arab cable TV carries an Egyptian court drama that shows the Egyptian legal system. People may know more about the Egyptian system, which has three judge panels instead of juries and many other differences, from the U.S. system. However, many Middle Easterners watched the O. J. Simpson trial, which provided some perspectives on the U.S. legal system.

DOMESTIC VIOLENCE PROCEEDINGS

Traditionally, domestic violence has been considered a family problem rather than a legal problem. Recently, however, focus group members reported that domestic violence is becoming a punishable crime in some Middle Eastern countries.

Because Muslim law traditionally has governed family law cases, it is hard for many Middle Easterners to understand the entry of domestic violence protection orders. "She's my wife, we were married in the mosque, and no court can change that unless we get divorced in the mosque" is sometimes the reaction of Middle Eastern respondents and even petitioners in domestic violence cases. Due to this feeling, it is very important for courts to take extra steps to ensure that both parties understand the proceedings.

One common pattern is for the victim to change her story during the proceedings by claiming she was the aggressor. Sometimes this occurs due to the extended family's pressure that the petitioner not put the respondent in jail or for economic factors. In these cases, the prosecutor often takes the position that the state will continue prosecuting the case. The courts should ensure that victims know at the beginning of the process that they may not be able to halt the proceedings if they change their minds. The meaning of and consequences of disobeying domestic violence orders should be fully explained to respondents. Otherwise, they may not accept the fact that an enforceable order has been entered and that they cannot have any sort of access to the petitioner.

SENTENCING AND ORDERS

Middle Easterners may be surprised by orders and sentences entered by U.S. courts. The focus group felt that counseling orders may provoke the response that "we're not crazy, we don't need it." Attorneys participating in the focus group explain to Middle Eastern clients what counseling entails, that it is to their benefit, and that it will prevent them from serving jail time. Community service can also be unknown. One attorney related a case in which his client, a traveling circus worker, was arrested for failing to fulfill a three-day community service order. The client, who had also been fined, was never aware of the community service order and had left the area the next day because of his job. Probation is also bewildering to Middle Easterners who have never heard of the concept and have no written order telling them where to go. In all areas, careful communication will enable clients to better participate in legal proceedings in the United States.

The Russian Federation

by Antti Korkeakivi and Maria Zolotukhina

The Russian Federation is the largest country in the world, occupying 17 percent of the world's land area and encompassing more than 11 time zones. The Russian Federation is a multinational state with approximately 150 million inhabitants and more than 120 ethnic entities. It is made up of 21 republics, 6 territories, 49 regions, and 2 cities with federal status.

EMIGRATION

Traditionally, Russia has been a major source of emigration. For instance, between 1901 and 1915, approximately three million people emigrated overseas from the Russian empire. This trend continued during the era of the Soviet Union, although the communist regime imposed strict emigration controls. Attempts to emigrate from the Soviet Union were often prompted by persecution, both political and religious.

Jewish Emigration

A major development was the emergence of the Jewish emigration movement. The Soviet Union tried to bar the emigration of Jews facing persecution, but it was pressured by the United States and others to eliminate restrictions on emigration. As a result, thousands of Jews were able to leave the Soviet Union. In 1979, for instance, 51,320 Jews departed. The Soviet Union often treated those leaving as traitors, stripping them of their citizenship.

The Soviet Union gradually relaxed emigration rules toward the end of the

---

Ed. note: The boxed quotations in the margins have been added by the editors and represent the opinions of focus group members or other quoted individuals and do not necessarily represent the views of the authors, editors, or publisher.

1980s. Exit and emigration were made possible on the basis of an invitation from any person and permission from the country of destination.[1] The Russian Federation has generally accepted these procedures.

Recent Emigration

Although there are still many bureaucratic obstacles in the way of implementation of the new, relatively liberal rules, emigration to Germany, the United States, and elsewhere in the West has been popular in recent years (albeit not as massive as many expected). In 1994, for instance, Russian authorities issued passports to 2.2 million people, 106,000 of whom reportedly left to take up permanent residence abroad. Many Russians, including a great number of professionals, have left their country for economic reasons. This has created "brain drain," a serious problem in the Russian Federation. Economic emigration is not about to end: the migration officials of the Russian Federation estimate that more than 600,000 Russians may emigrate to the West by the year 2000.

In addition to economic emigration, there are still individuals who flee persecution. The war in Chechnya, for example, has produced asylum seekers. Anti-Semitism also continues to be a major problem.

THE JUSTICE SYSTEM

The Constitution, which was adopted by a referendum in 1993, sets out the fundamental norms of the Russian legal system. A number of "constitutional laws"—adopted by a qualified majority in the legislature—have almost as high a status as the Constitution itself. In the Russian legal system, the Constitution ranks supreme, followed by international treaties and then federal laws adopted by the bicameral Federal Assembly. Presidential decrees, in turn, are not supposed to be in conflict with federal laws. In practice, however, presidential decrees and other norms of lower status are of essential importance, and they are often more pivotal and followed more carefully than federal laws. The same is true with regional and local norms.

The Judiciary

Within the Russian judiciary, most cases are decided by courts of general jurisdiction, of which there are approximately 2,500, presided over by 14,000 judges. There is a three-level judiciary system, which is comprised of courts of trial or general jurisdiction (they are also called "people's courts"), courts of appeal, and the supreme court. There are two levels of appeal at which the losing party may appeal a judgment of a court of general jurisdiction. The courts of appeal are called the Regional Courts or, in large metropolitan cities, the City Courts; the supreme court is called the Supreme Court of the Russian Federation.

Russian courts have inherited much of their practices from the Soviet Union, where the courts were far from independent, and, indeed, the whole concept of separation of powers was rejected. Additionally, the Russian courts were built primarily in accordance with the civil law tradition, and, therefore, many concepts inherent in common-law legal systems are lacking or are present in a completely different form.

Attitude toward the Judiciary. The attitude toward the judiciary over recent years has changed and, in general, become more respectful. This has happened partly due to changes resulting from the collapse of the Communist party in the early 1990s. As a result, courts have become more independent from the outside influences that were rather common under Soviet rule. For example, a Soviet judge would typically use the privacy of a consultation room to receive telephone calls from party authorities for instructions regarding the classification of the crime in question and an appropriate sentence. This practice was commonly referred to as "telephone justice."

The working conditions of judges and court personnel remain inadequate. A lack of decent courthouses and even basic office equipment makes it all the more difficult for

> **"One component in a democratic system is to adhere to laws, but in Russia, in the past and present, people try to avoid entanglement with the legal system."**
> – *Russian focus group*

them to gain respect as an authoritative "third power" in society. It is not surprising, then, that in many regions it has been extremely difficult to find qualified lawyers willing to pursue a career as a judge. In addition, many courts are struggling with enormous caseloads, and this can make the duration of proceedings excessive. Indeed, the All-Russian Council of Judges reported in June 1996 that the fact that courts have received less than one-fifth of the sums required to cover their administrative costs has forced a number of courts to stop hearing cases altogether.

Corruption in the Judiciary. The judiciary is vulnerable to attempts to gain influence through money, partly due to the fact that the salaries of Russian judges are very low. Also, physical threats to judges dealing with criminal cases are difficult to oppose since the security provided for judges and court-houses is often deficient. In addition to pressures from affluent and/or powerful parties to a case, the independence of judges may be challenged by local authorities, who have traditionally controlled benefits and working conditions of judges.

In the Soviet Union, the selection process of judges also was often subject to improper influence by both party officials and members of regional soviets, who formally elected judges. To avoid pressure from local officials, the Russian Federation has tried to lift judicial selection to the federal level. The 1993 Constitution states that the President appoints judges in "federal courts" (with the exception of the Constitutional Court, the Supreme Court, and the Supreme Arbitration Court, the members of which are nominated by the President but need the approval of the Federation Council). The term "federal courts" is, however, not defined in the Constitution, and the reach of presidential appointment powers is, therefore, still being debated.

"Many people think the legal system must be cleaned up....
– Russian focus group

Attorneys

The lack of qualified advocates creates delays in processing cases. Those who have resorted to free legal aid, frequently considered "low-priority" clients, have often had to wait for months before their attorneys are ready to go to trial. Avoiding low-quality free legal aid and turning to more qualified lawyers is expensive. As a result, many end up seeking legal help from less expensive non-lawyers with no adequate experience or qualifications. All in all, according to the 1996 report of the Presidential Commission on Human Rights, approximately 80 percent of all cases in Russian courts are heard without the participation of lawyers.

The relative number of attorneys in Russia is less than one-tenth of that in some developed western countries. According to one estimate, there are 180 districts in Russia that have no lawyers at all. Traditionally, the scarcity of lawyers was primarily due to the complete subjugation of the courts to the authority of the Soviet party so that the attorneys served limited purposes in influencing predetermined court decisions. Furthermore, the fact that the Soviet Union rejected market economy meant that there was usually no need for legal counsel to determine relations among competing property rights. An additional reason for the relative scarcity of attorneys was the absence of respect for the law in the Soviet state structures. The written law did not correspond to the actual conduct of the state. The impotence of the law and the futility of asserting legitimate interests in court led citizens to seek informal avenues in order to exercise legal objectives and settle disputes. Instead of taking their cases to a court, individuals often preferred to turn to party officials or to the powerful procuracy.[2] In general, the ineffectiveness of courts elevated the importance of personal contact with state officials.

> **Regarding a Washington State murder trial of a Russian defendant:**
> **"No one thought he did it. Most people thought he was convicted because he got a free lawyer. One guy told me, 'Don't be fooled, if the government wants to close the file, they'll give him a free lawyer— who won't do any work.'"**
> *— Russian focus group*

Advocatura

The Russian "Bar Association," Advocatura, is a nongovernmental organizational unit of advocates that maintains the right to admit and disbar its members. Its mission includes rendering legal assistance to citizens and organizations and defending their legitimate interests and rights. Membership in the Bar is not, however, a precondition for litigating. In noncriminal cases in Russia, anybody with a power of attorney can represent a client in a court, although a draft law would restrict this. Also, the Bar is only one of many professional organizations of lawyers in Russia; judges, for instance, have their own association.

Criminal Law and Procedure

The criminal law of the Soviet Union was in many ways very distant from the one applied in the United States. Some of the differences were prompted by rejection of the market economy. For instance, activities such as speculation, middleman work, and production of artificial goods were all criminalized. Other differences reflected the fact that human rights were "guaranteed" only when they did not clash with the interests of the state. Toward the end of the 1980s, some of these rules were abolished. As a result, infamous provisions such as the ones on anti-Soviet propaganda and circulation of falsehoods about the Soviet state were eliminated from the Criminal Code. This trend was further strengthened with the 1996 adoption of the new Criminal Code, which, in most respects, meets the standards of corresponding laws in the West.

The Code of Criminal Procedure of the Russian Federation. The Code of Criminal Procedure of the Russian Federation established the following safeguards of the rights of the accused: (1) presumption of innocence, (2) no conviction without a fair trial, (3) no retroactive application of the harsher previous criminal law, (4) confrontation and cross examination of adverse witnesses, (5) protection against arrest and detention, (6) prompt judicial determination or right to a speedy trial, (7) right of appeal, (8) right to be represented by an attorney, and (9) right against compulsory self-incrimination.

> **"If you had a problem, you worked things out by talking or ... going to the authorities."**
>
> — *Russian focus group*

The Code of Criminal Procedure has introduced the right to be released on bail. This right has been on the books for a long time, but for a number of reasons (including the inability of most of the accused to post a substantial security bond during the Soviet era), it was rarely applied. The reinstated bail mechanism was recently applied in the case of Richard Bliss, a U.S. citizen accused of espionage in 1997.

While federal authorities have decriminalized many previously forbidden acts, regional and local norms still impose sanctions on many of these acts. Indeed, regional rules frequently attach fines on actions that are expressly "guaranteed" in the Constitution. For instance, despite the constitutional provision on the freedom to choose one's place of residence, major cities in Russia continue to fine residents who have not been able to obtain expensive residence permits.

Crime in Russia. Whereas crime rates were relatively low in the Soviet Union, there is a sense of lawlessness in today's Russia. The number of registered crimes in Russia grew 239 percent between 1976 and 1993, and the growth has continued since then. Especially grave crimes such as murder are committed much more frequently than before: the number of murders reported in the country increased from 15,500 in 1990 to 31,500 in 1995. New freedoms, the beginning of the private sector, and problems in law enforcement have all been blamed for the increase in crime, which often takes organized forms. Still, the crime rate in Russia remains considerably lower than that of the United States.

Conflict in Laws and Norms. Although a number of Russians violate laws deliberately, one reason for failure to follow norms is the fact that the norms are not properly publicized. This is especially true with regard to thousands of governmental, ministerial, and regional regulations. Even when an individual succeeds in finding the relevant norms, different pieces of legislation often provide contradictory norms. Another reason for a relative disrespect for the law is that Russian legislation still contains a number of rules that were inherited from the Soviet era but are not being implemented. Keeping these ignored rules on the books means that one must differentiate between "real law" and these "dead norms." When reacting to lawlessness, Russian authorities have also undermined their cause by issuing norms, in the name of fighting crime, that themselves go against the Constitution and federal laws.

> "A police goal is to catch people who are rich. Cops are poor—this is their major income."
>
> — *Russian focus group*

The Police. In addition to negative attitudes toward the judiciary, the popular view of police practices is far from positive. Minorities, in particular, generally perceive the police as a hostile force that harasses them arbitrarily and demands bribes. One indicator of the relationship between the police and the public at large is that, according to one study, only 37 percent of the population would "in principle" be willing to assist the police in their work. The status of the police has also suffered from the fact that many of the most qualified police officers have left their low-paying positions to join the rapidly expanding ranks of private security companies. Corruption is rampant in the police system.

Reform of Criminal Procedures. One of the most urgent objectives of judicial reform has been to bring the criminal procedure into conformity with constitutional requirements. However, this will require a period of adjustment and, in some cases, considerable financial investment. Meanwhile, many laws adopted during the Soviet era remain in force. For example, the permissible period of detention without charge remains 72 hours instead of 48 hours as required by the Constitution. This situation is aggravated by the inconsistent policies of the government, including the adoption of unconstitutional decrees. One of the most striking examples is a presidential edict of 1994,[3] which extends to 30 days the term of preliminary detention without a court order. During this time, the defendant is denied the right to be presented with the indictment and to know the grounds upon which he is being charged or the offense for which he has been detained.

Nevertheless, some progressive amendments have been made to the Code of Criminal Procedure. Thus, when a defendant, a procurator or an advocate objects to the lawfulness of a detention or arrest, the court must pronounce a judgment and release the detainee who has been kept in custody unlawfully. According to the Code of Criminal Procedure, the investigation has two months from the time of arrest in which to build a case against the detainee or he or she will be released. However, if the preliminary investigation cannot be completed during this period, the term of arrest can be extended by a higher-ranking prosecutor for up to 18 months, after which the defendant must be released from prison. The aforementioned limitation on detentions applies only to the period of the preliminary investigation and does not apply to post-investigative trial preparation or the trial itself, which can drag on for years. This often means that a defendant must serve a virtual sentence without the benefit of trial, a result that violates, *inter alia,* the constitutional principle of the presumption of innocence.

Criminal Process

The Russian procedure for charging a person with a criminal offense and the process of presenting a person with an accusatory instrument indicating the formal charge radically differ from U.S. criminal procedure. The main characteristic of the Russian model is the nearly total exclusion of court interference at the preliminary stages. Instead, prosecutors supervise criminal investigations and play a prominent role. The authority to initiate an accusation rests exclusively with investigative bodies, an individual investigator acting as an agent. An investigator must have sufficient evidence to indicate the guilt of a person prior to formally accusing a suspect. In contrast to a criminal defendant in the United States, a Russian accused is not informed about the evidence collected by an investigator until the preliminary investigation is completed. Consequently, the accused is deprived of any opportunity to respond to government accusations during the evidence-gathering stage.

Only after all possible evidence has been collected by an investigator, the accused is informed that the preliminary investigation has been completed and materials are presented to the accused. At this phase, the accused has the right to file motions with investigative bodies seeking consideration of additional evidence, changing the

> **"If you're arrested, you should first argue, and second, recite your connections. If your connections are good enough, the authorities will say your arrest was a mistake."**
> – *Russian focus group*

classification of the offense, moderating a restrictive measure, or moving for complete dismissal of an action. The investigator has complete discretion to grant or to decline these motions, which are not subject to review. After considering all motions, an investigator may issue an "accusatory conclusion" (bill of indictment). The accusatory conclusion is a document containing a comprehensive, enumerated analysis of all evidence confirming the guilt of the accused, and this document then becomes the foundation of the court trial. It is filed with the court, with a copy delivered to the accused. Criminal justice protections found in U.S. criminal law, such as the preliminary appearance or grand jury indictment, do not exist in Russian criminal procedure.

Criminal Trials. After receipt of the accusatory conclusion, the court will summon the accused to trial. At this stage, parties may again file motions, upon which a judge may hear arguments and decide whether to hand the accused over to the justice system, return the case to an investigator for additional investigation, suspend the case, or dismiss it. If the accused files a motion requiring a jury trial (in the regions where it is available), a court must set a date for a preliminary hearing, at which the presence of the parties is obligatory. The preliminary hearing is then held behind closed doors to resolve issues similar to those determined before a non-jury trial. If the judge concludes during the preliminary hearing that the evidence collected by the investigator is sufficient, the judge schedules the case for a jury trial.

Criminal Defense Attorneys. During the Soviet era, the role of the criminal defense attorney was especially complicated due to the official ideology that considered crime a residual of capitalism. The Soviet ideology held that with the building of the new com-

> A U.S. District Court judge spent two hours trying to convince the Russian defendant, who cannot speak English, that he needs an attorney. "I don't have money to hire a lawyer like Mr. [O. J.] Simpson," he said through an interpreter. "I don't believe any lawyers who are assigned by the court."
> — Spokesman Review, Spokane, WA, Jan. 27, 1996

issued by an investigator or a prosecutor. Court control over the validity or lawfulness of an arrest has become a widely used tool for advocates in their fight for human rights, and it has strengthened the prestige of advocates among the Russian citizens.

> **"In Soviet Russia, you could get acquitted only if you were rich or had connections."**
> *—Russian focus group*

Juries. An example of the strengthening of the attorneys' role is their influence in jury trials, which have been gradually introduced for criminal cases in nine regions in the Russian Federation since 1993. The number of acquittals in jury trials has been approximately 17 percent versus 0.7 percent in non-jury trials. Jury trials have, however, met with strong resistance from conservative forces in Russia, and it is unclear whether they will be expanded to other parts of the Federation as planned. Russian jury trials differ in many respects from the ones in the United States, and the roots of many rules of the 1993 law on juries can be found in the jury trials of pre-Revolutionary Russia. For instance, a guilty verdict can be reached by a majority of 7 out of 12 jurors.

Admissibility of Evidence

According to the Code of Criminal Procedure of the Russian Federation, evidence is any relevant material legally obtained. Information is relevant if it might assist in forming the basis on which an investigator or court could establish the presence or absence of a socially dangerous act or the guilt of the person who is accused. The requirement that a logical relationship exist between the evidence and the fact it helps to establish is similar to the American doctrine of relevancy. Factual data can only be derived from sources strictly determined by law, including testimony (of witnesses, victims, suspects, or experts), real evidence, records of investigative or judicial actions, or by any other document generally. Russian law also establishes specific criteria for admissibility of evidence, which are limited to the character of evidence offered. The three categories of evidentiary limitations are as follows: the scope of persons who could be interrogated as witnesses, the character of information acquired, and the method of obtaining the evidence.

Privileged Communications. The first of these limitations applies to persons whom the investigator may not interrogate, similar to privileges in American law of evidence. Russian "privileges" differ in that they prevent an investigator from even posing questions about protected topics to protected persons. They are more limited in that they apply only to attorneys and only to circumstances learned through the actual fulfillment of the obligations. Moreover, these privileges are available only to a criminal defense counsel or any representative of a professional labor organization (who may not be questioned with regard to circumstances known in connection with their representation). In the event that such prohibited questions are asked and answered, statements of these persons are inadmissible as evidence.

Hearsay. The second type of limitation refers to the character or source of information acquired. The Russian Code of Criminal Procedure refers to this category of excluded evidence as secondhand information, somewhat similar to the American hearsay rule. Unlike the complex application of the American hearsay rule, that of the Russian "secondhand information" rule is very simple. Any witness's testimony that includes secondhand information is inadmissible in a Russian court if the witness is unable to indicate the source of the information or if the original declarant is unavailable for cross-examination.

No Leading Questions. The third and most important category of limitation refers to the manner in which the evidence was obtained. In order to protect witnesses from intellectual or psychological influence, the law does not allow leading questions that, in their wording, contain the model of the anticipated response. Leading questions are so repugnant to Russian evidentiary law that an answer given to a leading question would be excluded regardless of when it was given. This protection, although powerful in law, is mute in application as it has not been rigorously observed in Russian preliminary investigations or court practice.

Evidence by Coercion. Evidence obtained by "threat of violence, coercion, or through other unlawful acts" is also prohibited by law, although it is often disregarded. During the preliminary investigation, which might last years, detainees are usually under the domination of investigative officers and they are routinely deprived of any opportunity to present a defense or communicate with counsel. Until recently, a defense attorney could not monitor or influence the course of the investigation. As a result, threats of violence, or actual torture, often forced defendants to confess their alleged guilt.

> **"At the point of pleading guilty (in U.S. cases) ... it seems like defendants are really confounded."**
> —*Russian interpreter*

New Exclusionary Rule. A revolutionary improvement in the procedure for admissibility of evidence was made by the adoption of a constitutional provision establishing that evidence acquired in violation of federal laws is inadmissible.[4] The adoption of this principle is helping to put an end to arbitrary acts of investigative bodies and to improve the quality of the administration of justice in the Russian Federation.

Confessions. To prevent forced confessions that result directly in sentencing, Russian law does not allow sentencing without a trial and conviction. In accordance with Russian law, an acknowledgment of guilt by a defendant could become the basis for the conviction only if such admission is confirmed by the totality of evidence in a case. Any doubt provided by the evidence would be theoretically interpreted in favor of the accused. There is no Russian analogy to the American guilty plea. However, inconsistency between laws and their application determine the nature of justice in the Soviet Union. In practice, a confession of guilt is tantamount to proof of guilt. After neglecting legal requirements and forcing confessions of guilt, investigators would conclude the investigation, not bothering to collect any additional evidence as the confession would foreclose the possibility of any subsequent appeals by the accused.

Imprisonment

There are approximately 1 million prisoners in Russia today. One reason for this large number is that arrest and detention still remain the most commonly used measure's to ensure a defendant's appearance at trial. In 1994, arrest and detention were used as a restrictive measure toward over 40 percent of those accused. This is common even when a person has allegedly committed a crime for which the injuries do not exceed an amount equivalent to $2. Experts of the Council of Europe were astonished, during their 1994 visit, to encounter a woman imprisoned while awaiting trial for stealing three cucumbers.

Human rights violations such as punitive arrest and detention are widespread. At the same time, many reform attempts have not advanced from paper to practice. For instance, release on bail, common in the United States, is not generally available to detainees. Recent legal reforms have, in theory, introduced the use of bail, but it is still limited to cases involving minor offenses.

Lengthy Confinement. In addition to the frequent use of pretrial detention, the high level of incarceration is caused by the practice of imposing long prison sentences for even minor crimes—especially for thefts. In the late 1980s, criminal law reformers started to emphasize the need to curtail the number and length of prison sentences, but met with mixed success: imprisonment remains the most commonly used form of punishment. The tendency to use imprisonment has been supported by the 1960 Criminal Code (which was still in force in 1996): 85 percent of its articles carry prison sentences. In contrast, noncustodial sentences are often rejected by both courts and the majority of the Russian public. Fines, for instance, constituted only 10.2 percent of the sentences given in the Russian Federation in 1992.

Overcrowding. As a result, jail and prison cells are now tremendously overcrowded, with a large percentage of the detainees being held under suspicion of minor crimes. In Moscow's largest pretrial jail, Matrosskaya Tishina, for example, a cell intended for 35 persons typically houses over 100 prisoners. According to current statistics for major city jails, each prisoner has less than one square meter of living space; prisoners in such cells cannot sleep or even stand at the same time.

Pretrial Facilities Worse. Russia has historically maintained two categories of penitentiaries: custodial jails to hold suspects during pretrial investigation and prisons/labor camps for those convicted by the court. The conditions in pretrial jails are even more inhumane than in labor camps. The larger pretrial facilities in Moscow and St. Petersburg were built in the 18th and 19th centuries and have not been properly renovated. The lack of even rudimentary sanitary conditions (a 100-occupant cell will have only one lavatory pan and one washstand), poor ventilation, and overcrowding result in endemic skin diseases and tuberculosis. (The mortality rate from tuberculosis is 17 times higher in jails than among the general population.) These inhuman conditions are aggravated by the often unlawful conduct of pretrial jail administrators and employees. In 1994, 2,537 employees were found guilty of crimes committed against people in custody.

Jail Conditions. There are no specific laws concerning Russian jails. The only regulations are those issued by the Ministry of Internal Affairs. Consequently, there is no real accountability for the miserable conditions or mistreatment of detainees, and rights are often violated. For example, jail administrators might put detainees on reduced diet (torture by hunger) or in cells inadequately ventilated/heated in winter (torture by cold). These inhumane jail conditions may even result in death.[5] In Moscow alone, nongovernmental organizations (NGOs) receive hundreds of complaints monthly of torture and beatings. The greatest number of complaints, made by convicts in labor camps, protest the conduct of Spetsnaz (special forces units of the Ministry of Internal Affairs), which has been given the task of maintaining order and security in labor camps. The true extent of tortures and beatings cannot be determined because of governmental inactivity and the inability of NGOs to monitor the situation. Recent public opinion surveys conducted by NGOs indicate that many torture victims have not filed complaints due to the threat of even greater victimization.

Death Penalty

When it joined the Council of Europe in March 1996, Russia was expected to impose a moratorium on death penalties. Instead, death penalty sentences have reportedly increased. In April 1998, according to Amnesty International, there were as many as 894 individuals on death row in the Russian Federation. The list of crimes punishable by death—which used to contain 22 crimes—has, however, been shortened in recent years and, for instance, economic crimes have been eliminated from the list. The newly adopted Criminal Code continues this trend. It follows the principles of the

> **Civil cases: "People didn't file civil cases much. That's because they had no property, no car insurance, no medical insurance."**
> — *Russian focus group*

1993 Constitution, which states that the death penalty can be used only to punish grave crimes against life. Minors and the elderly are excluded from this punishment.

Civil Procedure

In the Soviet Union, civil disputes could be decided outside the structure of the courts by quasijudicial institutions such as the State Arbitration Board and the Comrades' Courts. Most civil trials related to housing and tenants' rights, divorces and child support, and labor relations. The role of attorneys in civil cases grew with the commencement of economic reforms. The process of privatization and the establishment of private property required reformation of the State Arbitration Board, a part of the executive branch with jurisdiction over disputes involving industrial or commercial entities attached to governmental ministries. Cases before the State Arbitration Board were determined through an inquisition approach, and parties lacked many legal rights and protection. The State Arbitration Board was recently transformed into Arbitration Courts and became a part of the federal court system. Parties were granted fundamental rights such as the right to appeal, which also enhanced the role of attorneys in Russian civil procedure.

During the Soviet era, the Comrades' Courts had jurisdiction over petty

> **The (Comrades') court's mandate was to create a situation of intolerance to any antisocial offenses through "persuasion and social pressure."**
> — *Robert Rand,*
>   Comrade Lawyer, *1991*

housing disputes, lesser factory conflicts, and some minor criminal offenses. They were composed of members elected from factory employees or housing tenants. The idea of Comrades' Courts reflected the official socialist ideology about the determinant role of the collective in improving and educating people. During the course of judicial reform, the operations of Comrades' Courts were discontinued and their roles were assumed by trial courts.

Arbitration Panels. In some areas of Russia, new forms of arbitration panels have been created. All in all, there are approximately 300 such panels in the Russian Federation, specializing in questions ranging from security markets to labor disputes. These panels are, however, not familiar to the public at large and they suffer from lack of qualified personnel and a firm legislative basis.

Office of the Procuracy. One important way for Russian citizens to solve conflicts with the state is the procuracy. Although victims of alleged human rights violations can now bring complaints against state organs and officials to the judiciary, many prefer to bring their complaints to the procuracy. The procuracy cannot issue binding decisions but only protests, but complaints to the procuracy are still ten times more common than complaints to the judiciary. The traditional ineffectiveness of Russian courts is not the only reason for this; a complaint to the procuracy is also a cheaper alternative to bringing a case to a court.

Human Rights Committee. In contrast to the United States, the Russian Federation has given individuals within its jurisdiction the right to appeal also to international human rights monitoring bodies, the most important of which is currently the Human Rights Committee, which monitors states' compliance with the Covenant on Civil and Political Rights. Although this option has existed since 1992, the first Russians are only now beginning to use it. A more effective international mechanism will become available when Russia ratifies the European Convention on Human Rights.

CULTURAL NORMS

Significant cultural and political differences between the Russian Federation and the United States are manifested in their respective legal systems. These influences are also pertinent to two aspects of the conduct of a trial: the ideology and psychology behind the trial. During more than 70 years of Soviet statehood, official ideology opposed any public values not rooted in Marxist "class" ideology and rejected all moral or ethics norms except "socialist moral" norms.

Professional Ethics of Attorneys and Judges

Adherence to official policy had a decisive impact on developing professional ethics norms generally, and the professional ethics norms of judges and attorneys in particular. The effect of this policy was so significant that the prominent scholar M. C. Strogovich, author of *Fundamental Works of Soviet Criminal Procedure* and a spokesman for the democratization of the Soviet judicial system, stated, in the early 1970s, the following:

> The idea of professional ethics [of attorneys and judges] cannot be considered acceptable. Such an idea may lead to the conclusion that attorneys have a special ethic that differs from a common ethic and socialist moral. It means that an attorney may have an ethic that differs from the ethics of all Soviet people. We have disposed of the question of attorneys' professional ethics long ago. Our society accepts only one ethic, which is a Socialist ethic.

The disregard of professional ethical norms by Soviet—and now by some Russian—jurists further results from a general disregard of the law itself. The professional ethics and behavior of American judges generally reflect an attitude that the law is the only authority that should determine their conduct. Russian judges, on the other hand, have inherited conditions created by an anti-democratic regime. The entire judicial system of the Soviet Union was subservient to the will of the Soviet Communist Party, and the courts often acted as an instrument of repression.

> **"[The judge] was the grand inquisitor of the courtroom proceedings. It was her job to pry facts from both friendly and hostile witnesses."**
> — *Robert Rand,*
>   Comrade Lawyer, *1991*

Judge as Prosecutor

The conduct of a Russian judge during a trial reflects the most significant cultural difference between the two judicial systems. The Soviet government viewed the institution of the court as an instrument in fighting crime, thereby recasting the judge as a prosecutorial figure. As Soviet judges often acted like prosecutors, prosecutors themselves did not necessarily even have to attend trials. Indeed, according to one estimate, approximately 40 percent of all criminal trials in the Soviet Union were conducted without a prosecutor. In the current post-Soviet era, the judge remains the most active figure during the court sittings. For instance, the judge is the first to interrogate defendants, witnesses, and experts, and the parties have the right to ask questions only after the judge has finished his or her interrogations. Furthermore, a judge may at any moment interrupt the interrogations of the parties and continue with his/her own interrogations.

Role of Psychology in Trials

Trial psychology has always been of great importance in the United States due to the character of the jury trial. Parties to a trial often concentrate on influencing the psychological perceptions and emotions of the jurors. For this reason, cultural norms of behavior within the society have always been of great importance in the trial process. In Russian courts, trial psychology has not played a significant role. A primary reason is that judicial determinations were made strictly by professionals. Cases were officially decided by a professional judge and two lay assessors (nonprofessionals). The decision was actually made, however, at the sole discretion of the professional judge. An additional reason for the insignificance of trial psychology is the predominant role of the documents provided by the preliminary investigation rather than presentations in courtrooms. Since the introduction of the jury court in selected parts of the Russian Federation in the beginning of 1993, attention to cultural norms and jury psychology has gradually grown.

Distrust of Justice Figures

Furthermore, Russian immigrants may involuntarily bring a distrust of justice figures to the court. In a 1994 poll, 60 percent of respondents registered distrust in the courts. These attitudes have been acquired through decades of exposure to disregarded, arbitrarily applied, or abused laws and may result in an uncooperative or generally defensive demeanor on the part of parties or witnesses. In Russia, such an approach is still common even in the power elite of the society. For instance, in 1995, then Defense Minister Pavel Grachev refused to follow a court order to appear for a trial, stating that it would clash with his vacation plans. The low status of judges and courts also erodes the force of their decisions and means that court rulings are routinely ignored. Indeed, the Justice Minister of the Russian Federation stated, in February 1996, that only approximately 50 percent of the court rulings are actually implemented.

SUMMARY

When dealing with immigrants from the Soviet Union or the Russian Federation in the United States, one must keep in mind that their images of the judiciary and experiences with legal systems are likely to be dramatically different from those of the average U.S. resident. In particular, individuals whose experiences with the legal system are limited to the Soviet courts are likely to have difficulties in understanding the workings of the courts in the United States.

Russian immigrants may doubt even the ultimate principles of the court procedures. In criminal cases, they may suspect that the outcome of a case has been predetermined and that the proceedings are something close to a formality. Also, an immigrant with no experience in courts other than in Russia is likely to see the role of a judge differently than a U.S.-born individual. The impartiality and independence of a judge are hard to conceive when one has seen judges with clear accusatorial bias, who to an outsider may seem more like prosecutors than judges.

> **"People don't know their rights—the Russian government tried to keep them under wraps. It's hard for Russians to learn about the law system in the U.S."**
> — *Russian focus group*

Many features of the U.S. legal system are likely to be totally new to a recent Russian immigrant. For instance, although jury trials are now being conducted in selected regions of the Russian Federation, this concept is still new to a vast majority of Russians. Bail is another concept that is only now being introduced in Russia and is therefore new to many Russian immigrants. In a civil case, an immigrant may see the whole court process as less meaningful than it actually is. After all, in their native country, court rulings are frequently ignored and authorities are only rarely able to react to such a practice.

Vietnamese Immigrants in American Courts

by Tai Van Ta

Vietnam is on mainland Southeast Asia, bordering on China, Cambodia, Laos, and the South China Sea. An area of 329,560 square kilometers contains a population of 77 million people, of whom 65 percent work in agriculture and 35 percent in industry and service. Population density is high in the Red River delta in the north, particularly around Hanoi, the capital (pop. 3 million), and around Ho Chi Minh City (formerly Saigon, pop. 4 million) in the south.

The majority ethnic group is the Vietnamese (90 percent), who originally migrated from southern China and northern Vietnam to the northern delta some 4,000 years ago. They established a kingdom that was later colonized by the Chinese, who remained in power for a thousand years (111 BC – 938 AD). From the 11th to the 19th century, the Vietnamese pushed southward to take over the Champa Kingdom (now Central Vietnam) and the southern part of the Khmer Empire (now Southern Vietnam)—until they themselves were vanquished by the French, who imposed a colonial regime in Indochina at the end of the 19th century.

The other 10 percent of Vietnam's population is ethnic Chinese, most of whom migrated to Vietnam after the Manchu took over China from the Ming Dynasty (consequently, the Chinese in Vietnam are called Minh Huong, "people from Ming land"), Montagnards (mountain people, consisting of many tribes), and Khmer (Cambodian) minorities. Vietnamese, which is the primary language, has a Roman-alphabet writing system imported by Christian missionaries. Many Vietnamese are also adept in French, English, or Chinese as second languages. The literacy rate is relatively high (about 82 percent).

Ed. note: The boxed quotations in the margins have been added by the editors and represent the opinions of focus group members or other quoted individuals and do not necessarily represent the views of the authors, editors, or publisher.

After the Japanese overthrew the French colonial system during World War II and then surrendered to the Allies, Ho Chi Minh and his followers declared Vietnamese independence in 1945. A French attempt to return in 1946 caused the Indochina War, which ended in 1954 with the Geneva Accords and the division of Vietnam into two parts. The United States, which had given military assistance to the French in their war against Ho Chi Minh, became more deeply involved in 1954 when President Eisenhower ordered vessels to move nearly a million refugees from North to South Vietnam. The United States also provided aid directly to South Vietnam, which it considered to be "the last bastion of freedom in Southeast Asia" due to its ongoing fight against Asian Communism. After South Vietnam refused to carry out reunification elections in 1956, North Vietnam, which was determined to unify the country, started southern insurgency in 1960, which gradually escalated to a full-scale air and land war with the deep engagement of American combat troops in 1965. After the 1968 "Tet" Offensive by the Communists on Lunar New Year's Day, American public opinion caused Congress to begin winding down the American role in the war. "Vietnamization" of the war began phasing out the American presence from 1970 until 1973, when the Paris Peace Agreement permitted the United States to bring American war prisoners home. South Vietnam finally collapsed in March and April 1975 when the Communists conducted an all-out offensive against South Vietnam.

VIETNAMESE REFUGEES AND IMMIGRANTS

In 1975, after the collapse of South Vietnam, remaining American personnel evacuated thousands of Vietnamese refugees from Saigon Airport and rooftops in just a few days. Subsequently, the 7th Fleet picked up Vietnamese who had fled by boat to the South China Sea. A total of about 130,000 refugees arrived in the United States in May 1975. The 1975 exodus was the first real "wave" of Vietnamese refugees into the United States. The majority were from educated, urban classes, many with gold or money in their bags, although some others were from fishing villages along the coast. Earlier in the Vietnam War, Vietnamese immigrants were primarily the wives and children of American military service and civilian personnel returning from Vietnam.

The second wave of Vietnamese immigrants to the United States were the "boat people." They left Vietnam in the late 1970s after experiencing harsh Communist treatment such as confinement in "reeducation" (concentration) camps and the suppression of "bourgeois capitalists" (business people). Thousands took to the sea in crowded and barely seaworthy boats, or were sent out on big boats by Communist cadres who took over their properties. They initially went to Southeast Asian countries as "first asylum countries." Later, the United States accepted the majority of them as refugees. Eventually, the more the United States and other countries processed the boat people as refugees, the more they flooded into the Southeast Asian first asylum countries. The Office of the United Nations High Commissioner for Refugees (UNHCR) held the Geneva Conference in 1979 to pressure Vietnam to stem the flow of boat people. Still, Vietnamese kept exiting, and in both 1980 and 1981, the number of Vietnamese emigrants peaked at 85,000. Among the second wave were Vietnamese of ethnic Chinese origin who fled during the Vietnam-China Border War in 1979. This second wave was more representative of the Vietnamese population: it included not only urban and educated people but also peasants, fishermen, working people, and former military men.

The third wave of Vietnamese immigrants came under the "Orderly Departure Program" that the UNHCR negotiated with Vietnam in 1979. Under this program, which operates today, the American government accepts for immigration into the United States former reeducation internees, people connected with American war efforts (such as American business or embassy employees), and Amerasian children who are offspring of American personnel. At the present time, boat people are no longer accepted in Hong Kong or Southeast Asian countries, but orderly departure applicants are being continuously processed into the United States, as are relatives of American citizens. About 20,000 new Vietnamese immigrants enter the United States each year.

The great majority of the more than one million Vietnamese immigrants in the United States are documented; in fact, many are citizens. Except for a few who might have crossed the Canadian border without papers or over-stayed their visitor's visa from Europe, Vietnamese immigrants came, in a sense, at the invitation of the U.S. Congress.

Once in the United States, the Vietnamese engaged in secondary migration from one state to another. The population is concentrated in California, Texas, New York, Washington, Virginia, Illinois, and Massachusetts.

Because of the harsh circumstances surrounding the exodus of the second wave of immigrants, including pirates and ocean storms, a disproportionately large percentage of Vietnamese immigrants are men (about 60 percent), and the majority of them are young to middle-aged (60 percent 18 to 44, 23 percent under 17). Once settled in the United States, Vietnamese immigrants have been eager to remake their lives. Notably, they especially seek upward social mobility through education, a tradition dating back to the Confucian centuries: 60 percent are high school graduates and 20 percent are college graduates.

THE ECLECTIC CROSSROADS OF LEGAL CULTURES

Through the centuries, there have been many outside influences on the Vietnamese legal culture: traditional Chinese, French, Communist, and American.

Traditional Sino-Vietnamese Legal System

During the long traditional period from the beginning of recorded history to the arrival of the French at the end of the 19th century, Vietnam, like other societies on the periphery of China, experienced the many-faceted impact of Chinese civilization. During centuries of Chinese colonial rule, the Chinese imposed Chinese law codes[1] on Vietnam. However, the resilient Vietnamese never gave up their particular ways. The law codes of traditional Vietnam, especially the Vietnamese Code of the Le Dynasty (1428–1788), have both Chinese and Vietnamese features.

There are three common Sino-Vietnamese features. First, there is a preference for codification of laws in general and, in particular, for the criminal law principle that there cannot be a penalty without a specific statute. Mandarins were punished if they handed down a judgment without citing a statute. The preference for codified laws continued throughout Vietnam's history up to the present time, and it distinguishes Vietnam from the traditional common law system. Second, the influence of the legalist school of Chinese thought is evidenced in an overwhelmingly penal orientation throughout the law codes. This is revealed in the codes' standard phraseology, "Whoever does A shall receive punishment B"; the five-penalty system (beating with the light stick, the heavy stick, penal servitude, exile, and death); and the principle of group responsibility, which imposes liability on the household head for serious crimes committed by household members. Third, the Confucianization of the law meant that infractions of the Confucian moral code were treated as criminal violations. There was an emphasis on social harmony through mediation and conciliation, evidenced in such sayings as *di hoa vi qui,* "conciliation is the best policy," and *vo phuc dao tung dinh,* "woes fall on those who have to go to courts."

Some of the features of this traditional legal culture still influence many Vietnamese Americans who, for example, prefer clear rules in any given situation, readily accept the family's role in rehabilitation of criminals (including juveniles), or say that they prefer mediation and conciliation over litigation.

In addition to its Chinese characteristics, the Sino-Vietnamese legal system included two distinctively Vietnamese features. First, Buddhism had a humanizing influence on substantive criminal law and the penal administration. Second, civil laws and civil rights of private persons were emphasized, such as the imposition of standards for restrictions on the behavior of state officials; a compensation system for civil wrongs against persons, reputation, or property; procedural due process for criminal defendants; and equality between men and women.

Some of these features continue to influence the modern Vietnamese legal system. The French recommended the adoption into the Civil Codes of the customary laws formerly incorporated in the Le Dynasty Code, such as equality of rights for women. Vietnam's current family law provides that children and grandchildren must respect and support their parents and grandparents, filial duties that trace back to Confucianism. Also, Vietnamese in America say that Vietnamese women in the U.S. are more assertive about their rights in family relations and in domestic violence situations than other Indochinese women.

Influence of the French Civil Law System

In a "divide and rule" stratagem, the French split Vietnam's territory and legal system into three parts during their colonial rule: South, Central, and North Vietnam. Each had a separate criminal law code and civil code.

French influence lingered after the French left, both in non-Communist South Vietnam and Communist North Vietnam. In the southern Republic of Vietnam, the legal system's five major codes were chapter-by-chapter copies of French codes. In the Democratic Republic of (North) Vietnam, French influence was and is still strong; concepts and principles of the civil law system have been perpetuated by French-trained Vietnamese lawyers. The French tried to reinforce their remnant influence in Vietnam with the signing of an agreement to provide legal development assistance during President Mitterand's February 1993 visit to Hanoi.

South Vietnamese Criminal Procedure (Prior to 1975)

The Constitutions of 1956 and 1967 of South Vietnam were influenced by American law and provided a rather independent status for the courts. The Supreme Court regulated the courts and had an autonomous budget. Judges had life tenure and could only be removed in cases of physical or mental incapacity.[2] Moreover, following the American model, the Supreme Court was empowered to interpret the Constitution, and to decide on the constitutionality of all laws and decree-laws, and the constitutionality and legality of decrees, arrêtés, and administrative decisions.[3]

According to the 1967 Constitution, the rights of the defendant in arrest, detention, and trial consisted of the usual due process guarantees of arrest with warrant, damages from the state for wrongful detention, the presumption of innocence (confessions obtained by threat or coercion were not to be considered valid evidence), the right to counsel at every stage of the criminal process, and the right to trial by an impartial court.[4]

At the operational level, the criminal process was run by lawyers and judges who were trained by the French in the tradition of the continental civil law system.

Influence of the Socialist-Communist Legal System

After unification of Vietnam in 1976, a remarkable law reform commenced. The Vietnamese government declared a plan to incorporate formerly discrete laws into five major codes: criminal, criminal procedure, civil, civil procedure, and labor. A new 1980 Constitution was written (and amended in 1992) as well as other fundamental laws such as those creating the institutions of the state, including the National Assembly and the court system. Since the 1986 *Doi Moi* (Renovation) policy, law reform has been accelerated. The five codes have been completed, as well as a mind-boggling number of statutory laws on investment and trade and other economic matters.

Russian influence is apparent in the criminal and criminal procedure codes, in addition to inspiration from other legal systems and international law. Their basic structure is similar to that of the European civil law systems codes, but with a Communist flavor. While committing to the inviolability of the person, health, property, honor, and dignity of citizens, and such principles as presumption of innocence, no arrest without warrant, right to counsel, and independence of judges, the codes still severely punish political and economic crimes to protect the socialist legal system. Though references to "Marxism-Leninism" or "dictatorship of the Proletariat" have been deleted, the codes still preserve extrajudicial sanctions, including reeducation camps and administrative detention and administrative control.

In addition to Russian influence, since 1986, the law reform program of the Socialist Republic of Vietnam has been assisted by international law advisors.

CURRENT VIETNAMESE LEGAL INSTITUTIONS AND LAWS

Under the 1980 Constitution as amended, Vietnam has a typical socialist system of unified government under its all-powerful National Assembly.

Assembly members are elected by universal suffrage. They are the theoretical repositories of popular sovereignty. However, actual power belongs to the Communist Party, which ensures through the electoral process that the majority of Assembly members are Party members. There is no clear separation of powers into legislative, judicial, and executive branches. The Assembly, as "the ultimate representative body of the people and the highest organ of state power," makes and amends the Constitution and all laws.[5] The Assembly also regulates all state agencies, elects and removes all officials, decides issues of war and peace, and ratifies international agreements.[6]

The Standing Committee of the Assembly, elected from among its members, interprets the Constitution and all laws, issues decree-laws on matters entrusted to it by the Assembly when in recess, and supervises the implementation of the Constitution, laws, and resolutions of the Assembly and its Standing Committee. The Standing Committee also suspends those written orders of the Government, the Supreme Court, and the Supreme Procuracy that contravene the Constitution and laws. Thus there is no judicial review by a coequal judiciary.

The Assembly elects the Chairman of the State, whose powers are somewhat equivalent to those of the president in a presidential regime.[7] The Assembly elects the Prime Minister from the Assembly membership; it also elects the Chief Justice and Chief Procurator (the latter is responsible for enforcement of the law and prosecution of crimes).

The Government, headed by the Prime Minister, collectively issues decrees. The Prime Minister, ministers, and high agency heads, such as the Governor of the State Bank, issue circulars, directives, and decisions for implementing laws and decrees.[8] Provincial People's Committees also issue local ordinances to supplement national laws and regulations.

The Dominant Communist Party

Behind the formal government structure, the Communist Party exercises dominating power by employing any available measure to capture the majority of the National Assembly membership. Potential candidates must apply to the Party-controlled Patriotic Front for permission to run for National Assembly, which is restricted to Party or Party-approved candidates. In the July 1997 elections, only three independent candidates were elected to the 450-member Assembly. Moreover, voter choice among candidates is limited.[9] The Communist Party dictates who will be elected State Chairman and Prime Minister, as well as many lower-echelon officials. In September 1997, only one nomination for each of the above high posts was forwarded by the Politburo for the rubber-stamp approval of the Assembly. Party personnel, policies and programs are widespread in every governmental branch. Political expedience prevails over constitutional and legal principles.

For example, when the Party wanted to accelerate the law reform Renovation Program in the late 1980s, the Standing Committee responded by rapidly issuing decree-laws formulated with the aid of young assistants on such important subjects as citizenship, the civil procedure code, contracts, inheritance, and taxes, substituting this "quick and flexible" process for the normal National Assembly process.[10]

The Judiciary

Vietnam's judiciary, which consists of the Supreme People's Court, lower people's courts, and military courts, is not an independent coequal branch of government. The Chief Justice is nominated by the State Chairman and elected by the National Assembly for only a five-year term and may be removed at any time by the Assembly. The associate justices of the Supreme People's Court and the judges in the lower courts are appointed by the State Chairman for five-year terms and may be removed by him.

On every level of court, two "people's assessors" sit next to the judge and exercise equal powers. Decisions are made by the majority. People's assessors are appointed by people's councils for local courts, or by the Standing Committee for the People's Supreme Court. Under the Constitution and laws, judges and people's assessors are obligated to independently render decisions and follow the law in making judg-

> **"There is a dispute about whether any judges in Vietnam had integrity and were fair."**
>
> — *Vietnamese focus group*

ments.[11] However, since they are appointed for limited terms, can be removed at any time, and receive salaries through the Ministry of Justice, they are not as independent as U.S. judges. Stories are told about judges and assessors making decisions only after consulting with party hacks at their respective workplaces (the phrase *thinh an* means "asking for the judgment").

> **"The phrase meaning 'The king's law loses out to the village's custom' ... means that the law on the books has its own implementation at the local level."**
>
> — *Vietnamese focus group*

In Vietnamese courts, the defendant stands at a lower level while prosecutor, clerk, and judge sit together above the defendant. Vietnamese defendants in American courts are afforded a sense of equality before the law by being placed at the same level as the prosecutor. This sense is reinforced by a realization that, unlike Vietnamese courts, American courts are not dominated by political directives.

Vietnamese Laws

In Vietnam's civil law system, like those of Europe, codifications are important, but case precedent is not. Since 1986, Vietnam's law reform has resulted in a mind-boggling promulgation of laws, decree-laws, decrees, and circulars.[12]

Along with the proliferation of new laws, there has been a remarkable effort to publicize them. Popular journals, magazines, newspapers, academic and professional journals, and compendia of laws and regulations have joined the *Official Gazette,* the government legal publication, in publishing information about laws. This concerted effort is in contrast to the previous Communist tradition of providing only enough copies of laws for government agencies.

Implementation of the new substantive laws, however, lags behind the legislation and publication efforts. The primary reasons for the gap are corruption and bureaucratic inertia. There are thousands of almost-completed cases for which judgment has been entered but enforcement is still ignored. The Ho Chi Minh City Court, the largest court in the country, reportedly enforced only 11,594 cases out of 32,803 cases, according to statistics up to 1992.

The Criminal Process: Principles and Realities

The 1988 Criminal Procedure Code reenacts the principles found in the 1980 Constitution and various statutes, decrees, and circulars. In contrast to the previous version of the Constitution, which declared that Vietnam was a state or proletarian dictatorship with the Communist Party as the only leading force, the amended Constitution of 1992 declared that the government was restrained by the rule of law. Chapter V of the Constitution, entitled Citizens' Rights and Obligations, confers race and sex equality; the right to vote and stand for elections; the right to work; property rights, basic education and health care; freedom of movement, speech, assembly, association, and religion; and the inviolability of the person, health, honor and dignity, home, and correspondence. These constitutional rights are not unconditional. Article 51 requires citizens to comply with their obligations toward the state and society as a condition to enjoying their rights.

The Criminal Procedure Code repeats the above basic principles for protecting the citizens' lawful rights (while defending the socialist regime) and adds the right of presumption of innocence, the right to counsel, and the right to public trial by an impartial court, which renders majority decisions made by the assessors and the judge and which bases its decision solely on the law. The right to bring complaints against unlawful acts of the police, the procuracy, and the court is also conferred.

Arrest and Detention for Investigation. Arrest warrants approved by judges, procurators, or police chiefs (whose warrants must be approved by procurators) are required for almost all arrests. The warrant must be read to the accused in front of the local administrative chief and a neighbor.[13] The arresting authority must inform the accused's family, his village or town, and his work unit. Only in emergency situations (e.g., when serious crimes are about to be committed), and *in fragrante delicto,* can the police or military officer or any citizen make a warrantless arrest, but it must be reported

> **"In practice in Vietnam, arrested people are presumed guilty. So that here, arrested persons don't ever think of proving their side."**
>
> — *Vietnamese focus group*

to the procurator immediately.[14]

Temporary detention for three days must be reported to the procurator in 24 hours and cannot be extended.[15] Two to four months' temporary confinement can be ordered (and renewed) for very serious crimes, leading to a more than one-year imprisonment sentence if the defendant is particularly prone to ab-

> **"Bail is generally viewed in Vietnam as the end of the case. It is the payment of money that solves the legal problem."**
>
> *— Vietnamese focus group*

sconding or committing further crimes. Although the accused cannot be subject to torture,[16] and has the right to family visits and receipt of gifts and must be released when temporary confinement is no longer necessary, the Supreme Procuracy can further extend the confinement for national security reasons—which is sometimes used as a measure against political detainees.[17] The accused may be bailed out with the guarantee of two individuals or one organization, or, if he or she is a foreigner, for money bail in an amount to be determined by the investigating police with the approval of the procuracy.[18]

Trial. The accused is presumed innocent until proven guilty. The burden of proof is on the prosecution, which must present exculpatory and extenuating evidence in addition to incriminating evidence. The accused has the right to counsel. The judge, the people's assessors, and the procurator and investigator must recuse themselves if there is reason to assume that they may not be impartial. Judges and people's assessors have the duty to decide cases independently, in accordance with the law.[19]

Deviations from Idealistic Legal Standards. The actual operation of the criminal legal system deviates from the laws' idealistic standards. In detention, for example, an accused may be subject to threat or abuse. An accused may be detained past the authorized period,

> **"The trial is the opening and closing, with little questioning of the witnesses or defense. The lawyer's job is to offer questions to the judge, but there is no direct questioning of the witnesses or clients. Lawyers in Vietnam plead for mercy, they do not show evidence."**
>
> *— Vietnamese focus group*

especially on the ground of national security. Even though physical torture to obtain confessions is illegal, the KGB taught many Vietnamese police officers refined ways of extorting confessions, such as requiring repeated writing of autobiographies so that contradictions might be used during lengthy, oppressive interrogations. Police misconduct can reach extremes. Hanoi was swept by scandal in 1993 after a brutal police officer killed an innocent man who was only a messenger for others.

Though defense counsel's presence is required during interrogations, the requirement can be waived by the procuracy in cases involving national security.[20] The defender in Vietnamese criminal proceedings need not be an attorney-at-law, but rather may be chosen from among laymen at the accused's workplace, "people's defenders,' or relatives. Attorneys are members of the government-run bar association, which collects fees and provides cases and payment to member attorneys.[21] There is no tradition of private attorneys or specialized public defenders who put up a vigorous fight for the defendant. Many attorneys just ask for leniency or "go by the back door," as one Vietnamese lawyer put it, to try to help their clients. In reality, they have to go by the back door, because many judges themselves decide cases by asking Party hacks in their work units to indicate what kind of judgment they should hand down (*thinh án*), especially in political cases. One consequence of this experience of being "railroaded" through the criminal process in Vietnam is that some Vietnamese in America may be too easily persuaded to plead guilty by lazy appointed counsel even though there may be a good chance the client could win on the basis of the evidence. One such lawyer in Massachusetts has been nicknamed "Mr. Guilty" by Vietnamese defendants.

"I know a lawyer in Vietnam ... she reports that she is not there to defend the defendant. Her role is siding with the judge and asking the defendant to apologize and ask for mercy."
— Vietnamese focus group

The government's most serious deviation from constitutional and criminal law standards is reeducation in labor camps. Detainees are arrested without specific criminal charges and without trial or any other due process guarantees. Such detainees are released only after camp authorities decide they have been "reformed" in thought and action. The justification for such practice is the 1961 Resolution No. 49—NQTVQH of the Standing Committee of the National Assembly in North Vietnam. In violation of the 1946, 1959, 1960, and 1980 Constitutions of Vietnam, this resolution has been used in all of Vietnam since 1975. Since the late 1970s, Amnesty International and Human Rights Watch/Asia have issued critical reports on these camps and other extra-legal measures, such as administrative detention.

> "Defense attorneys can explain the American process, but it's hard to get it across. The defendant keeps wanting the defense attorney to ask for sympathy and mercy."
>
> — *Vietnamese focus group*

The general situation has been improving in the 1990s.[22] Former South Vietnamese political detainees in reeducation camps have been allowed to emigrate to the United States under the Orderly Departure Program. In addition, prominent political detainees have been given trials to make a show of lawful conformity with the Constitution and Criminal Procedure Code.[23] As Vietnam currently is making a transition to a market economy, the population is no longer depending on government rations and is independent from restrictions on their livelihood. Individuals and organizations, including religious ones, no longer fear the government and have become more demanding of citizens' rights. As Vietnamese meet foreigners and visiting overseas relatives, who take basic human rights for granted, or obtain new ideas from outside world information through mass media, despite government efforts to restrict its flow, they have become more apt to assert their rights. For example, in September-November 1997, thousands of residents of Thai Binh, Thanh Hoa, and Dong Nai Provinces successfully revolted against unpopular officials, incarcerating and injuring them in protest against corruption and infringement on property. Party membership is only 3 percent of Vietnam's 77 million people, and the Party is losing control, in the same manner that "a basket cannot cover a growing elephant" (Vietnamese proverb).

Civil Cases and Alternative Dispute Resolution

The Family Law of 1986, the Civil Code of 1995, and the 1989 Decree-Law on Civil Procedure make up a complete set of rules to resolve civil cases. Conciliation, mediation, and arbitration may precede court action.

After the lower court has entered a judgment, it can be appealed to the appellate court for a partial review or a complete retrial wherein new and old evidence will be presented.

Civil matters originating in Vietnam that have reached the American courts include divorce, division of the marital estate, and validity of documents such as divorce papers, marriage, and birth certificates, etc.

CULTURAL FACTORS AFFECTING ATTITUDES IN COURTS

The legacy of the traditional extended family of the Vietnamese, consisting of the nuclear family plus grandparents, uncles and aunts, and cousins, has an impact on their living patterns in the United States. This cultural trait is another facet of the concept that the head of the household was, under the traditional codes, responsible for crimes committed by household members. In America, no court would hold the household chief liable for individual members' offenses, but the social pattern of extended family still has some legal and social consequences.[24] Courts can rely on the extended family's cohesion to entrust it with the rehabilitation of criminal offenders, especially juveniles. Many elderly people prefer to live with their younger offspring, ideally in an in-law apartment next to the main building or in a nearby dwelling, to rely on them for their English language proficiency or moral support.

> **"Vietnamese family and society are influenced by Chinese perspectives. There is the hierarchy of the father, the mother-in-law, and the wife."**
> — *Vietnamese focus group*

Peaceful Settlement of Disputes

As stated above, the social motto "harmony is the best policy" was incorporated in the Le Dynasty Code with its long articles on conciliation and mediation. Before the Westerners came, the Vietnamese had been imbued with the culture of Buddhism, which valued respect and tolerance of all living creatures (*tu bi hi xa*), and the culture of Confucianism, which treasured self-improvement, cohesion in the family, law and order in the nation, and peace in the world (*tu than, te gia, tri quoc, binh thien ha*). As a result, many Vietnamese like negotiation and mediation and have a distaste for legal combat in the court. They fit in with the new American preference for alternative dispute resolutions. On the other hand, they also need to be encouraged to assert their rightful interests in court when necessary.

> **"Rural dwellers rely ... on elders to solve problems ... and there is a no-fault system for torts. If a dog bites a person, ... the person will go to the owner's house to be taken care of and fed. This makes the tort feasor lose face and pressures the tort feasor to pay."**
> — *Vietnamese focus group*

Respect Through Body Language

In old Vietnam, people bowed their heads to show respect to their interlocutor and bowed further, even prostrated to the ground, to show respect to the emperor. In America, if the Vietnamese look to the ground, avoid eye contact, and otherwise act with indirectness, they should be understood as showing reverence and tactfulness and not undue shyness or guilt.

Fear of Authority

The Vietnamese have long suffered all kinds of police oppression: French colonial, Communist, and feudalist-militarist. Throughout history, once they were in police hands, the thorough investigation of the investigating magistrates or the confession coerced by the police most often led to a guilty verdict in

> **"The Vietnamese have a hard time showing emotions, especially emotions of remorse and guilt.... 95 percent of Vietnamese decline to speak at sentencing after being invited to speak by the judge."**
> — *Vietnamese focus group*

the court. That historical baggage brought to America has resulted in the fact that most Vietnamese are careful and law-abiding in dealing with the police; on the other hand, sometimes they may seem to be evasive in cooperating with the court and the police as victims/witnesses, or may be wrongly suspected of guilt and treated roughly by the police. This impression is worsened by the language barrier. Many Vietnamese defendants need to have a combative defense attorney to help them fight an equal court fight with the police or the prosecutor in this adversarial system so unfamiliar to them.

Westernization and Downward Social Mobility

Due to their long involvement with Western countries, the Vietnamese are among the most westernized in East Asia. Vietnam was exposed to Western ideas of liberty, equality, and fraternity early during French colonization, and to American modernism during the 20-year period of the war. In addition, linguists have said that due to the Vietnamese use of the Roman alphabet, Vietnamese children quickly become literate in English.

Despite their relative westernization, once they have been transplanted out of Vietnam to a strange country that is still somewhat racially discriminatory, many Vietnamese experience culture shock and difficulty adapting. A number have succeeded, but some have become discouraged and fallen into social and emotional troubles. Some are elder war veterans, who lapse into unresolved grief and anxiety because they are near the end of their active lives and feel it is too late to re-create their place under the American sun. Others are husbands who have lost their careers and status, and become emotionally unstable or perhaps even prone to domestic violence against their wives and offspring who may seem to succeed better with their jobs or education. Another vulnerable group is disadvantaged children who were lacking in

> "Authorities blame cultural differences, language, unpleasant experiences with corrupt police in native lands and an intense fear of retaliation ... [for standing] between peace officers and the growing refugee community."
> – Los Angeles Times,
> Oct. 21, 1990

educational background in Vietnam and give up school to join gangs because they can't keep up. Despite the fact that the news portrays a popular image of outstanding Vietnamese American (and Asian American) whiz kids, the image needs to be complemented by the reality of the unsuccessful and wretched flotsam and jetsam of the Vietnam War.

Application: Presiding Over Cases Involving Immigrants

by Judge Paul J. DeMuniz and Joanne I. Moore

In order to identify problems commonly encountered in court proceedings involving immigrants, surveys and interviews were conducted with 40 judges, attorneys, and interpreters in several states. The results can be found in Appendix 1. The problems they identified reflect legal system differences and other factors discussed in the foregoing chapters. Some of the difficulties that immigrants experience are described below, along with recommended approaches for addressing them.

ADVICE OF RIGHTS ISSUES

Judge's observation: I don't think [immigrant] defendants begin to understand the importance or meaning of the rights they are given before arraignment....

Recently arrived immigrants usually have very little knowledge of the vocabulary or substantive features of the U.S. legal system. Their expectations are largely based on the legal system of their native country and most first-time immigrant defendants hear about their rights for the very first time when the Advice of Rights is read to them in court.

Therefore, Advice of Rights concepts should be carefully explained to immigrants by the court and by their attorneys. Some courts have created short videos in various languages, which explain criminal defendants' rights. An explanation of defendants' rights translated into Arabic, Chinese, Russian, Spanish, and Vietnamese is located in Appendix 2.

BAIL

Judge's observation: Some immigrants seem to believe that bail is a final disposition of the case, and misunderstand the concept of bond and the purpose of bondsmen's fees.

Bail or other forms of pretrial release do not exist in many countries and are rarely granted in others. Immigrants from such countries often do not understand what bail is and/or that they are required to return to court for further proceedings.

A brief, simple explanation of the bail system by the judge will help to prevent misunderstandings. The defendant can be advised that bail will allow release only until the next hearing, that the case is not finished, that the defendant's money will be retained by the court and returned at the end of the case, and that if the defendant does not have sufficient funds to pay the bail amount, bail might be obtainable through a bail bonds company. Attorneys representing immigrant defendants should repeat the bail explanation if necessary.

In addition, if possible, a brief, translated document explaining bail and naming the next hearing date should be given to a defendant who is bailing out. A sample bail explanation translated into Arabic, Chinese, Russian, Spanish, and Vietnamese is located in Appendix 2.

EXPEDITIOUS RESOLUTION OF COURT PROCEEDINGS

Judge's observation: In a number of cases they [immigrant defendants] keep repeating, "I just want to pay and get this done." Even after an explanation of the potential of jail and a fine, they still say, "I just want to pay" ... they will also keep insisting on paying when I've already sentenced them to jail—it's almost as if they think I might change my mind.

Many immigrant defendants come from countries where minor cases are resolved by the payment of a fine at the first court appearance. In addition, some immigrants come from countries where governmental corruption is common, and they may be familiar with legal systems in which cases can be favorably resolved by making a payment to the judge or prosecutor. Therefore, many immigrant defendants expect to resolve minor criminal charges during their first appearance, especially if they have not been involved in the criminal justice system previously. Often they are not aware that the normal U.S. criminal process consists of several court hearings.

Immigrant parties who seek to resolve their cases through payment may need more clarification as to the U.S. legal system than can be given during court proceedings. Defense attorneys should be encouraged to talk about important due process features of the proceedings and related topics with their clients and to carefully explain what they can expect in upcoming court proceedings.

Since the U.S. legal system requiring multiple hearings differs fundamentally from many countries' legal systems, an affirmative program to provide accurate information to immigrant community groups is often needed in addition to in-court explanations. Judges and attorneys can enhance an immigrant community's resources for understanding the U.S. court system by making presentations about the courts to local immigrant and refugee groups or to English as a Second Language (ESL) classes, writing brief articles for immigrant newsletters, or taking other opportunities to communicate with immigrants. Presentation resources are located in Appendix 4.

RIGHT TO AN ATTORNEY

Judge's observation: Immigrants who are less "sophisticated" in regard to the criminal system seldom request a public defender, even after being advised of their rights through an interpreter.

Judge's observation: The defendant will ask questions that I cannot answer [but] refuse an attorney who could answer the questions.

In many countries, criminal defense lawyers' representation is limited to pleading for leniency rather than contesting guilt and to excluding defenses that are perceived as contradicting the interests of society. In other legal systems, court-appointed attorneys are not provided for indigent defendants. In countries where attorneys are appointed for criminal defendants, their role is often perceived as serving the interests of the government first, and their clients second.

It is recommended that judges give a simple explanation that it is in an immigrant defendant's best interest to have an attorney in U.S. legal proceedings and that the court-appointed attorney will be required by law to keep everything said confidential and to conscientiously and thoroughly defend the defendant against the charges. Attorneys should be encouraged to carefully, and, if appropriate, repeatedly explain their role to immigrant clients.

In many countries, public aversion to court-appointed attorneys is deep. Detailed discussions of the role of attorneys in the United States during presentations to immigrant groups will help disseminate accurate information about them within immigrant communities.

PLEADING GUILTY

Judge's observation: Plea bargaining—there's lots of confusion. Immigrants give odd looks regarding "pleading guilty to a lesser charge."

An immigrant may have no understanding of the concept of plea bargaining or pleading guilty to a lesser included crime. Judges can help ensure that immigrants are not confused by the plea bargain process by explaining the process in court and by directing attorneys to review it carefully with the defendant and explain the paperwork in an understandable fashion.

IMMIGRATION

Attorney's observation: I'm so scared that I'll unknowingly advise a defendant to make decisions which will lead to deportation....

Many defendants do not understand that a criminal conviction is a ground for deportation, exclusion from the United States, or denial of naturalization. In order to make knowledgeable decisions regarding their cases, they often need an informational warning from the judge and/or specific and detailed information from their attorneys about impending immigration consequences.

THE JUDGE'S ROLE

Judge's observation: There isn't always a realistic perception of what the judge can and can't do—[they think the] judge can do anything.... English speakers more easily understand the limits.

In many countries the judicial branch is not independent. Political party membership may be a prerequisite to being appointed judge, and a primary role of the courts may be to uphold political order. In some countries, the judge takes something of a prosecutorial role, doing most of the questioning of witnesses.

Judges and attorneys should explain some of the role differences of judges in the United States when these issues arise during proceedings. Examples are the judge's limited discretion in sentencing, the judge's general inability to punish or fine people who are not parties to the action, or the judge's apparent detachment during a jury trial.

IMMIGRANTS' UNFAMILIARITY WITH JURIES

Interpreter's observation: Most immigrant defendants ignore the jury ... most of them think the judge is the only one hearing and deciding the case.

Juries do not exist in many countries. Many defendants do not know what a jury trial is or understand the role of the jury in deciding the case. Before waiving a jury trial, many defendants need an explanation of the jury's role during the Advice of Rights.

If an immigrant party seems confused during a jury trial, the judge should direct defense counsel to explain the jury system in a meaningful way, thus informing the party of how important it is to pay an appropriate amount of attention to the jury.

IMMIGRANTS' PARTICIPATION IN COURT

Judge's observation: Immigrants' apparent comprehension of the proceedings varies. They are so anxious, they agree to things they may not understand or accept ... participation of immigrants should be better.

Many immigrants demonstrate difficulty in comprehending legal proceedings. Immigrant parties are often silent when given an opportunity to address the court and are often likely to agree to the entry of orders against them.

Judges and attorneys can ensure immigrant parties better understand the proceedings by periodically asking if the party understands particular parts of the proceedings and by offering short, simple explanations of what is going on in the courtroom or asking counsel to do so.

IMMIGRANTS' DEMEANOR

Judge's observation: [It is] difficult ... to evaluate the defendant's demeanor or remorsefulness due to cultural differences.

Different countries have a wide range of body language considered appropriate for very serious situations such as court. Immigrant parties are likely to exhibit different body language and eye contact patterns than would most U.S.-born parties. Information about a particular country's culture may be available to courts from local immigrant and refugee agencies or churches. Professionals such as anthropologists may also provide accurate information.

Juries often are unfamiliar with demeanor differences among different people. These issues may be addressed during voir dire or at other points in the trial, such as jury instructions.

DOMESTIC VIOLENCE PROCEEDINGS

Judge's observation: A particular area of concern [is] domestic violence....

Interpreter's observation: Domestic violence is considered personal; they think the state has no reason to be involved.

Domestic violence is considered a nonlegal matter in many countries. In those countries, domestic violence problems may be resolved within the extended family or possibly the community, and certainly are considered to be outside the jurisdiction of the courts. This can cause victims of abuse to be reluctant to seek protection, respondents to not take protective orders seriously, or other problems. If one or both of the parties is undocumented, the fear of deportation can complicate the issues.

Domestic violence proceedings and orders should be carefully explained to the victim when initiating the action, and to both parties during proceedings, and when orders are entered. Enforcement of orders should also be explained.

It is important that translated written orders be provided to both parties, if possible, so they know what the orders say and will be able to follow them.

Judges' presentations on domestic violence laws and proceedings at immigrant and refugee agencies or other forums can dramatically increase newcomers' understanding of domestic violence laws and local domestic violence proceedings and resources. See information on Immigration Status and Battered Immigrants in Appendix 5.

SENTENCES

Judge's observation: In sentencing, there are issues regarding receptivity to counseling or other affirmative conduct areas of probation.

Noncustodial sentences are virtually unknown to a large number of immigrants. In many countries, alternate sentences ordering defendants to perform community service, attend counseling or substance abuse treatments, or participate in work release or similar programs do not exist. Fines and parole do exist in some countries.

In the United States, litigants are commonly ordered to participate in various kinds of treatment programs, particularly in domestic or criminal cases. As many judges have noted, serious language problems arise from drug treatment, alcohol treatment, or counseling orders if programs do not have bilingual capability. Bilingual counselors can be very effective, because they can talk directly to their clients and are likely to be culturally sensitive; professional interpreter services are another option. Before ordering treatment programs for non-English-speaking parties, courts should determine if local treatment providers have the appropriate bilingual capability and encourage them to develop it if not.

When an affirmative conduct sentence is ordered, it is especially important that the non-English-speaking party receive a written translation of the conditions of the order, if at all possible. Non-English-speaking parties furnished with unfamiliar English orders are often unable to remember important aspects of the order they heard once in court, read it, or obtain an accurate translation of it on their own.

CONCLUSION

It is commonly said that crowded court calendars make it impossible for judges and attorneys to spend extra time on individual cases. This may be one of the reasons that a lack of adequate communication is the main obstacle to a fair trial in many cases involving immigrants.

As observed in a court interpreter case heard by the Second Circuit Court of Appeals in 1970, the justice system needs to insure that defendants are capable of understanding court proceedings:

> Considerations of fairness, the integrity of the fact-finding process, and the potency of our adversary system of justice forbid that the state should prosecute a defendant who is not present at his own trial ... otherwise, '(the) adjudication loses its character as a reasoned interaction ... and becomes an invective against an insensible object.' *United States ex rel. Negron v. New York,* 434 F.2d 386 (2d Cir 1970), quoting *81 Harv.L.Rev.* 454, 458 (1969).

By providing a sufficient amount of information, judges and attorneys can change a litany of unknown words into discourse that is meaningful to immigrant parties, thus providing them the opportunity to participate in their own cases. The explanations suggested in this book often need be no more than one or two sentences long. Judges and attorneys who take a little extra time to give immigrant parties notice of their rights and of what is expected of them can enormously improve the fairness of their court proceedings.

Summary of Survey Results: Application Chapter

Forty judges, attorneys, and interpreters in Washington, California, Oregon, Michigan, Massachusetts, Minnesota, Utah, and Florida were surveyed and interviewed about their observations concerning immigrants' participation in court hearings. Judges who preside over a significant number of cases involving immigrants were contacted because of their expansive experience with the issues. In addition, attorneys who represent a high number of immigrant parties, hear their clients' thoughts and reactions, and are cognizant of communication and cultural problems were interviewed. A wealth of in-depth observations of immigrants in court from a bicultural perspective was also tapped through interviews with interpreters, who are often put in the frustrating position of being aware of confusion and communication problems but unable to remedy them due to ethics prohibitions against giving legal advice or otherwise interfering with the case. These interviews yielded many comments about the thousands of court proceedings involving immigrant parties in which the interviewees had participated.

The first problem point noted by interviewees occurs during defendants' first court appearances in U.S. courts. At that time, defendants are generally advised of their important constitutional rights such as the right to an attorney, to a jury trial, to plead guilty or not guilty, and so forth. Most U.S.-born defendants entering court for the first time are relatively well prepared in terms of their familiarity with much of the vocabulary in an Advice of Rights, the necessity of making decisions such as whether to plead guilty or not guilty, and the concept of waiving certain rights. American television includes many courtroom shows, television news frequently discusses court cases or broadcasts them, criminal trials are common subjects for newspaper articles, and many people are introduced to the legal system and/or its history at school.

Since many immigrants cannot speak English when they arrive, many are unable to understand the English media, and many do not have comprehensive educational experiences in the United States. In contrast to an American-born person's expectations, a recently arrived immigrant is likely to have very little knowledge of the vocabulary or substantive features of the U.S. legal system.

Bail

Judges who participated in the survey were split as to whether they perceived immigrants to be confused about bail and thus unaware of their obligation to return to court. Some judges felt immigrants are often bewildered regarding bail; others reported seeing no difference between immigrants and non-immigrants. Some judges saw high rates of "failure-to-appear" (FTA) charges against immigrants; others had not observed a difference. Several judges stressed that careful explanations regarding bail in court along with the setting of the return date can prevent bail misunderstandings.

The interpreters *all* indicated that immigrant defendants find the concept of bail very confusing. Several interpreters reported that, consistent with the court process followed in their native legal systems, immigrant first-time offenders think they're paying a fine. "A lot of them have the Mexican system on their minds. [They] think in Mexico bail is the same thing as paying a fine—so there's a lot of confusion that paying bail [here] is the same.... It would make a difference if someone really explained [statements like] 'you can get out on your personal recognizance—or have a bail hearing.' Judges and attorneys must understand that interpreters can't explain." Interpreters indicated that generally, when describing bail, judges and attorneys tend to speak quickly, which may add to immigrant defendants' confusion.

Interpreters indicated that other factors may contribute to failures to appear. "I think FTAs happen because people move—they live with friends and may not know their addresses. Then they don't give a forwarding address." Some of the interpreters pointed out that in rural areas, many people do not know their street addresses. They describe their residences by giving directions.

Confusion can also result from court procedures. For example, one interpreter pointed out that when defendants have two charges with two hearings at different times, they are likely to go to only one. Consequently, "they get an FTA on the other charge. I've seen this over and over."

Statements of Defendants

Attorneys and interpreters representing several different languages believe that admissions of guilt and full confessions are favored in some countries. These may be coerced or even extracted by torture by the police. One attorney observed that "many incriminating statements made by immigrants are unreliable ... experience and understanding informs them that if they don't admit to what they have been arrested/detained for, they will be coerced." An interpreter noted that "for suspects, the notion is expressed explicitly, even in [Russian] movies: sincere confession will minimize your guilt." Another interpreter described what she's seen in the United States: "Immigrant defendants are very nervous, and they want to cooperate—they think they'll be better off. Most do speak and many say, 'Yes, I did it, so I have to tell it.' By the time the defense attorney is there, it's too late. Sometimes they didn't have the intent or have a defense, but since they've already talked, their fate is probably sealed." One judge raised the important issue of interpreter quality during pretrial statements; interpreters also raised this language issue, noting that some Miranda warning translations are very poor, and they may be "read by police who mispronounce many words or have intonation problems. They are not understandable." Interpretation quality of the immigrant suspect's statements can also be a problem.

Although the interviewed attorneys and interpreters all felt that immigrant defendants' incriminating statements are often unreliable, many of the judges who were interviewed were not aware of any particular difference between immigrants' statements and others' statements.

To prevent the admission of unreliable statements by the immigrant defendant, courts have heard motions to exclude them based on the defendant's legitimate lack of understanding due to expectations based on the defendant's native legal system. To remedy Miranda warning language issues, it was suggested that courts discuss with law enforcement agencies the necessity of obtaining good, standard translations and using certified or qualified interpreters to read them to defendants.

Right to an Attorney

Several judges agreed that defense attorneys are often not sought by first-time immigrant defendants. The interpreters unanimously reported a deep level of mistrust of court-appointed attorneys. "After a recent murder case where an immigrant was convicted, everyone in the Russian community said, 'Of course, it was a court-appointed attorney, what do you expect?' They don't trust attorneys—they think they're working with the prosecution. If I pay, I own the attorney; if I don't, the prosecutor does!" They are judging attorneys by the court systems in their own countries—and "you know you can't trust anyone there."

An interpreter reported, "Most Chinese immigrants are skeptical of government-appointed personnel, thinking they naturally would side with the government against them." On the other hand, several judges who were interviewed indicated that many U.S.-born defendants believe that court-appointed attorneys are in league with the prosecutor and felt that there is nothing unique about immigrant defendants' behavior.

Interpreters emphasized that immigrant defendants do not have any idea of the attorney's role in representing the defendant. They suggested that to effectively advise defendants, judges could briefly describe the attorney's role in court. Subsequently, the attorney should carefully go over the attorney-client relationship, the hearing process, and upcoming hearings, and repeat the process briefly before hearings. Pressed public defenders are often very confusing in their communications to immigrant defendants. One interpreter reported, "Immigrants don't understand the system and the attorney won't let them speak to the judge.... Usually the attorney says, 'Don't tell me, let me tell you what they are saying,' and then reads the police reports, what the prosecutor says, etc. This creates a bad feeling—the immigrants don't know why the attorneys won't listen." These and similar communication problems caused by too little time were described by most interpreters.

Pleading Guilty

Most judges did not report seeing a difference between immigrant and nonimmigrant defendants in the understanding of plea bargaining and pleading guilty. One judge noted that "more often I have Hispanic defendants who are reluctant to plead not guilty at arraignment. Usually they want to plead guilty, don't understand that they plead not guilty and then may change it later." Regarding plea bargaining, one judge observed that "sometimes immigrants turn down really good plea offers—this is distressing." Another judge also noted that the "judge assumes attorney has thoroughly explained to defendant; doesn't seem to be a problem."

Interpreters reported that many immigrant defendants are confused. "They don't understand negotiations and don't understand the standard ranges of sentences," said one interpreter. Another observed, "The concept of plea bargaining is very foreign. After the charge is reduced, they say, 'How can I plead guilty to something I didn't do?' They think it's a trick." Interpreters also noted that the accompanying paperwork can seem contradictory to immigrant defendants. "There's lots of confusion, for example, guilty plea forms talk about trial and trial rights. They say, 'I thought we weren't going to trial.'"

For first-time offenders who are immigrants, judges can help ensure that they aren't confused by the process by directly asking attorneys to review and explain the paperwork in an understandable fashion, and by explaining the process in court. This can prevent misunderstandings such as those reported by one interpreter: "They often think that after pleading guilty the case is completely over. They don't understand probation ... the court usually explains things too fast."

Judge's Role

Interpreters and attorneys observed that many immigrants see judges as having far more discretion than they actually do. This may come out during the proceedings. For example, a few judges noted that some immigrant defendants believe judges have unlimited discretion; as evidenced by requests that the court order nonlitigants to do or refrain from doing things, or, in sentencing, persistent requests that the judge change a jail sentence to a fine.

Almost every interpreter and attorney interviewed brought up immigrant parties' confusion about juries when discussing the judge's role. "They think judges are really in charge—they don't know what the jury's role is," noted one. Another interpreter said, "Most Chinese immigrant defendants ignore the jury, thinking they are just like the media.... Most of them think the judge is the only one hearing and deciding on the case." Immigrant parties' misunderstanding about the jury's role can hurt their credibility. "It is so difficult [for attorneys] to persuade the defendants/witnesses to have eye contact with the jurors—they ... look at the judge or the interpreter whenever they speak," explains an interpreter.

One attorney noted that it is usually important for judges, lawyers, interpreters, and court personnel to address parties correctly and rather formally during court proceedings and interviews. Interpreters suggest that judges and attorneys can improve communication by devising effective explanations of the jury system for immigrant defendants that are sensitive to their backgrounds. One interpreter recounts how several attorneys, when trying to explain the jury system, have asked immigrant defendants if they've seen *L.A. Law* and been dumbfounded that they haven't, or have described solely where the jury sits in the courtroom, rather than its function. It was suggested that the judge ask defendants if they understand how jurors are picked, whether they ask questions, and who makes the decision. If the defendant does not understand the purpose of the jury, the judge should direct defense counsel to explain the jury system in a meaningful way.

Immigrants' Apparent Comprehension of the Proceedings

Interpreters felt that many immigrant parties' comprehension is often poor. "Some are really alert during voir dire, etc., but many others don't even pay attention because they don't get it at all. If they're better educated, e.g., [have been to] high school, they understand explanations and it's easier for them. Many are not educated—they have only some years or so of elementary school. It is really difficult for them." One interpreter illustrated immigrant defendants' lack of comprehension and eagerness to agree with the court by contrasting immigrants' reactions to a complicated form with U.S.-born court personnel's reactions:

> There's a horrible form regarding collateral attack and appeal rights that absolutely no one understands—even attorneys and interpreters—except the immigrant defendants always say they do [understand the translated version]. This puts into question everything they say—every waiver and agreement—because they say that they understand, when in fact they don't.

In response to the topic of the defendant's comprehension, several judges reported the importance of the interpreter and the judge's appearance in the proceeding. [The court] "needs simultaneous interpretation. This puts a burden on the judge to be more responsive through intonation, body expression," said one judge. "[It is] critical we insist on qualified interpreters even for agreed orders," noted another. Interpreters reported that immigrant defendants constantly ask them for advice, which interpreters are not permitted to give. "They won't object to bad interpreting because they have great fear of authority."

Interpreters suggested that judges and attorneys can help immigrant defendants understand the proceedings by, once again, offering short, simple explanations of what is going on in the courtroom. An interpreter related that one effective judge inquires periodically, when the jury is not present, whether the defendant understands the various stages of the trial.

Jurors' Awareness of Cultural Differences

While a few judges perceived no difference in jurors' perceptions of immigrant and U.S.-born parties, most reported difficulties. Several judges raised problems with evaluating the non-English-speaking defendant through an interpreter: "Jurors have a very difficult time judging credibility when the interpreter is interpreting. They cannot detect tone of voice and body language." Interpreters have reported hearing juror complaints regarding evaluating credibility through interpreters.

In addition to interpreter issues, both judges and interpreters raised issues about jurors' perceptions of immigrant parties. Perceived problems were often based on the jury's probable lack of knowledge about the type of eye contact and body language factors discussed in several chapters. One judge observed:

Do judges have a duty to raise the issue of juries not using body language, etc., of immigrants/refugees in determining credibility? This is done with race in other cases. When I ask attorneys whether they object to the raising of the race issue, they never object. I have never raised the culture issue, but am considering it.

One judge suggested that "judges should make sure the jury is looking at the [immigrant] witness—otherwise they don't see the expressions at the same time they hear the words. Languages and their loudness can differ also. Jurors really have to be alert." This judge suggested that a question or two on interpreter issues be asked by judges during the general voir dire period and that judges use a jury instruction regarding the use of interpreters.

Domestic Violence

Judges reported a variety of observations regarding domestic violence cases. Some noted basically no differences between hearings involving immigrant and nonimmigrant parties. Others reported that immigrant respondents are far more likely to agree to the entry of a domestic violence protection order. Some noted that some immigrant respondents' attitude is, "I'm not going to follow this order."

Interpreters and attorneys reported that both victim and respondent may not have much confidence in the enforceability of decisions. "Victims think,

'Nobody can protect me once I am out of this courtroom.' Unfortunately, the [respondents or] defendants also share this conviction." This may especially be a problem in cases involving parties from countries where domestic violence is not a criminal act and may be tacitly accepted. The role of the domestic violence advocate is very important in helping the victim overcome what are often enormous pressures not to seek a protective order. The advocate can explain the laws and the process to the victim through an interpreter. An interpreter notes that respondents, who are often unrepresented, may be unfamiliar with their obligations in the proceeding:

> I do a lot of protection orders. Usually the victim meets with the advocate first, and has a long interview, which works well [to advise the victim of the process]. The respondent doesn't have anyone to explain. "Serving" is not very clear.... A question is: Do the respondents know they have to come to court?

In other instances, interpreters feel the parties are unaware of the consequences of domestic violence proceedings:

> Domestic violence is considered personal, they think the state has no reason to be involved ... it should be resolved in the church or family only. [After the legal process has been going for awhile, both parties think] "the charges should be dropped and we can get together again." Many violate orders because they need each other—he needs a place, she needs money.

Deportation is usually an important issue if one or both of the parties is undocumented. The victim and children may be economically dependent on the batterer and thus unwilling to risk deportation by pursuing a protection order. However, consistent with United States domestic violence protection laws, judges remarked that the serious nature of domestic violence outweighs such factors in many cases and courts should take extra time to question the parties carefully.

Domestic violence procedures should be thoroughly explained to both parties. In addition, bilingual counseling should be available, as one interpreter noted that "once the matter is brought to court, the family harmony seems to never come back; thus, domestic violence counseling must be provided for and attended by everyone involved including both victims and defendants and related family members."

Sentencing and Orders
One interpreter observed, "I think a fine is the only real penalty they comprehend. 'Suspended sentence' is very difficult. They think it's gone—not suspended . . . counseling for DUI—they understand if it's explained to them . . . ." Several interpreters felt that immigrants' problems in understanding orders and sentences could be ameliorated through written translations. "They feel bad, saying they don't understand orders . . . for community service, they understand better if there are real specifics re: dates, etc., and if the interpreter translates everything for them. If they don't know where to go, they don't show up." Judges also mentioned problems with English orders:

> The judgment and sentence with all conditions are written in English.... The Department of Corrections or the court interpreter could translate it, especially special conditions. The bottom line for court is that [without translations] ... immigrant defendants won't come out with an understanding— and we have to depend on follow-up (by attorneys or Corrections).

Many judges see serious language problems arising from drug treatment, alcohol treatment, or counseling orders if the programs do not have bilingual capability. This problem was articulated by several judges; one noted being "very concerned about the lack of Spanish-speaking treatment providers, which I think is fundamentally unfair."

Bilingual counselors are usually most effective, because they can talk directly to their clients and are likely to be culturally sensitive. Treatment through a professional interpreter supplied by the treatment provider is an acceptable alternative, though using unprofessional interpreters is risky, especially in family law cases, since they are likely to be biased and unlikely to be able to follow interpreter ethics rules. Judges noted that before ordering treatment programs for non-English-speaking parties, courts should determine if local treatment providers have the appropriate bilingual capability and encourage them to develop it if not. One judge reported that in DUI and domestic violence cases, "I inquire whether bilingual services are available. I have on occasion waived counseling when, due to language issues, no services were available that would be helpful." For a longer-term solution, however, communities should develop appropriate bilingual resources, so non-English-speaking parties are able to access equal services.

Many of the legal professionals interviewed stressed that the judges' and attorneys' efforts to communicate effectively with immigrant parties seem to dramatically improve immigrants' ability to fulfill sentences and otherwise respond to the requirements of the legal system.

Translated Explanation of Important Legal Concepts

Two problematic areas for many immigrants appear at the beginning of criminal cases. Ordinarily, a standard Advice of Rights is spoken or read to criminal defendants to advise them of their criminal procedure rights. The language of an Advice of Rights is usually abbreviated and dense. Defendants are assumed to be familiar with a number of common legal terms contained in rapidly delivered statements.

Since numerous immigrant defendants are unfamiliar with many American legal concepts, two explanatory documents were drafted and translated into five languages. The first, "Explanation of Some Important Rights," defines important terms and describes with some detail important rights, which defendants must exercise or waive. The second, "Paying Bail and Going to Court in Your Case," describes some important aspects of the bail system.

The documents have been translated into Spanish, Russian, Arabic, Vietnamese, and Chinese.

Where useful, these documents are meant to be shown to non-English-speaking defendants. However, while these documents have been carefully reviewed by a number of attorneys and professional translators, they are not meant to be a substitute for a court Advice of Rights, which would contain other additional information. Rather, they were designed to be a supplement to aid the defendant in understanding important rights in criminal cases.

For permission to reproduce these translated documents for distribution to non-English-speaking parties or for other use, write to the University of Washington Press, P.O. Box 50096, Seattle, WA 98145.

Explanation of Some Important Rights

If you are accused of a crime for which you may be sent to jail:

1. You are considered innocent of any charge. Before the court can decide if you are guilty, the prosecutor must prove guilt beyond a reasonable doubt.

2. Before your trial, you will be asked to plead guilty or not guilty:
   - Pleading not guilty is a formal statement to the court that you did not commit the offense charged or that you have a defense for it. If you plead not guilty, the judge will set another court date for your next appearance.
   - Pleading guilty is a formal statement to the court that you committed the offense charged. If you plead guilty, the court will sentence you.

3. You have the right to a speedy trial. This means that your trial must be held within the time set by law. You must be brought to trial within a reasonable amount of time. You can ask the judge or your attorney how much time your trial will take.

4. You have a right to a jury trial. A jury trial is one in which a number of ordinary people from the community listen to the evidence and decide whether you are innocent or guilty. If you specifically give up your right by waiving it, you will not have a jury trial.

5. During the trial, you have the right to see, hear, and question all witnesses who testify against you.

6. You have the right to call witnesses on your behalf at the trial. You may ask the court to legally obligate witnesses to appear at the trial and testify on your behalf.

7. You will have to make a choice about whether to testify or remain silent. You have the right to testify on your own behalf. Or, if you wish, you have the right to remain silent by not giving testimony for your case. If you remain silent, your silence cannot be used against you.

8. You have the right to be represented by an attorney. You may hire one, or, if the judge determines that you cannot afford an attorney, one will be provided for you. Even if you do not have a lawyer to represent you at this moment, you will continue to have the right to an attorney at any later proceeding.

9. Your attorney's job is to represent you and not the government, even if the government is paying the fees. Your attorney may not reveal your secrets to anyone, unless you give your permission. You have the right to decide whether to plead not guilty or guilty, waive a jury trial, or testify in your trial.

10. You have the right of appeal from any judgment of guilty entered by this Court. An appeal asks a higher court to review the judgment. The judge or your attorney can tell you when your appeal must be filed.

11. If you are not a citizen, pleading guilty or being convicted of a crime may result in your deportation, exclusion from admission to the United States, or denial of naturalization pursuant to the laws of the United States. Your attorney should be able to advise you of possible immigration consequences.

Paying Bail and Going to Court in Your Case

Your next court date is _____ .

1. People who are charged with a crime in the United States usually go to court two or more times before their cases are finished. It is mandatory that you attend all court appearances.

2. At the beginning of your case, you will probably be given the opportunity to make a deposit of bail money to the court.

3. The only purpose of bail is to provide the court with insurance that you will come back to court for hearings on dates set by the court.

4. The judge will determine the amount of bail and will consider things like your address, employment status, and whether you have relatives in the area.

5. *Your case is not finished* when you pay bail money. This is true even if the bail amount equals hundreds of dollars.

6. If you pay bail before or during your first court hearings, you will be released and given a date for the next hearing.

7. If you do not appear for the court date, the court will forfeit (keep) your bail. The court also may have you arrested again for not appearing at the court hearing.

8. If you do appear for all court hearings, the court will give back the bail money if you are found innocent. If the court finds that you are guilty, the court may use the bail money for all or part of a fine.

9. Real estate or other property owned by you or your relatives can sometimes be pledged to guarantee that you'll return to court. If so, you must come to court for your appearances, or ownership of the real estate or other property will be forfeited to the court.

10. Sometimes persons accused of a crime use a bail bonds business. The accused person pays the bail bonds business a percentage of the bail amount, which is not refunded. Then the bail bonds business pays the entire bail amount to the court for the accused person. The accused person is released from jail, but must appear for all court hearings in the case.

Explanation of Some Important Rights   **(Spanish)**

EXPLICACIÓN DE ALGUNOS IMPORTANTES DERECHOS
Si es acusado de un delito por el cual le podrían mandar a la cárcel:

1.   Usted es considerado inocente de cualquier cargo. Antes de que el tribunal pueda decidir si es culpable o no, el abogado fiscal tiene que probar que no existe ninguna duda razonable en cuanto a su culpabilidad.

2.   Antes de comenzar el juicio en su contra, se le pedirá que se declare no culpable o culpable:
   -- El declararse no culpable es una declaración formal ante el tribunal de que usted no ha cometido el delito del que se le acusa o que tiene una defensa en contra de dicho cargo. Si se declara no culpable, el juez fijará la fecha en la que tendrá que presentarse nuevamente ante el tribunal.
   -- El declararse culpable es una declaración formal ante el tribunal de que usted ha cometido el delito del que se le acusa. Si se declara culpable, el juez le impondrá una condena.

3.   Tiene derecho a un juicio sin demora. Esto significa que su juicio debe realizarse dentro del plazo establecido por la ley. Se requiere que el juicio se lleve a cabo dentro de un período razonable de tiempo. Puede preguntarle al juez o a su abogado cuánto tiempo tardará el juicio.

4.   Tiene derecho a un juicio por jurado. En un juicio por jurado varias personas comunes y corrientes de la comunidad escuchan todo el testimonio y deciden si usted es inocente o culpable. Si usted indica específicamente que renuncia a este derecho, no tendrá un juicio por jurado.

5.   Durante el juicio, usted tiene derecho a ver, escuchar y hacer preguntas a todos los testigos que den testimonio en su contra.

6.   Tiene derecho a llamar a testigos para que den testimonio a su favor durante el juicio. Usted puede pedirle al juez que obligue legalmente a los testigos a presentarse al juicio y dar testimonio a su favor.

7.   Tendrá que decidir si desea dar testimonio ante el juez o si prefiere guardar silencio. Usted tiene derecho a dar testimonio en su propio favor. O bien, si lo prefiere, usted tiene derecho a guardar silencio y no dar testimonio en su caso. Si guarda silencio, este silencio no puede ser utilizado en su contra.

8.   Tiene derecho a ser representado por un abogado. Puede contratar a un abogado o, si el juez determina que usted no tiene los recursos necesarios para pagarle, el tribunal le proporcionará un abogado. Aunque no tenga un abogado en este momento, siempre tendrá derecho a tener un abogado para cualquier procedimiento jurídico posterior.

9.   El trabajo de su abogado es representarlo a usted, y no al gobierno, aunque el gobierno pague los honorarios de su abogado. El abogado no puede revelar a nadie los secretos que usted le confíe, a menos que usted mismo le dé permiso para hacerlo. Usted tiene derecho a decidir si desea declararse culpable o no culpable, si desea renunciar a su derecho a tener un juicio por jurado, o si desea dar testimonio durante su juicio.

10.   Tiene derecho de apelar cualquier determinación de culpabilidad decidida por este tribunal. Una apelación es una petición a un tribunal superior para que revise la determinación del caso. El juez o su abogado puede indicarle cuándo se debe presentar la apelación.

11.   Si usted no es ciudadano estadounidense y se declara culpable o si ha recibido un fallo condenatorio por algún delito, podrían haber otras consecuencias que incluyen ser deportado, no ser admitido nuevamente en los Estados Unidos de América, o negársele la naturalización, según lo ordenan las leyes de los Estados Unidos de América. Su abogado podrá indicarle si existen otras posibles consecuencias con el servicio de emigración.

Explanation of Some Important Rights - Spanish

Paying Bail and Going to Court in Your Case   **(Spanish)**

PAGO DE LA FIANZA Y CITA PARA PRESENTARSE EN EL TRIBUNAL

Su próxima cita para presentarse en el tribunal es el _____.

1. Las personas acusadas de un delito en los Estados Unidos de América generalmente deben presentarse en el tribunal dos o más veces antes de que se terminen sus casos. Es obligatorio que usted se presente cada vez que se le cite para comparecer ante el juez.

2. Usted probablemente tendrá la oportunidad de depositar una fianza en el tribunal cuando comience el caso.

3. El único propósito de la fianza es asegurarle al tribunal que usted se presentará nuevamente en el tribunal en las fechas establecidas por juez.

4. El juez determinará la cantidad de fianza requerida y tomará en cuenta circunstancias como la dirección de su residencia, si tiene trabajo o no, y si familiares suyos viven en el área.

5. *Su caso no se da por terminado* cuando usted paga la fianza, aunque la cantidad sea de cientos de dólares.

6. Si paga la fianza antes o durante su primera audiencia ante el juez, será puesto en libertad y se fijará una fecha para la próxima audiencia.

7. Si no se presenta en la fecha fijada, el tribunal se quedará con la fianza. El juez también puede mandar que se le detenga otra vez por no haberse presentado para su audiencia.

8. Si se presenta a todas las audiencias ante el juez y se le declara inocente, el tribunal le devolverá la fianza. Si se le declara culpable, el tribunal podrá usar la fianza para pagar alguna multa, o parte de ella.

9. A veces se pueden dejar en prenda, como garantía de que regresará al tribunal, bienes inmuebles u otra propiedad de su pertenencia o que le pertenezcan a sus familiares. En este caso, deberá volver al tribunal para las audiencias; de otra manera, el tribunal se quedará con sus bienes inmuebles o propiedades.

10.   A veces las personas acusadas de un delito usan un servicio de fianza. El acusado paga al servicio de fieanza un porcentaje de la fianza, el cual no se le devolverá. En dicho caso, el servicio de fianza pagará toda la fianza al tribunal en nombre del acusado. El acusado es entonces puesto en libertad pero tendrá que presentarse ante el tribunal para todas las audiencias que se relacionen con su caso.

Paying Bail and Going to Court in Your Case - Spanish

РАЗЪЯСНЕНИЕ НЕКОТОРЫХ ВАЖНЫХ ПРАВ

Если Вы обвиняетесь в совершении преступления, за которое Вас могут послать в тюрьму:

1. Вы считаетесь невиновным в любом предъявленном обвинении. До того, как суд решит, что Вы виновны, обвинитель должен доказать вину при отсутствии обоснованного в том сомнения.

2. Перед рассмотрением Вашего дела в суде Вас попросят признать себя виновным в предъявленном обвинении или заявить о своей невиновности.

    ♦ Заявление о невиновности - это официальное заявление суду о том, что Вы не совершали преступления, в котором обвиняетесь, или у Вас есть возражения по обвинению. Если Вы заявите о своей невиновности, то судья назначит Вам другую дату явки в суд.

    ♦ Признание себя виновным - это официальное заявление суду о том, что Вы совершили преступление, в котором обвиняетесь. Если Вы признаете себя виновным, то суд вынесет в отношении Вас приговор.

3. У Вас есть право на безотлагательное рассмотрение дела. Это означает, что судебный процесс по Вашему делу должен состояться в сроки, установленные законом. Ваше дело должно подвергнуться рассмотрению в суде в течение разумного периода времени. Вы можете спросить судью или своего

4. адвоката, сколько времени будет длиться судебный процесс по Вашему делу.

5. Вы имеете право на рассмотрение дела судом присяжных. Суд присяжных - это когда группа обычных людей, живущих в данной местности, выслушивает доказательства и решает, виновны Вы или невиновны. Только при условии, что Вы прямо откажетесь от этого права, Ваше дело не будет рассматриваться судом присяжных.

6. Во время судебного процесса у Вас есть право видеть и слышать показания любых свидетелей, которые свидетельствуют против Вас, и задавать им вопросы.

7. Во время судебного процесса Вы имеете право вызывать свидетелей, дающих показания в Вашу пользу. Вы можете попросить суд по закону обязать свидетелей явиться в суд и дать свидетельские показания.

8. Вам нужно будет решить, будете ли Вы давать показания или не будете отвечать на вопросы. Вы имеете право свидетельствовать в свою пользу, или, если Вы этого захотите, Вы имеете право не отвечать на вопросы и не давать показаний по своему делу. Если Вы не будете отвечать на вопросы, то Ваше молчание не может быть использовано против Вас.

9. Вы имеете право пользоваться помощью адвоката. Вы можете нанять адвоката или, если судья определит, что Вы не можете позволить себе нанять адвоката, Вам

Explanation of Some Important Rights - Russian

будет предоставлена помощь адвоката. Если даже у Вас сейчас нет адвоката, Вы будете продолжать иметь право пользоваться помощью адвоката при дальнейшем рассмотрении дела в суде.

10. Обязанности Вашего адвоката состоят в том, чтобы представлять Вас, а не государство, даже если государство и оплачивает услуги этого адвоката. Ваш адвокат не может разгласить кому-либо доверенные Вами тайны, если Вы не дали на то разрешения. Вы имеете право решить, признать ли себя виновным или заявить о своей невиновности, отказаться от рассмотрения своего дела судом присяжных или свидетельствовать по своему делу.

11. Вы имеете право апелляции (обжалования) на судебное решение о признании виновным, вынесенное этим судом. Апелляция представляет собой обращение в вышестоящий суд о пересмотре судебного решения. Судья или Ваш адвокат могут сказать Вам, когда нужно подать апелляцию.

12. Признание себя виновным в совершении преступления или осуждение в некоторых случаях повредит Вашему иммиграционному статусу. Ваш адвокат должен разъяснить Вам возможные иммиграционные последствия.

Explanation of Some Important Rights - Russian

ВНЕСЕНИЕ ЗАЛОГА И ЯВКА В СУД ПО ВАШЕМУ ДЕЛУ

Дата Вашей следующей явки в суд _____

1. Лица, обвиненные в совершении преступления в Соединенных Штатах Америки, обычно должны явиться в суд два или три раза до того, как дело завершено. Явка в суд является для Вас обязательной.

2. В начале судебного разбирательства по Вашему делу Вам, вероятно, будет дана возможность внести в суд определенную сумму денег в качестве залога.

3. Единственная цель залога - дать гарантию суду в том, что Вы явитесь в суд на слушания по Вашему делу в дни, установленные судом.

4. Судья определит сумму залога и примет во внимание Ваш адрес, имеете ли Вы работу, и есть ли у Вас родственники в этом регионе.

5. Когда Вы вносите залог, это не значит, что *Ваше дело завершено,* даже если сумма залога составляет сотни долларов.

6. Если Вы внесете залог до или во время первого слушания по Вашему делу, то Вы будете освобождены из заключения, и будет назначен день следующего слушания.

7. Если Вы не явитесь в суд в назначенный день, то суд конфискует (удержит) Ваш залог. Суд может также решить подвергнуть Вас повторному аресту за неявку на судебное слушание по Вашему делу.

8. Если Вы явитесь в суд на все судебные слушания по Вашему делу, то суд вернет Вам сумму залога, если Вас признают невиновным. Если Вас признают виновным, то суд может использовать залог в качестве всей суммы штрафа или ее части.

9. Недвижимость или другое имущество, которым владеете Вы или Ваши родственники, иногда может быть отдано в залог в качестве гарантии того, что Вы явитесь в суд. В этом случае Вы должны явиться в суд, иначе право владения этой недвижимостью или имуществом будет передано суду.

10. Иногда лица, обвиненные в совершении преступления, пользуются услугами компаний, которые предоставляют поручительство за явку ответной стороны в суд. Обвиняемый в совершении преступления выплачивает такой компании определенный процент суммы залога, который ему не возвращается. Тогда компания, предоставляющая поручительство, выплачивает суду всю сумму залога за этого обвиняемого. В этом случае обвиняемый освобождается из заключения, но должен являться на все судебные слушания по своему делу.

Paying Bail and Going to Court in Your Case - Russian

Explanation of Some Important Rights   **(Arabic)**

شرح لبعض ا قوق الهامة التي تعنيك

في حال اتهمت بجريمة قد تؤدي إلى إدخالك الـ جن:

١. يعتبرك القانون بريئاً من أي تهمة. وقبل أن تـ ت يـ ا كمة أن تقرر ما إذا كنت مذنباً، يتوجب على المدعي العام أن يثبت ذنبك بلا أي شك معقول.

٢. وقبل محاكمتك، سوف يـ لـب منك أن تقر بالذنب أو أن تنكر التهمة:

– إنكار التهمة هو بيان رسمي توجه إلى ا كمة بأنك لم تقترف الجرم الذي اتهمت بـ ، أو بأنـ لديك دفا في شأنـ . وفي حال أنكرت التهمة يحدد القاضي موعداً لجلـ ة تالية للنظر في قضيتك.

– الإقرار بالذنب هو بيان رسمي توجه إلى ا كمة بأنك اقترفت الجرم الذي اتهمت بـ . وفي حال أقررت بالذنب، تقوم ا لدارا كم عليك.

٣. لك ا ق في ا اكمة العاجلة، أي أن محاكمتك يجب أن تجري ضمن الفترة الزمنية التي يحددها القانون. ويجب أن تجري محاكمتك خلال فترة معقولة من الزمن. ويجوز لك أن تـ أل القاضي أو ا امي عن الوقت الذي قد تـ تغرؤ محاكمتك.

٤. لك ا ق في ا اكمة أمام هيئة محلفين. و تتم ا اكمة أمام هيئة محلفين بالشكل التالي: يـ تمـ عدد من أفراد المجتمـ إلى الأدلة وا جج ويقررون ما إذا كنت بريئاً أو مذنباً. أما إذا تنازلت تحديداً عن هذا ا ق بالتخلي عـ فلن تحصل على محاكمة أمام هيئة محلفين.

٥. أثناء ا اكمة، لك ا ق في أن ترى جميـ الشهود الذين يدلون شهادات ضدك (شهود الإدعاء)، وأن تـ تمـ إليهم وأن تـ تجوبهم.

٦. لك ا ق في أن تـ تدعي شهوداً لصا لك في ا اكمة. ويجوز لك أن تـ لـب من ا كمة أن تصدر أمراً لازماً يرغم الشهود على المثول أمام ا كمة والإدلاء بالشهادات لصا لك.

٧. عليك أن تختار بين الإدلاء بشهادتك أو إلتزام الصمت. لك ا ق بأن تدلي شهادتك لصا لك. أو، إذا شئت، لك ا ق بالتزام الصمت وعدم الإدلاء بالشهادة في قضيتك. وفي حال التزمت الصمت، لا يجوز مؤاخذتك على متك واستعمال ضدك.

٨. لك ا ق بأن تعيّن محامياً يمثلك. يمكن أن تكلف محامياً بنف لك، أو، في حال أقر القاضي أ لي بمقدورك أن تتحمل كلفة محامي، تقدم لك ا كمة محامياً. وحتى إذا لم يكن لديك محام في الوقت ا اضر، يبقى لك ا ق في توكيل محام يمثلك في أي إجراءات لاحقة.

٩. من واجب ا امي وكيلك أن يمثلك أنت، لا أن يمثل الدولة، حتى وإن كانت الدولة تدف أجرة . ولا يجوز للمحامي وكيلك أن يفشي أسرارك لأي كان، إلا إذا كان ذلك بإذن منك. ولك ا ق في أن تقرر ما إذا أردت أن تنكر التهمة أو تقر بالذنب، وأن تتخلى عن حقك با اكمة أمام هيئة محلفين أو لا، وأن تدلي بشهادتك أو لا.

١٠. يحق لك أن ت تأنف الدعوى إذا ا ادرت هذ ا اكمة عليك حكماً بالذنب. و لب الاستئناف من محكمة أعلى أن تراج ا كم وتنظر في مجدداً. يخبرك القاضي أو محاميك متى يجب عليك أن تقدم لب الاستئناف.

١١. في حال لم تكن من حملة الجن ية الأميركية، قد يؤدي الإقرار بالذنب أو الإدانة بجريمة إلى ترحيلك من الولايات المتحدة، ومنعك من الدخول إليها، أو منعك من ا صول على الجن ية فيها بمقتضى القانون الأميركي. من واجب محاميك أن ي لمك على التبعات ا تملة فيما يتعلق بم ائل الهجرة.

Explanation of Some Important Rights — Arabic

Paying Bail and Going to Court in Your Case   **(Arabic)**

دف الكفالة والمثول أمام ا كمة في قضيتك

موعد الجل ة التالية للمحكمة للنظر في قضيتك : ─────────────

١. في الولايات المتحدة يحضر الأشخاص المتهمون بالجرم أمام ا كمة مرتين أو أكثر قبل أن تنتهي قضاياهم. إن حضورك لجميع الجل ات هو أمر إلزامي لا خيار لك في .

٢. عند افتتاح قضيتك، الراج أن ت ذ لك الفر ة لإيدا الكفالة المالية في ا كمة.

٣. الغرض الوحيد من الكفالة هو تقديم الضمان للمحكمة بأنك ستعود إلى ا كمة ضور الجل ات في المواعيد ا ددة من قبلها.

٤. يحدد القاضي مبلغ الكفالة آخذاً بعين الاعتبار عنوانك وسواء كنت تعمل أو لا وسواء كان لك أقرباء في المن قة أو لا، وما شاب ذلك.

٥. لا تنتهي قضيتك بمجرد قيامك بدف الكفالة. ي ري هذا الشر حتى وإن بلغت الكفالة المئات من الدولارات.

٦. إذا دفعت الكفالة قبل الجل ات الأولى أو أثنائها، ي لق سراحك ويعيّن لك موعد الجل ة التالية.

٧. في حال لم تحضر جمي الجل ات، تصادر (تحتفظ) ا كمة بالكفالة التي دفعتها. كما قد تأمر ا كمة بإلقاء القبض عليك مجدداً لعدم حضورك جل ة ا كمة.

٨. أما إذا حضرت جمي جل ات ا كمة، ف وف تعيد إليك ا كمة الكفالة في حال ثبتت براءتك. أما في حال إدانتك، فقد ت خر ا كمة الكفالة لدف جزء من الغرامة المتوجبة أو كاملها.

٩. يجوز في بعض الأحيان إيدا الأملاك العقارية وغيرها من الأملاك التي تملكها أنت شخصياً أو التي يملكها أقاربك كرهينة لضمان عودتك إلى ا كمة. في هذ ا ال، يجب عليك أن تمثل أمام ا كمة في المواعيد ا لددة وإلا تصادر ا كمة تلك الأملاك العقارية أو غيرها من الأملاك.

١٠. في بعض الأحيان يعمد الأشخاص المتهمون بالجرم إلى أحد المكاتب التي تتاجر بـ ندات الكفالة، حيث يدفـ المتهم إلى المكتب التجاري نـ بة مئوية من مبلغ الكفالة غير قابلة للاسترجا . عندها يدفـ المكتب التجاري مبلغ الكفالة بكامل إلى ا كمة نيابة عن المتهم. بعد ذلك يتم إ لاق سراح المتهم، غير أن يتوجب عليـ المثول أمام ا كمة في جميـ الجلـ ات المتعلقة بالقضية.

Paying Bail and Going to Court in Your Case — Arabic

GIẢI THÍCH VỀ MỘT SỐ QUYỀN HIẾN ĐỊNH QUAN TRỌNG
Nếu quý vị bị truy tố về một trường hợp phạm tội có thể bị tống giam:

1. Quý vị vẫn được xem là vô tội về các tội cáo buộc. Trước khi tòa có thể quyết định quý vị có tội, công tố viên phải chứng minh mà không còn mối hoài nghi hợp lý nào nữa là quý vị có tội.

2. Trước phiên xử, quý vị sẽ được hỏi là có nhận tội hay không nhận tội:

   -- Không nhận tội là lời tuyên bố chính thức trước tòa rằng quý vị đã không phạm tội đang bị truy tố hoặc quý vị có lý lẽ biện minh. Nếu quý vị không nhận tội, thẩm phán sẽ ấn định ngày khác để quý vị ra tòa lại.
   -- Nhận tội là lời tuyên bố chính thức trước tòa rằng quý vị đã phạm tội đang bị truy tố. Nếu quý vị nhận tội, tòa sẽ tuyên án quý vị.

3. Quý vị có quyền được xét xử nhanh chóng. Điều này có nghĩa là phiên xử quý vị phải được tổ chức trong thời hạn luật định. Quý vị phải được đưa ra xét xử trong một thời hạn hợp lý. Quý vị có thể hỏi thẩm phán hoặc luật sư của mình là phiên xử sẽ kéo dài bao lâu.

4. Quý vị có quyền được đưa ra xử trước bồi thẩm đoàn. Một phiên xử có bồi thẩm đoàn là khi có một số người thường trong cộng đồng sẽ nghe các bằng chứng trình bày và quyết định xem quý vị vô tội hay có tội. Nếu quý vị chọn từ bỏ quyền này thì quý vị sẽ không được xử trước bồi thẩm đoàn.

5. Trong phiên xử, quý vị có quyền nhìn, nghe và chất vấn tất cả các nhân chứng đưa lời khai chống lại quý vị.

6. Quý vị có quyền đưa ra nhân chứng cho chính mình trong phiên xử. Quý vị có thể xin tòa về pháp lý bắt buộc các nhân chứng phải ra tòa để khai làm chứng cho quý vị.

7. Quý vị có quyền chọn tự mình ra khai hoặc giữ im lặng. Quý vị có quyền khai làm chứng cho chính mình. Hoặc, nếu muốn, quý vị có quyền giữ im lặng không làm chứng cho vụ của mình. Nếu quý vị giữ im lặng thì việc giữ im lặng đó không được xử dụng làm cớ chống lại quý vị.

8. Quý vị có quyền có luật sư đại diện. Quý vị có thể thuê luật sư hoặc, nếu thẩm phán quyết định rằng quý vị không có khả năng thuê luật sư, quý vị sẽ được cung cấp luật sư. Dù lúc này quý vị không có luật sư, quý vị vẫn có quyền có luật sư trong bất cứ phiên tòa nào sau đó.

9. Công việc của luật sư quý vị là đại diện cho quý vị chứ không phải cho chính phủ, dù cho chính phủ trả tiền lệ phí cho luật sư đó. Luật sư của quý vị không được phép tiết lộ bí mật của quý vị với bất cứ người nào khác, trừ phi được quý vị cho phép. Quý vị có quyền quyết định có nhận tội hay không nhận tội, có từ bỏ quyền được xử trước bồi thẩm đoàn hay không, hoặc có ra khai làm chứng trong phiên xử cho chính mình hay không.

10. Quý vị có quyền kháng cáo bất cứ phán quyết nào của Tòa này khi nói rằng quý vị có tội. Kháng cáo là nhờ đến tòa trên xét lại phán quyết đó. Thẩm phán hoặc luật sư của quý vị có thể cho quý vị biết khi nào phải nộp đơn kháng cáo.

11. Nếu quý vị không phải là công dân, khi nhận tội hoặc bị kết án về tội nào đó có thể đưa đến việc bị trục xuất, không được cho nhập cảnh Hoa Kỳ, hoặc không được cho nhập tịch chiếu theo luật pháp Hoa Kỳ. Luật sư của quý vị có thể cố vấn cho quý vị về các hậu quả khả dĩ về tình trạng di trú.

Explanation of Some Important Rights - Vietnamese

ĐÓNG TIỀN BẢO CHỨNG TẠI NGOẠI VÀ RA TÒA TRONG VỤ CỦA QUÝ VỊ

Ngày ra tòa lần tối của quý vị là _____.

1. Những người bị truy tố về một trường hợp phạm tội tại Hoa Kỳ thường phải ra tòa từ hai lần trở lên trước khi xử xong vụ của họ. Quý vị bắt buộc phải tham dự tất cả các phiên tòa.

2. Khi bắt đầu vụ của quý vị, quý vị có thể được cơ hội đóng tiền ký quỹ bảo chứng tại ngoại cho tòa.

3. Mục đích duy nhất của việc bảo chứng tại ngoại là để bảo đảm với tòa rằng quý vị sẽ ra tòa vào những lần do tòa ấn định.

4. Thẩm phán sẽ quyết định số tiền bảo chứng tại ngoại, và sẽ cứu xét đến những yếu tố như địa chỉ của quý vị, tình trạng công việc làm, và quý vị có thân nhân trong vùng hay không.

5. Khi quý vị đóng tiền bảo chứng tại ngoại thì *không có nghĩa là vụ của quý vị đã xong*. Dù quý vị có đóng tiền bảo chứng tại ngoại đến hàng trăm đô la thì cũng vậy.

6. Nếu quý vị đóng tiền bảo chứng tại ngoại trước hoặc trong buổi ra tòa đầu tiên của mình, quý vị sẽ được phóng thích và ấn định ngày ra tòa lần sau.

7. Nếu quý vị không trình diện ở tòa vào đúng ngày ấn định, tòa sẽ tịch thu (giữ luôn) tiền bảo chứng đó. Tòa cũng có thể ra lệnh bắt quý vị lại vì đã không ra tòa.

8. Nếu quý vị ra tòa đầy đủ tất cả những lần ấn định, tòa sẽ trả lại tiền bảo chứng tại ngoại cho quý vị nếu quý vị được phán quyết là vô tội. Nếu tòa kết tội quý vị, tòa có thể xử dụng tiền bảo chứng tại ngoại để trừ vào tất cả hoặc một phần tiền phạt.

9. Đôi khi bất động sản hoặc tài sản nào khác của quý vị hoặc thân nhân quý vị có thể được dùng để bảo đảm quý vị sẽ ra tòa trở lại. Nếu thế, quý vị phải ra tòa vào tất cả những ngày quy định vì nếu không tòa sẽ tịch thu quyền sở hữu bất động sản hoặc tài sản nào khác đã được dùng để bảo đảm.

10. Đôi khi những người bị truy tố về một trường hợp phạm tội xử dụng một hãng lập giao kèo bảo chứng tại ngoại. Bị cáo đóng cho hãng bảo chứng một tỷ lệ phần trăm nào đó của số tiền bảo chứng, và số tiền này sẽ không được hoàn trả lại. Sau đó hãng bảo chứng sẽ đóng cho tòa trọn số tiền bảo chứng cho bị cáo. Bị cáo sau đó sẽ được phóng thích khỏi nhà giam, nhưng phải ra tòa lại vào tất cả những lần ấn định trong vụ của mình.

Paying Bail and Going to Court in Your Case - Vietnamese

Explanation of Some Important Rights　　　　　　**(Simplified Chinese)**

对一些重要的公民权利的解释

如果你被指控犯罪并可能入狱：

1. 对任何控告，你都被认为是无罪的。在法庭对你判决是否有罪之前，检查官必须按超出合理怀疑范围原则证明你有罪。

2. 在接受审讯之前，你将被问到是否认罪：

   —"不认罪"是你对法庭的正式陈述，表示你并无被控告的犯罪行为或你要对指控进行申辩。如果你不认罪，法官将为你安排下一次出庭日期。

   —"认罪"是你对法庭的正式陈述，表示你确有被控告的犯罪行为。如果你认罪，法庭将对你作出判刑。

3. 你有权要求加速审讯。这表示对你的审讯必须在法律规定的时间内进行。你必须在恰当的时间内被带往审讯。你可向法官或你的律师询问对你的审讯需要多长时间。

4. 你有权要求陪审团。陪审团是指一些来自社区的普通人到法庭听取证词，然后决定你是否有罪。如果你特别指明放弃这一权利，你就不会接受陪审团的审讯。

5. 在审讯过程中，你有权利听见和看到所有反对你的证人，并向他们提问。

6. 在审讯中你有权传召在你一边的证人到庭。你也可以要求法庭依法强制传召你的证人到庭为你作证。

7. 你必须在作证或保持沉默中作出选择。你有权为自己作证，或者，只要你愿意，你有权保持沉默，对案件不予作证。如果你选择保持沉默，则你的沉默不能被用来反对你。

8. 你有权要求律师代表你。你可以聘请律师，或者如果法官断定你承担不起请律师的费用，法官会为你提供免费律师。即使你目前没有自己的律师，但在以后的诉讼中你仍有权得到自己的律师。

9. 你的律师的任务是代理你而非代表政府，即使律师的费用是由政府支付。除非得到你的许可，否则你的律师不会将你的秘密揭示给任何人。在对你的审讯中，你有权决定认罪还是不认罪，放弃陪审或作证。

10. 对本法庭对你作出有罪的判决你有权提出上诉，要求上一级法庭重新审理这一判决。法官或你的律师会告诉你应在何时提出上诉。

11. 如果你不是美国公民，认罪或被判刑会有损于你的移民身份，例如驱逐出境，不准入境或根据法律拒绝你的入籍申请。你的律师应将犯罪对你的移民身份可能会产生的后果告诉你。

Explanation of Some Important Rights - Simplified Chinese

Paying Bail and Going to Court in Your Case (Simplified Chinese)

为你的案件支付保释金及上法庭

你下次出庭日为＿＿＿＿＿＿＿＿＿＿＿＿＿＿＿＿＿＿＿＿＿

1. 在美国被指控犯罪的人，在其案件结束之前通常要上法庭两次或更多。法律强制规定你必须出席每次开庭审判。

2. 开始审理案件时，你将有机会向法庭支付保释金。

3. 保释金的唯一目的是向法庭提供保证，保证你会在法庭指定的日期回到法庭出席听证。

4. 法官将决定保释金的金额的多少，并会考虑其它因素诸如你的住址、就业情况以及在当地有否亲戚等。

5. 支付了保释金并不意味着你的案件已经结束，即使你支付了保释金额高达上万元。

6. 如果在第一次法庭听证时或听证之前支付保证金，你会被释放，并给予下次到庭听证的日期。

7. 如果在开庭日缺席，法庭将没收（保存）你的保释金。法庭还会因你的缺席而再次逮捕你。

8. 如果你出席了所有的法庭听证而且被判无罪。法庭会将保释金如数退回。如果法庭判你有罪，则这笔保释金将会作为全部或部分罚金。

9. 你或你的亲戚拥有的房地产或其他财产有时可作为对你会出庭的保证。如果以动产作保，则你必须到庭听证，否则你对房地产或其他财产的拥有权就会被法庭没收。

10. 被控告犯罪的人有时可使用保释保证金业务机构。被告人支付给保释保证金业务机构一定百分比的保释金，这笔钱是不能退回的，然后保释保证金业务机构会为被告人向法庭支付全部保释金，这样被告人会获释出狱，但必须出席与这一案件有关的全部法庭听证。

Code of Professional Responsibility for Interpreters

CODE OF PROFESSIONAL RESPONSIBILITY FOR INTERPRETERS IN THE JUDICIARY

PREAMBLE

Many persons who come before the courts are partially or completely excluded from full participation in the proceedings due to limited English proficiency or a speech or hearing impairment. It is essential that the resulting communication barrier be removed, as far as possible, so that these persons are placed in the same position as similarly situated persons for whom there is no such barrier.[578] As officers of the court, interpreters help assure that such persons may enjoy equal access to justice and that court proceedings and court support services function efficiently and effectively. Interpreters are highly skilled professionals who fulfill an essential role in the administration of justice.

APPLICABILITY

This code shall guide and be binding upon all persons, agencies and organizations who administer, supervise use, or deliver interpreting services to the judiciary.

Commentary:

The black letter principles of this Model Code are principles of general application that are unlikely to conflict with specific requirements of rule or law in the states, in the opinion of the code's drafters. Therefore, the use of the term "shall" is reserved for the black letter principles. Statements in the commentary use the term "should" to describe behavior that illustrates or elaborates the principles. The commentaries are intended to convey what the drafters of this model code believe are *probable* and *expected* behaviors. Wherever a court policy or routine practice appears to conflict with the commentary in this code, it

---

578. A non-English speaker should be able to understand just as much as an English speaker with the same level of education and intelligence.

Reprinted, with permission, from the *New England Law Review*, vol. 30, no. 2, pp. 353-60.

is recommended that the reasons for the policy as it applies to court interpreters be examined.

CANON 1: ACCURACY AND COMPLETENESS

Interpreters shall render a complete and accurate interpretation or sight translation, without altering, omitting, or adding anything to what is stated or written, and without explanation.

Commentary:

The interpreter has a twofold duty: 1) to ensure that the proceedings in English reflect precisely what was said by a non-English speaking person, and 2) to place the non-English speaking person on an equal footing with those who understand English. This creates an obligation to conserve every element of information contained in a source language communication when it is rendered in the target language.

Therefore, interpreters are obligated to apply their best skills and judgment to preserve faithfully the meaning of what is said in court, including the style or register of speech. Verbatim, "word for word," or literal oral interpretations are not appropriate when they distort the meaning of the source language, but *every spoken statement, even if it appears non-responsive, obscene, rambling, or incoherent should be interpreted.* This includes apparent misstatements.

Interpreters should never interject their own words, phrases, or expressions. If the need arises to explain an interpreting problem (e.g., a term or phrase with no direct equivalent in the target language or a misunderstanding that only the interpreter can clarify), the interpreter should ask the court's permission to provide an explanation. Interpreters should convey the emotional emphasis of the speaker without reenacting or mimicking the speaker's emotions, or dramatic gestures.

Sign language interpreters, however, *must* employ all of the visual cues that the language they are interpreting for requires — including facial expressions, body language, and hand gestures. Sign language interpreters, therefore, should ensure that court participants do not confuse these essential elements of the interpreted language with inappropriate interpreter conduct.

The obligation to preserve accuracy includes the interpreter's duty to correct any error of interpretation discovered by the interpreter during the proceeding. Interpreters should demonstrate their professionalism by objectively analyzing any challenge to their performance.

CANON 2: REPRESENTATION OF QUALIFICATIONS

Interpreters shall accurately and completely represent their certifications, training, and pertinent experience.

Commentary:

Acceptance of a case by an interpreter conveys linguistic competency in legal settings. Withdrawing or being asked to withdraw from a case after it begins causes a disruption of court proceedings and is wasteful of scarce public resources. It is therefore essential that interpreters present a complete and truthful account of their training, certification and experience prior to appointment so the officers of the court can fairly evaluate their qualifications for delivering interpreting services.

CANON 3: IMPARTIALITY AND AVOIDANCE OF CONFLICT OF INTEREST

Interpreters shall be impartial and unbiased and shall refrain from conduct that may give an appearance of bias. Interpreters shall disclose any real or perceived conflict of interest.

Commentary:

The interpreter serves as an officer of the court and the interpreter's duty in a court proceeding is to serve the court and the public to which the court is a servant. This is true regardless of whether the interpreter is publicly retained at government expense or retained privately at the expense of one of the parties.

The interpreter should avoid any conduct or behavior that presents the appearance of favoritism toward any of the parties. Interpreters should maintain professional relationships with their clients, and should not take an active part in any of the proceedings. The interpreter should discourage a non-English speaking party's personal dependence.

During the course of the proceedings, interpreters should not converse with parties, witnesses, jurors, attorneys, or with friends or relatives of any party, except in the discharge of their official functions. It is especially important that interpreters, who are often familiar with attorneys or other members of the courtroom work group, including law enforcement officers, refrain from casual and personal conversations with anyone in court that may convey an appearance of a special relationship or partiality to any of the court participants.

The interpreter should strive for professional detachment. Verbal and non-verbal displays of personal attitudes, prejudices, emotions, or opinions should be avoided at all times.

Should an interpreter become aware that a proceeding participant views the interpreter as having a bias or being biased, the interpreter should disclose that knowledge to the appropriate judicial authority and counsel.

Any condition that interferes with the objectivity of an interpreter constitutes a conflict of interest. Before providing services in a matter, court interpreters must disclose to all parties and presiding officials any prior involvement, whether personal or professional, that could be reasonably construed as a conflict of interest. This disclosure should not include privileged or confidential information.

The following are circumstances that are presumed to create actual or apparent conflicts of interest for interpreters where interpreters should not serve:

1. The interpreter is a friend, associate, or relative of a party or counsel for a party involved in the proceedings;

2. The interpreter has served in an investigative capacity for any party involved in the case;

3. The interpreter has previously been retained by a law enforcement agency to assist in the preparation of the criminal case at issue;

4. The interpreter or the interpreter's spouse or child has a financial interest in the subject matter in controversy or in a party to the proceeding, or any other interest that would be affected by the outcome of the case;

5. The interpreter has been involved in the choice of counsel or law firm for that case.

Interpreters should disclose to the court and other parties when they have previously been retained for private employment by one of the parties in the case.

Interpreters should not serve in any matter in which payment for their services is contingent upon the outcome of the case.

An interpreter who is also an attorney should not serve in both capacities in the same matter.

Canon 4. Professional Demeanor

Interpreters shall conduct themselves in a manner consistent with the dignity of the court and shall be as unobtrusive as possible.

Commentary:

Interpreters should know and observe the established protocol, rules, and procedures for delivering interpreting services. When speaking in English, interpreters should speak at a rate and volume that enable them to be heard and understood throughout the courtroom, but the interpreter's presence should otherwise be as unobtrusive as possible. Interpreters should work without drawing undue or inappropriate attention to themselves. Interpreters should dress in a manner that is consistent with the dignity of the proceedings of the court.

Interpreters should avoid obstructing the view of any of the individuals involved in the proceedings. However, interpreters who use sign language or other visual modes of communication must be positioned so that hand gestures, facial expressions, and whole body movement are visible to the person for whom they are interpreting.

Interpreters are encouraged to avoid personal or professional conduct that could discredit the court.

Canon 5: Confidentiality

Interpreters shall protect the confidentiality of all privileged and other confidential information.

Commentary:

The interpreter must protect and uphold the confidentiality of all privileged information obtained during the course of her or his duties. It is especially important that the interpreter understand and uphold the attorney-client privilege, which requires confidentiality with respect to any communication between attorney and client. This rule also applies to other types of privileged communications.

Interpreters must also refrain from repeating or disclosing information obtained by them in the course of their employment that may be relevant to the legal proceeding.

In the event that an interpreter becomes aware of information that suggests imminent harm to someone or relates to a crime being committed during the course of the proceedings, the interpreter should immediately disclose the information to an appropriate authority within the judiciary who is not involved in the proceeding and seek advice in regard to the potential conflict in professional responsibility.

CANON 6: RESTRICTION OF PUBLIC COMMENT

Interpreters shall not publicly discuss, report, or offer an opinion concerning a matter in which they are or have been engaged, even when that information is not privileged or required by law to be confidential.

CANON 7: SCOPE OF PRACTICE

Interpreters shall limit themselves to interpreting or translating, and shall not give legal advice, express personal opinions to individuals for whom they are interpreting, or engage in any other activities which may be construed to constitute a service other than interpreting or translating while serving as an interpreter.

Commentary:

Since interpreters are responsible only for enabling others to communicate, they should limit themselves to the activity of interpreting or translating only. Interpreters should refrain from initiating communications while interpreting unless it is necessary for assuring an accurate and faithful interpretation.

Interpreters may be required to initiate communications during a proceeding when they find it necessary to seek assistance in performing their duties. Examples of such circumstances include seeking direction when unable to understand or express a word or thought, requesting speakers to moderate their rate of communication or repeat or rephrase something, correcting their own interpreting errors, or notifying the court of reservations about their ability to satisfy an assignment competently. In such instances they should make it clear that they are speaking for themselves.

An interpreter may convey legal advice from an attorney to a person only while that attorney is giving it. An interpreter should not explain the purpose of forms, services, or otherwise act as counselors or advisors unless they are interpreting for someone who is acting in that official capacity. The interpreter may translate language on a form for a person who is filling out the form, but may not explain the form or its purpose for such a person.

The interpreter should not personally serve to perform official acts that are the official responsibility of other court officials including, but not limited to, court clerks, pretrial release investigators or interviewers, or probation counselors.

CANON 8: ASSESSING AND REPORTING IMPEDIMENTS TO PERFORMANCE

Interpreters shall assess at all times their ability to deliver their services. When interpreters have any reservation about their ability to satisfy an assignment competently, they shall immediately convey that reservation to the appropriate judicial authority.

Commentary:

If the communication mode or language of the non-English-speaking person cannot be readily interpreted, the interpreter should notify the appropriate judicial authority.

Interpreters should notify the appropriate judicial authority of any environmental or physical limitation that impedes or hinders their ability to deliver interpreting services adequately (e.g., the court room is not quiet enough for the interpreter to hear or be heard by the non-English speaker, more than one person at a time is speaking, or principals or witnesses of the court are speaking at a rate of speed that is too rapid for the interpreter to adequately interpret). Sign language interpreters must ensure that they can both see and convey the full range of visual language elements that are necessary for communication, including facial expressions and body movement, as well as hand gestures.

Interpreters should notify the presiding officer of the need to take periodic breaks to maintain mental and physical alertness and prevent interpreter fatigue. Interpreters should recommend and encourage the use of team interpreting whenever necessary.

Interpreters are encouraged to make inquiries as to the nature of a case whenever possible before accepting an assignment. This enables interpreters to match more closely their professional qualifications, skills, and experience to potential assignments and more accurately assess their ability to satisfy those assignments competently.

Even competent and experienced interpreters may encounter cases where routine proceedings suddenly involve technical or specialized terminology unfamiliar to the interpreter (e.g., the unscheduled testimony of an expert witness). When such instances occur, interpreters should request a brief recess to familiarize themselves with the subject matter. If familiarity with the terminology requires extensive time or more intensive research, interpreters should inform the presiding officer.

Interpreters should refrain from accepting a case if they feel the language and subject matter of that case is likely to exceed their skills or capacities. Interpreters should feel no compunction about notifying the presiding officer if they feel unable to perform competently, due to lack of familiarity with terminology, preparation, or difficulty in understanding a witness or defendant.

Interpreters should notify the presiding officer of any personal bias they may have involving any aspect of the proceedings. For example, an interpreter who has been the victim of a sexual assault may wish to be excused from interpreting in cases involving similar offenses.

CANON 9: DUTY TO REPORT ETHICAL VIOLATIONS

Interpreters shall report to the proper judicial authority any effort to impede their compliance with any law, any provision of this code, or any other official policy governing court interpreting and legal translating.

Commentary:

Because the users of interpreting services frequently misunderstand the proper role of the interpreter, they may ask or expect the interpreter to perform duties or engage in activities that run counter to the provisions of this code or other laws, regulations, or policies governing court interpreters. It is incumbent upon the interpreter to inform such persons of his or her professional obligations. If, having been apprised of these obligations, the person persists in demanding that the interpreter violate them, the interpreter should turn to a supervisory interpreter, a judge, or another official with jurisdiction over interpreter matters to resolve the situation.

CANON 10: PROFESSIONAL DEVELOPMENT

Interpreters shall continually improve their skills and knowledge and advance the profession through activities such as professional training and education, and interaction with colleagues and specialists in related fields.

Commentary:

Interpreters must continually strive to increase their knowledge of the languages they work in professionally, including past and current trends in technical, vernacular, and regional terminology as well as their application within court proceedings.

Interpreters should keep informed of all statutes, rules of courts and policies of the judiciary that relate to the performance of their professional duties.

An interpreter should seek to elevate the standards of the profession through participation in workshops, professional meetings, interaction with colleagues, and reading current literature in the field.

Providing Information About the Law to Immigrants

As recommended in the application chapter (pages 158–65), judges can effectively disseminate information about the U.S. legal system by making presentations to groups of immigrants. Through these interactions, judges provide accurate information to, and can also become aware of possible misperceptions held by, immigrants. Additionally, the judge's presence in the immigrant community helps to underscore that judges and the justice system are accessible to everyone. Since recent newcomers' English ability is usually limited, an interpreter will often be required for presentations made to immigrant groups. To ensure that their words will be accurately conveyed, many judges prefer to bring experienced, certified or qualified legal interpreters with them.

Judicial Presentations

Traditionally, many judges have spoken to various kinds of community groups, including groups of immigrants. Judges often respond to requests that they speak, or offer to make presentations to organizations. The approaches discussed below are, for the most part, equally applicable to presentations arranged for judges and those made as part of a court project or by individual judges.

An effective court project for providing judicial speakers to immigrant groups on a regular basis, the Speakers Bureau was recently established by King County District Court.[1] Within a few months of its initiation, the Speakers Bureau provided judicial speakers for hundreds of immigrants at different community meetings in the Seattle area. Two persons have been instrumental in formally organizing the Speakers Bureau: the presiding judge and the court's interpreter coordinator.[2] Because thousands of immigrants have settled in Seattle and attend immigrant organization functions, many judges were interested in outreach once the idea was broached by the presiding judge. Throughout the duration of the program, the presiding judge has continued to enlist speakers.

In arranging for the meetings with community groups, the interpreter coordinator played a key role. To obtain names and addresses of immigrant organizations, he referred to a statewide directory of community organizations. Locally compiled directories are available in some cities. Telephone books also may list organizations in the yellow pages under "Community Organizations." The interpreter coordinator also had ties with numerous community groups through his coordinator role and acquaintance with interpreters of many languages. In addition, by virtue of his previous role in social services, he was acquainted with the staff of a number of immigrant groups.

In lining up presentations, the interpreter coordinator suggests that speaking to a group at a preexisting meeting is easiest to arrange. Church services are excellent; sometimes an announcement can be made during the service for a talk to be held immediately afterwards. Church services for immigrant groups are conducted in many towns and cities. Immigrant groups who regularly meet for other reasons, such as at senior citizen centers or social services agencies, are another good choice.

Agency employees should be consulted about what topics are of interest to group members. For example, family law, tort law, domestic violence, or other topics may be concerns. Topics that are selected in advance can be publicized by the agency before the talk. If important new topics surface during the presentation, a second presentation could be scheduled, perhaps including an attorney who specializes in the topic if it is complex, such as the effect of criminal convictions on immigration status.

As for any speaking engagement, preparation is important. During presentations, Speakers Bureau judges each bring their own style to the immigrant groups. For example, one judge found that reading about the Vietnamese legal system in advance and making reference to some of the differences communicated the judge's genuine concern and knowledge, which surprised the audience and led to significant dialogue. While speaking to a Cambodian group, another judge discovered the audience was particularly concerned with domestic violence and with juvenile court issues, and adjusted the presentation to address those issues. Telling stories derived from cases or the media to illustrate legal points was the way another judge stimulated a dialogue with another audience and effectively communicated legal doctrines such as the separation of powers. In general, straight lectures emphasizing formal legal concepts like jurisdictional limits, detailed descriptions of the U.S. trial and appellate process, and other abstract legal topics were found to turn off the audience.

The Speakers Bureau has attracted radio and newspaper media attention, both ethnic and mainstream press. Most important, the talks have spread accurate information and honed the participating judges' awareness of the concerns and needs of immigrants. In the past few months, other Washington courts have indicated their intention to begin similar speaking programs.

Classroom Settings

Judges throughout the United States have participated in teaching immigrant students in an organized educational setting. Three resources for assisting judges in these efforts are briefly described below. Following these descriptions, one lesson plan is reprinted from each of the two curricula.

Court Access: A Law-Related Education Curriculum for Limited English Speakers (317 pages) includes 58 lesson plans written for English as a Second Language (ESL) classes. The ideal model for this curriculum is to have judges paired with actual teachers of ESL in community colleges and immigrant and refugee assistance programs. As a team, the teachers and judges present interactive lessons, using ESL methods. The materials can also be used by judges speaking to groups. Funded by the State Justice Institute in 1993, the curriculum is available from the Office of the Administrator for the Courts, 1206 S. Quince St., P.O. Box 41170, Olympia, WA 98504-1170, (360) 753-3365.

It's Yours: The Bill of Rights (110 pages) includes eight units of lessons on the U.S. Bill of Rights for school-age students in English as a Second Language classes. Funded by the Commission on the Bicentennial of the U.S. Constitution, 1991, this curriculum is available from the Constitutional Rights Foundation of Chicago, 407 S. Dearborn Ave., Suite 1700, Chicago, Il 60605, (312)663-9057.

Through My Own Eyes: A Personalized Look at the United States Justice System. Available from the American Judicature Society in Arabic, Cantonese, English, French, Haitian, Khmer, Korean, Polish, Russian, and Spanish, and Vietnamese, this video sells for $12 plus $3.50 shipping and handling. It is 30-minutes long and comes with a facilitator's manual (English only). American Judicature Society, 25 E. Washington St., Suite 1600, Chicago, Il 60602.

Domestic Violence — The Law

Lesson 2: Order for Protection

Objectives

- Students will listen to and interact with a judge who will explain how the legal system handles cases of domestic violence.

- Students will role-play a meeting between Maria and her lawyers/counselors.

- Students will have the opportunity to speak, write, read and understand English.

Estimated Time

One 50-minute class period.

Materials

Copies of handout — The Law.

Vocabulary

- **Civil legal system** — the part of the court system that handles disputes between private citizens. Civil cases include divorces (dissolution), contract disputes, auto accidents, and consumer disputes.

- **Criminal legal system** — the part of the court system that prosecutes persons accused of crimes.

- **Prosecutor** — The lawyer who represents the government in criminal cases. The prosecutor files charges against the person who allegedly committed the crime.

Procedures

■ Tell students that they will be role-playing a meeting between Maria and lawyers or counselors.

■ Set up the front of the room for the role-play, with two chairs on either side of a table. The players will include: two lawyers/counselors from the center, Maria, Tina, and Maria's neighbor, who has agreed to accompany Maria to the center. She will help Maria ask and answer questions.

(You may play the role of one of the lawyer/counselors, or ask for students to play both of these roles. Discuss with the classroom teacher beforehand whether s/he thinks students will feel prepared to play these roles.)

■ Pass out the handout about the law, and review it briefly with students. Do not go into detail, as you can bring up points about the law when debriefing the role-play. Ask for volunteers to play the roles described. Tell "Maria" and "Tina" that they want to know what Maria can do. Should she ask for an Order for Protection? How else can the legal system help her? Tell the rest of the class to watch and write down the options the counselors suggest. Allow 10 to 15 minutes for the role-play.

■ After the role-play, first ask the volunteers how they felt about their roles. Did it feel realistic? Elicit feedback from the rest of the class. Did they think it seemed realistic? Did the advisors give Maria all of the information she needed to know? What else would you have wanted to know? What else would you have told Maria? Was Tina helpful?

Excerpt from *Court Access* curriculum, pp. 247-50.

Domestic Violence, The Law — Lesson 2

JUDGE'S LESSON

■ Tell students that it costs $20 to file for an Order for Protection. The fee can be waived if the person cannot afford to pay.

Your State
How much does it cost to file for an Order for Protection in your state?

■ Tell students that a Temporary Order for Protection can be issued immediately if the person needs *immediate* protection. Notice must be served on the Respondent, and the temporary order is effective until the time of the hearing. At the hearing, the Petitioner can then ask for a Protection Order that lasts for a year. If there is no immediate danger, the Petitioner waits approximately two weeks for a hearing, and then asks for an Order at that time. Explain that the Petitioner must be able to prove the information in the Petition to obtain an order. The Respondent may be present to respond at the hearing. If he or she does not appear, the Order may still be issued, as long as he or she was properly served. [The local law enforcement agency will usually help with service, by giving the Respondent a copy of the Petition, with the date of the hearing, at his or her place of residence or work.]

■ What exactly does the Order for Protection do? Review the law, pointing out that it can restrain the respondent from committing acts of domestic violence; keep the respondent away from the Petitioner's home; prohibit harassment; award temporary custody of minor children; and order the respondent to participate in counseling.

■ How does the petitioner enforce the Order? Tell them to call 911 immediately; h/she should also carry a copy with her at all times; give copies to the children's school and other caregivers; and keep a record of any violations.

■ After debriefing the role-play, explain to students about any other procedures and resources in your area for victims of domestic violence. A list follows of some resources statewide, but it would be helpful to localize.

Your State
What resources exist in your state for victims of domestic violence? How does your state's law compare with the law described above?

JUDGE'S LESSON

Getting Help for Domestic Violence Through the Legal System

Washington state law has special protections for victims of domestic violence. The laws protect individuals who are being abused whether the abuser is a spouse, former spouse, someone you live with or used to live with, someone you are related to by blood or marriage, someone with whom you have a child, or if you are 16 years old or over, someone with whom you have or had a dating relationship. *"Abuse"* means that the person is threatening to hit you, hitting you, or restraining your freedom of movement. Most victims of abuse are women. There are also cases of women abusing men, women abusing other women and men abusing other men.

A person who is being abused can seek help either through the criminal legal system or the *civil* legal system.

The Criminal Legal System

If an attack is taking place, the best thing to do is to call the police.
The police should take a report. They should also inform you in writing of your rights as a domestic violence victim, and make sure you are not in continuing danger. The police should give you information about shelters and other community resources to help you.

The police must also inform you that there is a statewide 24 hour toll-free hotline with information about shelter and alternatives to domestic violence. That number is **1-800-562-6025.**

The abuser can go to jail.
The police must *arrest* the abuser *if* there is reason to believe that the abuser assaulted you within the last four hours, and that you were injured by the assault. Even if the abuser is arrested, s/he may be out of jail within a few hours. Since that is the case, the judge can issue a *"no-contact"* order if there is a danger of further harm to the injured party. *The no-contact order commands the abuser not to contact the victim by phone or in person until the trial date.* If the abuser violates the no-contact order by harassing or harming the victim, s/he can be arrested.
If the abuser violates the no-contact order, you should call 911, and show the police a copy of the order.

JUDGE'S LESSON

Civil Legal System

The civil legal system can offer help to victims of domestic violence by issuing an *Order for Protection*. You can get an Order for Protection without a lawyer. There are two types of orders—emergency temporary orders, which last for up to two weeks, and full protection orders, which last for up to one year, and can be renewed. The filing fee is $20, but the fee can be waived (set aside) for low-income people. *An Order for Protection can command the abuser not to threaten, harass, or molest the victim and can exclude the abuser from the home for up to one year.* The Order can also award temporary custody of children and order that the abuser get counseling. An Order may be issued by any court, but only the superior court can award custody of children or order the abuser to move out of the house.

If the victim is married to or has children with the abuser and is bringing an action for dissolution, legal separation, or child custody, a temporary restraining order (TRO) can be issued as part of that case. The temporary restraining order provides the same protection as an Order for Protection, except that there can be no order for counseling. A temporary restraining order, can, however, award temporary child support and temporary use of property such as a car.

If the abuser violates an Order for Protection or a temporary restraining order, the police must arrest the abuser. Of course, these orders will only be enforced if the victim calls the police to report any harassment or abuse. Again, actual enforcement of these orders can be difficult.

If the abuser violates a court order, call 911 immediately. Show the police officer a copy of the Order.

Domestic Violence Resource List

Domestic Violence Hotline
Statewide 1-800-562-6025
(Information about shelters and what to do if you are a victim)

Washington State Coalition Against Domestic Violence
200 "W" Street SE, Suite B
Tumwater, WA 98501
206-352-4029

Asian Pacific Island Family Safety Center
(Information phone line and support group for Asian Pacific Island women)

Northwest Immigrant Rigths Project
(Assists with legal mattters)

Refugee Women's Alliance
(Has advocate for battered women)

Gideon v. *Wainwright*: **The Right to a Lawyer**

> **VOCABULARY:**   civil   provide

Any person accused of a crime has the right to have a lawyer represent him or her. But some people don't have money to pay a lawyer. In 1961 Clarence Earl Gideon said he did not get a fair trial because he did not have a lawyer. He did not have the money to pay a lawyer.

Accused of a crime

Clarence Earl Gideon, 51 years old, had no one to help him when he was accused of breaking into a bar in a small Florida town in 1961.

No free lawyer

He asked the court to **provide** one for him free. But the state of Florida only provided a lawyer for a person who could be put to death if found guilty. The crime that Gideon was accused of was not serious enough for that punishment. Most states provided free lawyers to people accused of serious crimes if they were not able to pay. Florida was one of five states that did not do this. The Florida legislature thought that providing free lawyers would cost the state too much money. Besides, the Bill of Rights did not say that a state had to pay for a lawyer for someone. It only said that people have the right to a lawyer when they are accused of a crime.

Clarence Gideon in the courtroom where his fight for a free lawyer began.

Gideon had to defend himself in his trial. He was found guilty and sent to prison for five years.

Supreme Court review

While he was in prison, Gideon wrote to the Supreme Court, asking it to decide his case. He did not get a fair trial, he said, because he did not have a lawyer. He was too poor to hire one. In 1963 the Court said it would decide Gideon's case.

Excerpt from *It's Yours: The Bill of Rights,* pp. 63-64.

Unit 5

WHAT DO YOU KNOW?
1. Why didn't Gideon hire a lawyer?
2. Why didn't the state of Florida provide a lawyer for him?
3. How did the Supreme Court find out about Gideon's case?

WHAT DO YOU THINK?
1. Do you think Gideon had a fair trial without a lawyer?
2. Do you think a state should provide free lawyers for people accused of a crime who are too poor to hire a lawyer? Explain.

Supreme Court Decision

After hearing Gideon's case, all of the Supreme Court Justices voted in favor of Gideon. They agreed that the states must provide free lawyers to all poor persons accused of a serious crime that could put them in prison. The Court thought that a person needed a lawyer in order to get a fair trial. Since the government has lawyers to prosecute an accused person, the accused person should have a lawyer, too.

This right comes in part from the Sixth Amendment, which says that in criminal cases, people accused of a crime have the right to be helped by a lawyer.

WHAT DO YOU KNOW?

Complete each sentence by choosing the correct ending.

1. When Gideon was accused of breaking into a bar, he
   a. hired a lawyer to defend him in court.
   b. left town as fast as he could.
   c. asked the state to give him a lawyer.

2. Gideon did not hire a lawyer to help him in court because
   a. he hated all lawyers.
   b. he was too poor to pay a lawyer.
   c. he did not know he would need a lawyer.

3. Gideon believed his trial was not fair because
   a. the judge did not like his religion.
   b. the state would not pay for a lawyer to help him.
   c. he was not told what the charge against him was.

4. In the Gideon case the Supreme Court said that
   a. in criminal cases, people should have the help of a lawyer.
   b. in criminal cases, people have the right to a lawyer only if they can pay for one.
   c. poor people cannot defend themselves in court.

Right to a Lawyer in Civil Cases

We know that a person accused of a crime such as murder has the right to a free lawyer. Does a person who wants a divorce or who is sued by another person have the same right?

These people do not have the right to a free lawyer because these cases are not criminal, they are **civil** cases. The Legal Services Corporation is funded to help people with legal difficulties in such things as housing, immigration, or family problems. Call your state or city bar association for the legal services program in your area and other organizations that can help.

Immigration Status and Battered Immigrants

Battering is viewed as a pattern of coercive control that one person exercises over another. Abusers use physical and sexual violence, threats, emotional insults and economic deprivation to dominate their partners and get their way. For immigrant women, the controlling behavior of the batterer can include isolating her from friends, family, or anyone who speaks her language. The batterer can also hide or destroy her important documents, including her passport. Very often, the batterer can threaten to report her to the Immigration and Naturalization Service or withdraw the petition to legalize her immigration condition.[1]

Immigrant women[2] are not only particularly vulnerable to spousal abuse but are also less likely to seek assistance.[3] In a 1990 study[4] of the service needs and overall experiences of 400 undocumented women in the San Francisco Bay Area, 35 percent of those surveyed had experienced some form of domestic violence. While some of these women had sought help from an agency or friends, in other cases, women were so isolated that they had never talked to anyone about their problem. The police were called in only 6 percent of the cases.

This failure to seek assistance was based on participants' fears in response to threats that their husbands or partners would abandon them, leave them for other women, use violence against them or refuse to help them legalize their immigration status. In addition, lack of fluency in English, lack of support from family and friends, and lack of access to basic social services deterred immigrant women from seeking help.

Until new laws were passed in the early 1990s, the immigration process tended to worsen the problems of immigrants experiencing domestic violence. Normally, under immigration law, immigrant women who marry U.S. citizens or lawful permanent residents obtain their lawful immigration status through the sponsorship of their spouse. Those who apply for permanent residency before the second anniversary of their marriage receive what is known as "conditional permanent residency" for two years. Within 90 days before this two-year waiting period ends, the couple must file a joint application to have the "condition" removed from the permanent residence status for the wife. The immigration requirements have commonly been used by abusers as a control tactic to continue to mistreat their spouses and keep them in the abusive relationships.

Congress passed two laws in the 1990s to allow battered women to file for a waiver of the joint filing requirement and to allow battered women married to U.S. citizens or resident spouses to file their own immigration papers. These laws only apply to individuals who are legally married to U.S. citizens (USC) or permanent residents (LPR). If a battered spouse who does not yet have status obtains a final dissolution from her batterer with status before she petitions under the Violence Against Women Act (VAWA), she loses her ability to self-petition.

The first law, the Immigration Marriage Fraud Amendment, applies to women whose husbands have already begun the immigration process for them and who have received a conditional residency card. It permits qualified immigrants who have been divorced from a good faith marriage, battered, or subjected to extreme cruelty in the United States to remove the "condition" from their permanent resident status without the assistance of their husbands.

The second law, the Violence Against Women Act, changes the immigration process for battered immigrants (and their children) who have not yet received a permanent residency card. Battered immigrants who qualify are excused from relying on their spouse to apply for residency with the INS but can instead petition directly on behalf of themselves and their children. Their spouses play no role in the process and do not need to even know that the battered immigrant is petitioning.

The unmarried children under age 21 of VAWA self-petitioners may be included as beneficiaries of their parent's self-petitions, and have the same immigration status as their parents. Immigrants who were never abused themselves can also self-petition to become permanent residents if their child was abused by their citizen or permanent resident spouse. Additionally, VAWA provides a defense to deportation called "cancellation of removal" for undocumented women battered by their USC or LPR spouse, if their child has been battered by the child's USC or LPR parent. If the victim qualifies for the cancellation of removal, the court may waive deportation and grant residency.

Undocumented persons married to permanent residents cannot get conditional or permanent residency immediately. They are subject to annual limits on immigrants from a particular country, meaning that once the limit for that country has been met that year, later applicants are shifted to following years in the order they applied.

Domestic violence is the crime least reported by recent immigrants, according to a recent national survey of police chiefs, prosecutors, and court administrators. Recent immigrants report crime less frequently than other victims do. Only 12 percent of the surveyed law enforcement and court officials believed that recent immigrants were as likely or more likely to report crimes as other victims were.[5]

More Information on Immigration Consequences

by Norton Tooby

Definition of Conviction

Only certain dispositions are considered to be "convictions" for immigration purposes. Diversion (if no plea of guilty has been entered), dispositions in juvenile proceedings, and convictions that are still on appeal are not considered "convictions."

Diversion. Completing a pre-plea diversion program and obtaining dismissal of the charges does not constitute a "conviction" under immigration *so long as there has been no plea of guilty or no contest entered at any time*.[1] Criminal cases dismissed after successful completion of a traditional diversion provision with no guilty plea requirement do not constitute convictions for immigration purposes.

Accessory After the Fact. Conviction as an accessory after the fact has been held not to be a drug offense for immigration purposes even when the principal offense involved drugs.[2]

Effects of Convictions and Sentences on Noncitizens

The Immigration and Naturalization Act of 1952 (INA), as amended, is the federal immigration statute.[3] It creates several categories for criminal offenses. The category under which a crime is placed, combined in some cases with the person's immigration status or equities, determines the immigration effect of a conviction. The four main categories are crimes that make a noncitizen deportable for an aggravated felony, deportable under other grounds, inadmissible, and ineligible to establish good moral character.

Deportable for Conviction of an Aggravated Felony. This category or type of conviction causes the greatest of all adverse immigration consequences. See 8 USC § 1101(a)(43). Even a long-term permanent resident who is convicted of an aggravated felony will almost certainly be quickly deported and permanently banished. In the last 10 years, Congress has put dozens of serious and even minor offenses (including some misdemeanors under state law) into the aggravated felony category.[4]

Deportable for a Non-Aggravated Felony Conviction. A person who is deportable for some reason other than conviction of an aggravated felony faces serious immigration consequences.[5] Even a long-term, lawful permanent resident can and often will be deported. Depending upon the type of conviction and the person's immigration status and history, the person may be eligible to apply in immigration court for some discretionary waiver of deportation.

Inadmissible, Ineligible to Establish Good Moral Character. A noncitizen who comes within one of the grounds of inadmissibility usually can be blocked from obtaining a green card or some other form of immigration benefit.[6] For example, if the person is undocumented but could get a green card through a family member, being inadmissible may prevent this. An inadmissible permanent resident who wants to travel outside the United States may be stopped at the border and not permitted to return.

A person who is inadmissible based on criminal problems usually will be held not to have "good moral character," which is a requirement for naturalization and some other forms of immigration relief.

The Effect of Sentence. In some but not all cases, obtaining a certain sentence may be sufficient to avoid adverse immigration results.

Besides the grounds of inadmissibility, a person can be blocked from establishing good moral character for having spent 180 days in jail as a result of one or more convictions during the required time period for which good moral character must be shown. This 180-day requirement for good moral character is the one immigration rule that depends upon time actually spent in jail, as opposed to the term of imprisonment formally ordered by the judge.

For other immigration purposes, a period of confinement ordered by a judge for an offense, "regardless of any suspension of the imposition or execution of that imprisonment or sentence in whole or in part," will be counted as the term of the sentence.[7] This changed the former rule, which was that if a court suspended imposition of sentence and ordered jail time as a condition of probation, the time would equal zero sentence for immigration purposes. Under current law, if imposition of sentence is suspended (so no particular state prison sentence is selected) and no custody time is ordered as a condition of probation, that counts as zero sentence for some immigration purposes; if the person receives six months' custody time as a condition of probation and was released from custody in four months, that counts as a six-month sentence for immigration purposes. If the defendant receives a five-year sentence, execution of which is suspended, and the defendant is placed on probation with no custody time, that counts as a five-year sentence. Concurrent sentences are evaluated as the length of the longest sentence, and consecutive sentences are added together.[8]

Aggravated Felonies. Defendants who are convicted of an aggravated felony and deported and then return to the United States illegally are subject to a potential 20-year federal prison term just for the illegal reentry.[9] These cases are increasingly being prosecuted.

In many cases, once informed of the immigration consequences, the defendant can knowledgeably participate in the defense. For example, for some offenses, such as theft, burglary, or a crime of violence, a sentence of 364 days or less may avoid the conviction being considered an aggravated felony.

As described in "Immigration Information for Criminial Cases in State Courts," pages 51–52, the offenses in 8 USC section 1101(a)(43) are aggravated felonies for deportation purposes regardless of the date the conviction was entered.[10]

In general, an aggravated felony includes:

1. The following offenses, but *only if custody of one year or more is ordered:*
   - A "crime of violence" as defined in 18 USC § 16 (the definition of a "crime of violence" is quite broad, even including misdemeanor driving under the influence)[11]
   - Theft
   - Burglary
   - Offenses involving commercial bribery, counterfeiting, forgery, or trafficking in vehicles with altered identification numbers
   - Perjury, subornation of perjury, or obstruction of justice
   - Using fraudulent documents to obtain an immigration benefit[12]

These offenses are not considered to be aggravated felonies if the sentence is less than a year. For example, conviction of three counts of theft, with a 364-day sentence for each to run consecutively, does not result in an aggravated felony conviction.

2. Any drug trafficking offense (e.g., possession for sale or sale of $10 of marijuana or even second-offense misdemeanor simple possession).[13]

An expungement or technical record clearance will not eliminate this conviction for immigration purposes. A plea to a state drug offense that is not a violation of federal law and does not involve trafficking would not be an aggravated felony but would still trigger deportation as a drug offense, although discretionary relief may then be available in immigration court.

3. Trafficking in firearms or destructive devices (bombs, grenades).[14]

4. Murder, rape, or sexual abuse of a minor.[15] Statutory rape probably will be held to constitute sexual abuse of a minor.

5. The following offenses, but only if the loss suffered by the victim or the government was $10,000 or more: money laundering, transactions involving proceeds from specified unlawful activity, offenses involving fraud or deceit, or tax evasion.[16]

6. Several offenses relating to operating a business of prostitution, slavery, or peonage.[17]

7. Offenses relating to revealing the identity of domestic or international undercover agents.[18]

8. A defendant's failure to appear for service of sentence if the underlying offense is punishable by a term of five years or more; or failure to appear before a court pursuant to a court order to answer to or dispose of a charge of a felony for which a sentence of two years' imprisonment or more may be imposed.[19] As with all aggravated felonies, conviction of the offense is required to make it an aggravated felony: merely failing to appear, without being convicted of the offense of failure to appear, does not have immigration consequences.

9. Alien smuggling, except for a first conviction in which the person smuggled was an immediate family member.[20]

10. RICO offenses in which a sentence of one year could have been imposed.[21]

Drug Offenses and Drug Abuse. As discussed above, most drug convictions will constitute aggravated felonies and trigger deportation. One clear exception is first conviction of simple possession, which is not an aggravated felony in most cases; however, this conviction is a basis for deportation (except simple possession of 30 grams or less of marijuana).[22] In many cases, statutory expungement will eliminate a single conviction for first offense simple possession.[23] A person can be found inadmissible—even without ever having been convicted—if the INS has "reason to believe" the person has ever been a drug trafficker or conspired or assisted in trafficking.[24]

A person who admits committing any drug offense, whether or not there has been a conviction, is also inadmissible.[25] This might occur, for example, if the person made a formal and knowing admission of a drug offense in court.

Drug addiction and drug abuse are a basis for exclusion and deportation.[26] The definition of abuse is in dispute. Currently some U.S. consulates are ruling that any drug use beyond mere "experimentation" (for example, one instance of use) within the last three years demonstrates drug abuse.[27]

Crimes Involving Moral Turpitude—Inadmissibility. A person who has been convicted of an offense involving moral turpitude is inadmissible,[28] meaning the person can be kept out of the United States or barred from obtaining a green card or other lawful status. Many minor and serious offenses can be classified as crimes involving moral turpitude. Generally, if an offense as defined by statute involves fraud, theft, intent to commit serious bodily harm, or in some cases lewdness, malice, or recklessness, the offense will be held to involve moral turpitude. It does not matter whether the offense is a felony or misdemeanor for this purpose. The fact that a state offense has been held under state law to involve or not to involve moral turpitude does not automatically mean that federal immigration authorities will reach the same conclusion.[29]

Since so many offenses can be classified as involving moral turpitude, many noncitizens are excluded for minor convictions. If a defendant comes within the "petty offense exception," the defendant will not be excluded. Under this exception, an alien is automatically not inadmissible if:

- The alien has committed only one crime involving moral turpitude;
- "Was not sentenced to a term of imprisonment in excess of six months (regardless of the extent to which the sentence was ultimately executed);" and
- The offense carries a maximum possible sentence of one year or less.[30]

Thus a person convicted of a misdemeanor first offense with a sentence of six months or less is not inadmissible under the moral turpitude ground. Note, however, that the defendant will be considered "sentenced to imprisonment in excess of 6 months" if ordered to serve in excess of six months, either as a condition of probation or straight sentence, even if execution is suspended.[31] If a term of imprisonment is imposed, suspended execution of sentence does not prevent the entire sentence from being counted as a sentence.[32]

Moral Turpitude Ground of Deportability. The defendant can become deportable in one of two ways:

- Conviction of one crime involving moral turpitude. A person is deportable who was convicted of a crime involving moral turpitude that was committed within five years of his or her last admission to the United States and that carries a potential sentence of one year or more.

- Conviction of two crimes involving moral turpitude. Conviction of two crimes involving moral turpitude is a basis for deportation unless the offenses represent a "single scheme of criminal misconduct." A 1971 and a 1997 conviction for misdemeanor petty theft, for example, will combine to make the defendant deportable.

Deportability for Firearms or Destructive Devices Offenses. Trafficking in firearms, destructive devices, or explosive materials is an aggravated felony and conviction is therefore a ground for deportation,[33] as is conviction of any of several federal firearms offenses listed in the definition of aggravated felony, including felon in possession of a firearm.[34] A noncitizen is also independently deportable for any offense relating to firearms or destructive devices.[35]

However, a firearms sentencing enhancement is not considered a firearms "conviction" for immigration purposes.[36] If the elements of the offense itself do not automatically involve firearms, a firearms sentence enhancement will not trigger deportation.[37] Conviction of a crime of violence with a sentence imposed of a year or more separately triggers deportation as an aggravated felony.

Some statutes encompass both acts that necessarily involve firearms and other acts that do not. If the statute is divisible or ambiguous, immigration authorities will not look beyond the "record of conviction" (charge, plea, judgment or verdict, and sentence) to determine whether the person was convicted of an offense relating to firearms.[38] A person deportable under the firearms ground might still be able to apply for some discretionary relief in immigration court, as long as the offense is not an aggravated felony.[39]

Domestic Violence, Child Neglect or Abuse. In 1996, Congress created a new, very broad ground of deportation based on a conviction of a state or federal crime of domestic violence, spousal abuse, stalking, and child neglect, abandonment, or abuse.[40] A person also is deportable whom a civil or criminal court has found to have violated a domestic violence protective order, even if there is no criminal conviction.

Conviction of a "crime of domestic violence" is a broad category of offenses defined as (a) "an offense that has as an element the use, attempted use, or threatened use of physical force against the person or property of another, or (b) any other offense that is a felony and that, by its nature, involves a substantial risk that physical force against the person or property of another may be used in the course of committing the offense."[41]

The defendant must be a current or ex-spouse, the parent of a victim's child, a person who cohabited as a spouse, or someone similarly situated under state domestic or family violence laws, or any other individual against whom such laws provide protection.[42] Thus, offenses such as vandalism or simple assault, which do not involve moral turpitude, might be held to be a basis for deportability if committed against a spouse, family member, girlfriend, or boyfriend.

Cancellation of Removal. Until recently, longtime lawful permanent residents who were convicted of certain crimes could apply for a waiver of deportation known as "section 212(c) relief," so called because it was then located in INA § 212(c). In cases brought to immigration court on or after April 1, 1997, section 212(c) has been eliminated and in its place permanent residents must apply for "cancellation of removal." If cancellation is granted, the person will not be "removed" (i.e., deported or excluded). The applicant must:

- Have been a permanent resident for at least five years;
- Have continuously resided in the U.S. for at least seven years after having been lawfully "admitted in any status";[43]
- Not have been convicted of an aggravated felony; and
- Not previously have received § 212(c) relief, suspension of deportation, or cancellation of removal.[44]

Defense of Non-Citizens in Juvenile Court

A juvenile adjudication does not constitute a conviction. Many of the most severe crime-related immigration consequences flow from criminal convictions. Since an adjudication of a criminal offense in juvenile court does not constitute a criminal "conviction" for immigration purposes, it will therefore not trigger any adverse immigration consequences that flow from a "conviction."[45]

There are, however, two situations—discussed below—in which a juvenile-court finding may trigger adverse immigration consequences: (1) a special immigration benefit called Family Unity may be barred by a crime of violence that constitutes an act of juvenile delinquency, and (2) a juvenile becomes deportable if a civil or criminal court finds the juvenile has violated a domestic violence protective order, on or after September 30, 1996.

A juvenile sentence does not constitute a sentence for immigration purposes, as juvenile incarceration does not constitute a "sentence to confinement." Certain adverse immigration consequences of criminal convictions depend upon a sentence or potential sentence of a certain length, each of which must flow from a conviction. Since a juvenile adjudication does not constitute a conviction, the length of incarceration flowing from a juvenile court disposition will not trigger any adverse immigration consequences.[46]

However, a conviction of a juvenile who has been transferred to adult court does constitute a conviction for immigration purposes. For example, a minor convicted in adult court of a crime involving moral turpitude may be inadmissible or removable if the juvenile court expressly finds the minor unfit for the existing juvenile proceedings and treats the minor as an adult offender.[47]

Some acts result in immigration consequences without a conviction; these apply with full force to juveniles. Although juvenile findings and dispositions do not trigger adverse immigration consequences, some immigration consequences flow from the fact that the immigrant juvenile committed acts considered to be wrongdoing. In general, minors suffer these misconduct-based disabilities just as fully as adult immigrants, with some specific exceptions discussed below.

Conduct-based grounds of inadmissibility for juveniles. Any of the following grounds of inadmissibility can bar an undocumented juvenile from obtaining lawful permanent residency and depend upon conduct, rather than a conviction:

- Admission of committing a drug offense
- Admission of committing a crime involving moral turpitude
- Giving the INS "reason to believe" the juvenile is or has been a drug trafficker
- Being currently a drug addict or drug abuser
- Engaging in prostitution
- Making a false claim of U.S. citizenship (on or after September 30, 1996)
- Lying or using false documents to get immigration benefits
- Illegally smuggling aliens or encouraging others to do so.

Conduct-based grounds of deportability of juveniles. The following grounds of deportability depend upon conduct, rather than a conviction. They therefore apply fully to juveniles:

- Being a drug addict or drug abuser at any time after entry
- Illegally smuggling aliens or encouraging others to do so
- Being found by a civil court to have violated a domestic violence protective order on or after September 30, 1996
- Engaging in, after "admission" into the United States, any activity to violate any espionage or sabotage law or to violate or evade any law prohibiting the export from the United States of goods, technology, or sensitive information, INA § 237(a)(4)(A); any other criminal activity that endangers public safety or national security INA § 237(a)(4)(A); or any activity a purpose of which is the opposition to, or the control or overthrow of, the government of the U.S. by force, violence, or other unlawful means, INA § 237(a)(4)(A)(iii).

Effect of juvenile violence on family unity benefits. Under new IIRIRA legislation, Congress now denies Family Unity benefits to persons who "commit an act of juvenile delinquency which if committed by an adult" would be a felony involving violence or the threat of physical force against another person.[48]

The legalization or amnesty programs under INA § 210, 245A, which provided lawful status for immigrants who have lived in the United States since 1982 and for agricultural workers, divided many families. For example, many parents qualified for amnesty but the children came to the United States too late to do so. The Family Unity program established by the Immigration Act of 1990, § 301, was designed to help such families by providing at least temporary status and work authorization to the non-legalized relatives. Many of these relatives will ultimately immigrate through family visa petitions, but rely on Family Unity for lawful status and work authorization during the years of waiting that may be required.

Family Unity stops deportation and provides lawful status for a fixed or indefinite period. Deportation is not stopped and the person is not eligible for Family Unity status if the person is deportable for a crime or convicted of three misdemeanors or one felony.

Juvenile violation of domestic violence orders. As noted earlier, in 1996, Congress created a new, very broad ground of deportation for those, including juveniles, who have convictions or civil findings of domestic violence.[49] A person also is deportable whom a civil or criminal court has found to have violated a domestic violence protective order, even without a criminal conviction. This deportation ground applies to juveniles, since it does not depend on the existence of a criminal conviction.

Political asylum and restriction on removal. If there is significant reason to suspect that an alien has committed a serious nonpolitical crime in the alien's country of origin, even if there is no conviction, the alien is barred from (a) receiving political asylum, see INA § 208(a)(2)(A)(iii), and 8 USC § 1227(a)(2)(A)(iii); and (b) receiving restriction on removal, see INA § 241(b)(3)(B)(iii) and 8 USC § 1227(1)(3)(B)(iii). Since this ground does not require a conviction, it applies to juveniles.

Special relief for juveniles eligible for long-term foster care. The Immigration Act of 1990 and subsequent amendments created a new option for juveniles. A juvenile can qualify as a "special immigrant," and therefore become eligible for permanent residency, if the juvenile: (i) has been declared dependent on a juvenile court located in the United States and has been deemed eligible by that court for long-term foster care, and (ii) for whom it has been determined in administrative or judicial proceedings that it would not be in the alien's best interest to be returned to the alien's or parent's previous country of nationality or country of last habitual residence.[50]

In appropriate cases, the juvenile court judge can issue an order making the necessary findings regarding court jurisdiction, long-term care, and inadvisability of return to the home country, and ruling that this is being done for the welfare of the minor.[51]

Special immigration relief for abused juveniles. Juveniles who have been abused by a permanent-resident or U.S.-citizen parent may be eligible for permanent residency under the 1994 Violence Against Women Act (8 USC §§ 1254(a)(1)(A)(iv), (B)(iii), 1254(a)(3)), even if they are not in dependency proceedings. An abused juvenile may also apply for a special form of cancellation of removal, requiring only three years' continuous presence in the United States (instead of ten years), good moral character, and extreme hardship. INA § 240A(b)(2).[52]

Effective Assistance of Counsel: A Suggested Standard for Notification of Immigration Consequences

When they are faced with unexpected immigration consequences after pleading guilty, immigrants often ask if it is possible to reverse the guilty plea. *People v. Soriano*[53] articulated the rule that defense counsel renders ineffective assistance when counsel does not investigate the immigration consequences facing a defendant, advise the defendant concerning them, and, consequently, attempt to protect the client against them. A number of other state courts also have concluded that the defense attorney's failure to warn the defendant of immigration consequences is ineffective assistance of counsel, resulting in a reversal of the defendant's conviction.[54]

While there is disagreement on whether failure to adequately warn the defendant means counsel is ineffective,[55] fairness to clients dictates that they should be informed of all important factors involved in their cases before making informed decisions on how to plead.[56]

In order to represent a noncitizen, counsel should take the following steps:

Obtain from the client the information necessary to formulate a strategy to avoid unnecessary immigration consequences.

Call an immigration expert or directly research the exact immigration consequences of any proposed plea or alternative. Ample resources—both expert legal resource offices and written information—exist to provide answers to immigration questions. Community agencies and immigration counsel often can offer assistance to persons with immigration problems.[57] Good secondary sources are also available.[58]

The specific immigration consequences to the client must be explained in an understandable manner. Many clients are advised that a disposition "might lead to deportation, exclusion, or denial of naturalization." While this general warning is sufficient to alert the defendant that there might be a problem, it is insufficient to inform the client of the chances that it will actually come to pass, or what must be done to avoid it.[59] In order to give the client an accurate warning, counsel should discover the actual consequences—e.g., disqualification from political asylum or naturalization, loss of permanent resident status, deportation, permanent ineligibility for lawful status, disqualification from waivers, and the like—and clearly explain them to the client.

Find out how high a priority the immigration consequences are for the client. Once the defendant understands what the immigration consequences are, he or she may not consider that a priority. Some defendants are not willing to risk more time in jail in an effort to safeguard their immigration status. Others place the right to remain with their families in the United States as their highest priority and would sacrifice almost any other consideration. These difficult choices must be made by the client, once fully informed.

If the client's immigration status is a high priority, the defense will be conducted with this in mind. Courts may see unusually vigorous criminal defense work—including strategies not normally used in defense of a minor charge. For example, the defendant may choose to take a minor case to trial, even if there is only a slim possibility of acquittal, if the alternative is certain deportation.

Notes

Introduction

1. The discussion about the *Ventura* case that follows is drawn primarily from my personal recollection of the reinvestigation I conducted as Ventura's post-conviction lawyer, the Ventura trial transcript, and a comprehensive article about the case by Peter Carlin, "What Becomes of the Resurrected?" *Los Angeles Times Magazine,* March 8, 1992, p. 22.

2. Because Ventura appeared to have been treated unfairly by the judicial system, the reinvestigation of Ventura's case eventually became the subject of intense media attention. Articles about the case appeared frequently in the *Oregonian,* Oregon's major newspaper. Local television news programs mentioned the case repeatedly. One local station did an hour-long feature on the case, even sending reporters to Ventura's home village in the remote mountains of southern Mexico. NBC sent a news crew to interview Ventura in prison and devoted five minutes to the story on the national evening news. Not to be outdone, Oprah Winfrey devoted most of a show to interviewing three of the Ventura trial jurors, while Ventura appeared via satellite from prison.

3. Carlin, "What Becomes of the Resurrected?" p. 22.

4. Ibid., p. 22.

5. This exchange from the *Ventura* trial transcript is reported in an essay by Lourdes De Leon, "The Mixtecs' Annual 3000-mile Journey," in Gamboa and Buan (eds.), *Nosotros, The Hispanic People of Oregon, Essays and Recollections* (Portland: Oregon Council for the Humanities, 1995), p. 119.

6. Ibid.

7. The Anglo participants did not know that young Mixtecs do not look directly at an elder or person of authority. Peter Carlin, "What Becomes of the Resurrected?" p. 22. Avoiding eye contact in this context is a respectful gesture in the Mixtec culture, not a display of excessive humility, untruthfulness, or guilt as can be perceived in the Anglo culture.

8. Carlin, "What Becomes of the Resurrected?" p. 22.

9. According to the U.S. Immigration and Naturalization Service, over 900,000 immigrants were admitted into the United States in 1996, 14 percent more than in 1995. During the 1990s, 75 percent of new immigrants are expected to be Asian or

Latino. Bill Ong Hing, "Addressing the Tension of Separatism and Conflict in an Immigration-Driven Multiracial Society," 81 *Cal. L. Rev.* 863, 865-66 (1993).

10. For discussions about the recent use of "cultural defenses" see Veronica Ma, "Cultural Defense: Limited Admissibility for New Immigrants," 3 *San Diego Justice Journal* 461 (1995); Nancy Kim, "The Cultural Defense and the Problem of Cultural Preemption: A Framework for Analysis," 27 *New Mexico Law Review* 101 (Winter 1997); Sharon M. Tomao, "The Cultural Defense: Traditional or Formal?" 10 *Georgetown Immigration Law Journal* 241 (Winter 1996).

11. For example in *Mak v. Blodgett*, 970 F. 2d 614 (9th Cir. 1992), supp. op. 1992 U.S. App. Lexis 17525 (9th Cir. 1992), cert denied. 507 U.S. 951 (1993), the 9th Circuit held that Mak's trial counsel was constitutionally ineffective at the penalty phase of a death penalty trial in failing to present a variety of mitigating evidence that included cultural dislocations that might have affected Mak's behavior. Specifically, the court noted that an expert could have discussed serious assimilation problems experienced by many Chinese who are moved during adolescence from Hong Kong to North America, and certain values in the Chinese culture of Hong Kong that could help explain Mak's involvement in criminal activities in this country. The court also pointed out that the expert's testimony could help explain Mak's apparent lack of emotion at the trial, not as evidence of disinterest or coldness, but consistent with cultural expectations of Chinese males. *Mak,* at p. 618.

Speaking of Culture: Immigrants in the American Legal System

1. For example, the elaborate parades of the Fourth of July or of Carnival in the Caribbean convey to their participants a sense of shared "community" whether they are conscious of it or not. American independence celebrations remind those on the sidelines of struggles for individual freedom within the community while the Carnival in Trinidad joyfully celebrates the multiculturalism of the nation.

2. Immigrant literature reflects the frustrations, sorrows, and joys of redefining one's self in a new place, as in Carlos Bulosan's *America Is in the Heart,* an autobiographical account of immigrants' lives in the United States (Seattle: University of Washington Press, 6th ed., 1984).

3. Immigrants are people who "choose" to leave their countries for a new land, and refugees are people who were "forced" to flee. Despite the legal distinctions between them, refugees and immigrants share many characteristics and circumstances. Unless specifically indicated, the term, "immigrant" and "refugee" will be used interchangeably.

4. Deborah E. Anker, "Determining Asylum Claims in the United States: A Case Study on the Implementation of Legal Norms in an Unstructured Adjudicatory En-

vironment," 19 *N.Y.U. Rev. L. & Soc. Change* 433 (1992), p. 513. In one case, the interpreter erroneously translated "pelogrosidad" as "dangerous" when it really was "a Cuban euphemism for a political crime." All court interpreter ethics codes require interpreters to guard against such mistakes and to ask the court for permission to inquire of the witness the meaning of such regional variants. See Appendix 3, "Code of Professional Responsibility for Interpreters," Canons I and VIII.

5. Christine Sleeter, "How White Teachers Construct Race," in Cameron McCarthy and Warren Cricholow (eds.), *Race, Identity and Representation in Education* (New York: Routledge, 1993), pp. 157-71.

6. John Tenhula, *Voices from Southeast Asia: The Refugee Experience in the United States* (New York: Holmes and Meier, 1991), p. 102.

7. Leo Chavez, *Shadowed Lives: Undocumented Immigrants in American Society* (Ft. Worth, TX: Jovanovich College Publishers, 1992).

8. Barry Stein, "The Refugee Experience: Defining the Parameters of a Field of Study," *International Migration Review,* Vol. 15, No. 1, 1981, p. 320.

9. Author interview with student, 1995.

10. Tenhula, p. 194.

11. "Second Generation," *The Iranian,* 1995, Internet Journal address, http:\\www.iranian.com.

12. This term characterizes Stein's third stage of acculturation and represents some of the experiences of many immigrants studied by Chavez before they reached the stage of integration.

13. Tehula, p. 115.

14. Ibid., p. 194.

15. "Prison Terms for Two Men Marrying Young Girls," *New York Times,* September 24, 1997, p. 14.

16. Tenhula, p. 146.

17. Tekle Woldemikael, "Assertion Versus Accommodation: A Comparative Approach to Intergroup Relations," *American Behavioral Scientist,* Vol. 30, No. 4, 1987, p. 411.

18. John Knudsen, "When Trust Is on Trial: Negotiating Refugee Narratives," in E. Valentine Daniel and John Chr. Knudsen (eds.), *Mistrusting Refugees* (Berkeley: University of California Press, 1995), pp. 26-27.

19. Nazli Kibria, *Family Tightrope: The Changing Lives of Vietnamese Americans* (Princeton, N.J.: Princeton University Press, 1993).

20. Ken and Ivory Levine, *Becoming American* (motion picture), WNET-13 (Franklin Lakes NJ: New Day Films, 1983).

21. Beth Goldstein, "Resolving Sexual Assault: Hmong and the American Legal System," in Glenn L. Hedricks, Bruce T. Downing, and Amoss Deinard (eds.), *The Hmong in Transition* (Staten Island, N.Y.: Center for Migration Studies of New York, 1986) p. 135.

22. Ibid., p. 140.

23. Author interviews with refugees and immigrants, 1997.

24. Ibid.

25. "Tragic Language Gap Costs Student His Life," *Chicago Tribune,* October 21, 1992.

26. Edward Hall, *Beyond Culture* (Garden City, N.Y.: Anchor Books Edition, 1976); and Edward Hall, *The Silent Language* (Greenwich, Conn.: Fawcett Books, 1959); Martha Miller, "Gender and Ethnic Differences in Non-Verbal Communication," lecture given at Trinity College, 1985.

27. Tenhula, p. 94. Editor's note: Behavior at odds with American expectations can be put into context by simply asking witnesses to explain why they behaved in a certain way, or, in cases involving substantial cross-cultural questions, by the appointment of experts on culture issues. "If it is a significant issue ... it may be worthwhile to call someone objectively familiar with the cultural setting to explain how a person from that particular ethnic background will have learned to respond to certain situations." Margery Hite, "Culture as a Legal Argument," in *Representing Refugee and Immigrant Clients: Crossing the Cultural Barriers* (Seattle: King County Bar Association, September 23, 1987).

28. *Interpreters: Their Impact in Court Proceedings,* video (Yakima County Bar Association, May 1984).

29. Tenhula, p. 102.

30. Michael Cole and Sylvia Scribner, *Culture and Thought: Its Psychological Introduction* (New York: John Wiley and Sons, 1974).

31. Anker, p. 525.

32. Ibid, p. 518.

33. Ibid.

34. Anker, p. 521. Judges felt that asylum applicants' answers were "vague, unresponsive, and evasive," often due to lapses in translation and the judges' insistence that applicants limit their answers to complex questions.

35. William Beeman, *Language, Status and Power in Iran* (Bloomington: Indiana University Press, 1986).

36. Author's interviews with refugees in asylum cases, 1992.

37 Tenhula, p. 93.

38. Janet Bauer, "A Long Way Home: Islam and the Adaptation of Iranian Women Refugees in Turkey and West Germany," in Asghar Fathi (ed.), *Iranian Refugees and Exiles Since Khomeini* (Contra Costa, Ca.: Mazda Publishers, 1991), pp. 77-100.

39. Anker, pp. 518, 521.

40. Ibid., p. 516.

41. Ibid.

42. Pierrette Hondagneu-Sotelo, "Overcoming Patriarchal Constraints: The Reconstruction of Gender Relations among Mexican Immigrant Women and Men," *Gender and Society,* Vol. 6, No. 5, 1992, pp. 393-415.

43. Colleen O'Neal, "When Teaching Differently Means More of the Same: Anglo Conformity in a Job Training Program for Immigrant and Refugee Women," ms. prepared for Janet Bauer (ed.), *Teaching Differently.*

44. Alice Yun Chai, "Freed from the Elders but Locked into Labor: Korean Immigrant Women in Hawaii," *Women's Studies,* Vol. 13, No. 3, 1987, pp. 223-34; Nazli Kibria, *Family Tightrope: The Changing Lives of Vietnamese Americans* (Princeton, N.J.: Princeton University Press, 1993).

45. Tenhula, p. 180.

46. Author interviews with refugees and immigrants, 1994.

47. John Ogbu, "Immigrant and Involuntary Minorities in Comparative Perspective," Margaret Gibson and John Ogbu (eds.), *Minority Status and Schooling: A Comparative Study of Immigrant and Involuntary Minorities* (New York: Garland Press, 1991), pp. 3-33.

48. Tenhula, p. 116.

49. Bruce Westfall, "Spitsyn Faces 10 to 14 Years in Prison," *The Columbian,* Vancouver, WA, May 16, 1997, p. 1.

50. Author interview with Connecticut lawyer dos Santos working with Portuguese immigrants on the East Coast, 1997.

51. *Spokesman Review,* Spokane, WA, January 27, 1996.

52. Leslye Orloff, Deeana Jang, and Catherine Klien, "With No Place to Turn: Improving Legal Advocacy for Battered Immigrant Women," 29 *Family Law Quarterly* 313, 316 (Summer 1995).

53. Dan Weikel, "Crime and the Sound of Silence," *Los Angeles Times,* October 21, 1990, p. 1.

54. Karen Haller, "Shadow People," *Connecticut Magazine,* Vol. 60, No. 6, June 1997, pp. 54-62.

55. Karol Ortiz, "Mental Health Consequences of Life History Method: Implications from a Refugee Case," *Ethos,* Vol. 13, No. 2 (1985), pp. 99-120.

56. Anker, pp. 487-96, 516-17.

Interpreters in Court Proceedings

1. This chapter will overview court interpreter issues and discuss some of the practical obstacles to providing accurate interpreting and methods for overcoming them. Several contemporary works give detailed overviews extensively discussing existing case law on court interpreters and how to work with interpreters in court: Judge Charles M. Grabau and Llewelen M. Gibbons, "Protecting the Rights of Linguistic Minorities: Challenges to Court Interpretation," *New England Law Journal* (Winter 1996); Judge Lynn W. Davis and William Hewitt, "Lessons in Administering Justice: What Judges Need to Know about the Requirements, Role, and Professional Responsibilities of the Court Interpreter," *Harvard Latino Law Review* (Fall 1997); see also Massachusetts Bar Association, *Ensuring Equal Justice* (1996); and for detailed overviews emphasizing the development of court interpreter programs for courts, Bill Hewitt, *Court Interpretation* (National Center for State Courts, 1995).

2. This cooperative testing and certification support bank originally consisted of founding members New Jersey, Washington, Oregon, and Minnesota. Washington and New Jersey contributed their existing collections of tests, which have been standardized and supplemented by new tests. Languages now tested include Spanish, Vietnamese, Korean, and Russian; tests for Hmong, Laotian, and Cantonese will be administered shortly.

3. Though a variety of Spanish interpreting courses, both degree programs and shorter-term programs are held in several states each year, they are unavailable to many aspiring interpreters. Interpreter education for languages other than Spanish is almost nonexistent. The dearth of training is one of the primary causes of the extremely low pass rate on certification exams, which average 10 percent or less.

4. See, e.g., the Washington State court interpreter statute, RCW 2.43, and the California state court interpreter statute, California Government Code 68561.

5. United States Bureau of the Census, 1990 Census of Population, CPHL-96 and CPHL-133.

6. Alejandro Portes and Ruben G. Rumbaut, *Immigrant America: A Portrait*, 2d ed., pp. 210-14 (Berkeley: University of California Press, 1996).

7. Ibid., p. 214.

8. Matthew Wald, "Professor Higgins Would be Pleased," *New York Times,* August 3, 1997.

9. Keo Capestaney, "Why Grandpa Has an Accent," unpublished paper, 1998.

10. See Janet Bauer, "Speaking of Culture," in this book.

11. John Tenhula, *Voices from Southeast Asia: The Refugee Experience in America* (New York: Holmes and Meier, 1991), p. 169, where a Vietnamese immigrant notes, "You know, there is functional English and there is good English. I think everyone

should be functional, but to speak good English, well, that takes a long time, a lifetime."

12. A 1977 study of legal proceedings by Dr. Roseann Gonzalez for the purpose of testing the English proficiency of Spanish-speaking persons appearing in court to determine whether they needed Spanish interpreters concluded that court language is extremely complex. These findings were later adopted by the federal court interpreter exam in setting the difficulty of court language at the 14th grade level for Spanish. Roseann Duenas Gonzalez et al., *Fundamentals of Court Interpretation: Theory, Policy and Practice* (Durham, N.C.: Carolina Academic Press, 1991). Other studies have concluded that court language is at the 12th-grade level plus technical legal language. Washington State Supreme Court Interpreter Task Force, *Interim Report,* 1991, Dr. Gilbert Sax, "Study of Washington State Legal Transcripts of Spanish, Cambodian, and Vietnamese Cases," unpublished, in the files of the Washington State Court Interpreter Program.

13. Bill E. Hewitt, *Court Interpretation* (Williamsburg, Va.: National Center for State Courts, 1995).

14. Michael Gardner and Judge Lynn W. Davis, "Justicia Para Todos: Ensuring Equal Access to the Courts for Linguistic Minorities," 9 *Utah Bar Journal* 21, 22 (February 1996).

15. Grabau and Gibbons, p. 270.

16. George S. Bridges, Ph.D., "A Study on Racial and Ethnic Disparities in Superior Court Bail and Pre-Trial Detention Practices in Washington," Washington State Minority and Justice Commission, 1997, p. 12.

17. Many courts provide quality interpreting for non-evidentiary hearings by arranging for telephone interpreting by certified interpreters. Some courts schedule arraignments or other pretrial hearings to be routinely interpreted by a prearranged in-state interpreter, or call the interpreter for unanticipated needs. Through such arrangements, courts can ensure a certified interpreter's services without paying travel expenses. An effective in-state telephone interpretation resource bank can be created by providing education to certified interpreters and judges on telephone interpreting, then circulating a list of willing certified interpreters to the courts. Commercial telephone interpreting services are also available and can provide quick access to interpreters. However, telephone interpreting services usually will not guarantee a certified interpreter, often disclaim responsibility for interpreter errors, and may charge hourly rates up to five times what is paid to in-person interpreters. Therefore they may be most useful for emergency situations or unusual languages. Whenever a telephone interpreter is appointed from any source, the judge needs to voir dire the interpreter regarding the interpreter's qualifications.

18. According to the various linguistic analyses performed for court language difficulty, a qualified court interpreter should have the equivalent of at least a 12th grade education in both languages. See note 12 and accompanying text.

19. Simultaneous interpretation is a precise contemporaneous reiteration of the proceedings for the benefit of the non-English-speaking party. In consecutive interpretation, used during the testimony of a non-English-speaking person, the interpreter waits until the speaker finishes a statement and then interprets it. Roseann Duenas Gonzalez et al., *Fundamentals of Court Interpretation: Theory, Policy, and Practice* (Durham, N.C.: Carolina Academic Press, 1991).

20. For example, Washington's oath is "I affirm that I as the interpreter will make a true interpretation to the party of all the proceedings in a language which the party understands, and that the interpreter will repeat the statements of the party to the court conducting the proceedings, in the English language, to the best of the interpreter's skill and judgment." RCW 2.43.050.

21. Bill Hewitt, *Court Interpretation* (Williamsburg, Va.: National Center for State Courts, 1995).

22. Grabau and Gibbons, p. 296, n.7.

23. Ken Kolker, "Trial and Errors," *Grand Rapids Press,* February 21, 1993.

24. Washington State Court Interpreter Task Force, "Evaluation of Spanish Interpreters in Washington Courts," *Final Report,* 1988.

25. Gardner and Davis, "Justicia Para Todos."

26. See, e.g., *Tomayo-Reyes v. Keeney,* 926 F.2d 1492 (9th Cir. 1991); reversed on other grounds, 112 S. Ct. 652.

27. Grabau and Gibbons, p. 233, citing *U.S. v. Mosquera,* 816 F. Supp 168, 175 (E.D.N.Y. 1993), affirmed without opinion, 48 F. 3d 1214 (2d Cir. 1994). One interpreter can interpret the entire proceeding, as long as the defendant hears all statements, *State v. Gonzales Morales,* 91 Wa. app. 420 § 958 (P. 2d 339), 1998.

28. The 1997 legislation did not pass, but the problem remains and various groups concerned with interpreting hope it will be reintroduced. Interview with Renee Veale, former president of the California Court Interpreters Association, November 25, 1997.

29. This arrangement tends to encourage attorneys to intensively prepare witnesses through an interpreter during pretrial interviews, then bring the interpreter to court, which will influence vocabulary used and presentation of the facts. Author's interviews with trial attorneys, 1995-1998.

30. Washington Interpreters and Translators Society, "Ethics Corner" *WITS Newsletter* (Winter 1997).

31. Susana Sawrey, presentations at Washington State Court Interpreter Program Workshops, 1997.

32. Author interviews, 1997.

33. *State v. Aquino-Cervantes,* 88 Wa. App. 699 (1997), rev. den., 1998 Wash. Lexis 425 (1998).

34. Susana Sawrey, presentations at Washington State Court Interpreter Program Workshops, 1997.

35. Bruce Westfall, "Spitsyn Faces 10 to 14 Years in Prison," *The Columbian,* Vancouver, WA, May 16, 1997, p. 1.

36. Washington State Interpreter Task Force, *Final Report,* 1988.

37. See, e.g., *Interpreters: Their Impact on Court Proceedings* (Yakima County Bar Association 1984), which recreates nonfictional scenes observed by attorneys of interpreters changing parties' language in order to enhance or detract from defendants' cases. The video "Working with Interpreters" (Washington State Administrator for the Courts and National Center for State Courts, 1994) depicts an attorney pressuring the interpreter to explain a legal document to her client.

38. *Interpreters: Their Impact on Court Proceedings* depicts arraignment scenes in which the court interpreter uses pressure and body language to guide the innocent defendant into pleading guilty.

39. Washington Interpreters and Translators Association, "Ethics Corner" *WITS Newsletter* (Summer 1997).

Immigration Information for Criminal Cases in State Courts

1. *Urbina-Mauricio v. INS,* 989 F.2d 1085, 1089 (9th Cir. 1993); *Avila-Murrieta v. INS,* 762 F.2d 733, 736 (9th Cir. 1985); *Ocon-Perez v. INS,* 550 F.2d 1153, 1154 (9th Cir. 1977).

2. *United States v. Garcia-Olmedo,* 112 F.3d 399 (9th Cir. 1997); *United States v. Zarate-Martinez,* 133 F.3d 1194 (9th Cir. 1998), interpreting 8 USC § 1101(a)(43)(B), petition for cert. filed June 1, 1998.

3. See Immigration and Nationality Act (hereinafter "INA") § 237(a)(2)(E), 8 USC § 1227 (a)(2)(E).

4. Cal. Penal Code section 1016.5 (1985); Conn. Gen. Stat. Ann. § 54-lj (West 1994); D.C. Code Ann. section 17-713 (1989); Fla. R. Crim. P. 3.172(c) (viii) (1989); Haw. Rev. Stat sections 802E-1 to 3 (1995); Mass. Gen. L. Ch. 278, § 29D (1992); Mont. Code Ann. § 46-12-210 (1995); N.C. Gen. Stat. § 15A-1022 (1988); N.Y. Crim. P. Law § 22.50(7); Ohio Rev. Code Ann. § 2943.031 (Baldwin 1993); Or. Rev. Stat. Ann. § 135.385 (1990); R.I. Gen. Laws § 12-12-22 (1956); Tex. Code Crim. Proc. Ann. Art. 26.13 (West 1989); Wash. Rev. Code § 10.40.200 (1990); Wis. Stat. Ann. § 971.08 (West 1985 & Supp. 1995).

5. *People v. Kadau,* 169 Mich. App. 278, 425 N.W.2d 784 (1988), recon. den. 523

N.W. 2d 629 (1994), quoting *United States v. Russell,* 222 U.S.App. D.C. 313, 686 F.2d 35, 42 (1982).

6. *Delgadillo v. Carmichael,* 332 U.S. 388, 68 S.Ct. 10, 92 L.Ed. 17 (1947).

7. *Morales v. State,* 910 S.W. 2d 642 (Tx. 1995), rev. ref. 1996; *Lotero v. People,* 203 Ill. App. 3d 160, 560 N.E. 2d 1104 (Ill. 1990); *State v. Lopez,* 379 N.W. 2d 633 (Minn. App. 1986), rev. den 1986; *People v. Pozo,* 746 P.2d 523 (Colo. 1987).

8. E.g., *Strickland v. Washington,* 466 U.S. 668 (1984).

9. For example, after a conviction was vacated on habeas corpus, on grounds counsel had failed to inform the defendant of the mandatory minimum custody before eligibility for release on parole, the courts in one California county routinely inquired of counsel whether they had so informed the defendant when taking future pleas.

10. *State v. Holley,* 75 Wash. App. 191, 876 P.2d 973 (1994), appeal after rev. 86 Wash. App. 1100 (1997), rev. den. 950 P.2d 476 (1988); *Daley v. State,* 61 Md. App. 486, 487 A. 2d 320 (Md. 1985); *State v. Ginebra,* 511 So.2d 960 (Fla. 1987); *People v. Huante,* 571 N.E. 2d 736 (Ill. 1991).

11. *State v. Ginebra,* 511 So.2d 960 (Fla. 1987).

12. The discussion of the immigration consequences of adult convictions that follows is largely drawn from K. Brady and N. Tooby, "Protecting Defendants from Immigration Consequences," in 24 *California Attorneys for Criminal Justice FORUM,* No. 3 (August 1997), p. 42, © 1997 California Attorneys for Criminal Justice, all rights reserved, reprinted by permission.

13. For a good list, see Chapter 11 in K. Brady, N. Tooby, et al., *California Criminal Law and Immigration* (Immigrant Legal Resource Center 1997).

14. *In re Batista-Hernandez,* Int. Dec. 3321 (BIA 1997). [But defendant must not be ordered to serve one year or more in custody—either as a condition of probation or state prison sentence (even if execution is suspended), or the conviction may trigger deportation as an obstruction of justice aggravated felony under 8 USC § 1101(a)(43)(S).]

15. 18 USC § 16 defines a "crime of violence" for this purpose to include any offense that (a) requires as an essential element "the use, attempted use, or threatened use of physical force against the person or property of another…," or (b) "by its nature, involves a substantial risk that physical force against the person or property of another may be used in the course of committing the offense." This determination is made on the basis of the elements in the abstract, without consideration of the actual conduct of the accused, which is held to be not relevant to the decision. (*United States v. Gonzalez-Lopez,* 911 F.2d 542 (11th Cir. 1990); *Matter of Alcantar,* Int. Dec. 3220 (BIA 1994).)

16. *In re Magallanes-Garcia,* Int. Dec. 3341 (BIA 1998) (DUI is a crime of violence).

17. See INA § 101(a)(43), 8 USC § 1101(a)(43)(F), (G), (J), (R), (S).

18. 8 USC § 1101(a)(43)(A).

19. See n. 2, *supra.*

20. See 8 USC § 1227(a)(2)(B)(i).

21. *Garberding v. INS,* 30 F.3d 1187 (9th Cir. 1994). The Board of Immigration Appeals held in accord. *In re Manrique,* Int. Dec. 3250 (BIA 1995).

22. See, e.g., *Wiedersperg v. INS,* 896 F.2d 1179 (9th Cir. 1990) (post-conviction writ vacating criminal conviction entitled alien to reopen deportation proceeding even after he had been deported); *Mendez v. INS,* 563 F.2d 956, 958 (9th Cir. 1977) (illegal to deport alien whose conviction had been vacated); *Estrada-Rosales v. INS,* 645 F.2d 819, 821 (9th Cir. 1981) (deportation of alien based on invalid conviction could not be considered "lawfully executed"); *United States ex rel. Freislinger on Behalf of Kappel v. Smith,* 41 F.2d 707 (7th Cir. 1930).

23. "Once a court grants a motion to withdraw a plea of guilty or a motion in the nature of coram nobis, however, the court's action will eliminate the conviction for most immigration purposes." D. Kesselbrenner and L. Rosenberg, *Immigration Law and Crimes* (1995), § 4.2(a), p. 4-4, citing *Matter of Sirhan,* 13 I & N 592 (BIA 1970); *Matter of Kaneda,* 16 I & N 677 (BIA 1979).

24. *Matter of Martin,* 18 I & N 226 (BIA 1982) (correction of illegal sentence); *Matter of H,* 9 I & N 380 (BIA 1961) (new trial and sentence); *Matter of J,* 6 I & N 562 (AG 1956) (commutation). Chapter 5 in K. Brady, N. Tooby, et al., for discussion of the immigration consequences of sentences and confinement.

25. State expungement under circumstances in which first-offender treatment would be granted under 18 USC § 3607 will eliminate a first-offense conviction for simple possession of a controlled substance. *Garberding v. INS,* 30 F.3d 1187 (9th Cir. 1994); *In re Manrique,* Int. Dec. 3250 (BIA 1995).

Law and Legal Culture in China

1. The discussion that follows is drawn in part from Derk Bodde and Clarence Morris, *Law in Imperial China* (Philadelphia: University of Pennsylvania Press, 1973); Sybille Van der Sprenkel, *Legal Institutions in Manchu China* (London: Athlone, 1966); Jerome A. Cohen, R. Randle Edwards, and Fu-mei Chang Chen (eds.), *Essays on China's Legal Tradition* (Princeton, N.J.: Princeton University Press, 1980).

2. The discussion that follows is drawn in part from Victor H. Li, "The Evolution and Development of the Chinese Legal System," in John M. H. Lindbeck, *China: Management of a Revolutionary Society* (Seattle: University of Washington Press, 1971),

p. 221; and Stanley Lubman, "Emerging Functions of Formal Legal Institutions in China's Modernization," in U.S. Congress Joint Economic Committee, *China Under the Four Modernizations* (Washington, D.C.: U.S. Government Printing Office, 1982), p. 235.

3. The discussion is drawn in part from "China's Legal Reforms," *The China Quarterly,* No. 141 (Special Issue); and Pitman B. Potter (ed.), *Domestic Law Reforms in Post-Mao China* (Armonk, N.Y., and London: M.E. Sharpe, 1994).

4. This discussion is drawn in part from Lazlo Ladany, *Law and Legality in China: The Testament of a China-Watcher* (Honolulu: University of Hawaii Press, 1992); Timothy Gelatt, *Criminal Justice with Chinese Characteristics: China's Criminal Process and Violations of Human Rights* (New York: Lawyers Committee for Human Rights, 1993); Shao Chuan Leng and Hungdah Chiu, *Criminal Justice in Post-Mao China* (Albany, N.Y.: State University of New York Press, 1985).

5. Amnesty International, *Torture and Ill Treatment of Prisoners in China* (London, UK: Amnesty International Publications, 1987).

6. For an English-language text of the Foreign Economic Contract Law, with analysis, see Jerome Alan Cohen, "The New Foreign Contract Law," in *The China Business Review,* Vol. 12., No. 4 (July-Aug. 1985), p. 52.

7. An English-language text of the A. L. L. appears in Pitman B. Potter, "The Administrative Litigation Law of the PRC," in *China Law and Government* (Fall 1991). Also see Pitman B. Potter, "Judicial Review and Bureaucratic Reform: The Administrative Litigation Law of the PRC," in Potter (ed.), *Domestic Law Reforms in Post-Mao China* (Armonk, N.Y.: M.E. Sharpe, 1994), p. 270.

8. A.L.L., Article 25.

9. A.L.L., Article 2.

10. This discussion is derived in part from the following sources: Pitman B. Potter, "Riding the Tiger: Legitimacy and Legal Culture in Post-Mao China," in 138 *The China Quarterly* 325 (1994), and "Socialist Legality and Legal Culture in Shanghai: A Survey of the Getihu," in 9 *Canadian Journal of Law and Society* 41 (1994); Stanley B. Lubman, "Studying Contemporary Chinese Law: Limits, Possibilities and Strategies," in 36 *Am. J. Comp. Law* 293 (1991); Godwin C. Chu and Yanan Ju, *The Great Wall in Ruins: Communication and Cultural Change in China* (Albany: State University of New York Press, 1993); Michael J. Moser, *Law and Social Change in a Chinese Community: A Case Study From Rural Taiwan* (Dobbs Ferry, N.Y.: Oceana Publications, 1982); Perry Link, Richard Madsen, and Paul G. Pickowicz (eds.), *Unofficial China: Popular Culture and Thought in the People's Republic* (Boulder, Co.: Westview, 1989) and Andrew Walder, *Communist Neo-Traditionalism: Work and Authority in Chinese Industry* (Berkeley and Los Angeles: University of California Press, 1986).

11. See Richard Solomon, *Mao's Revolution and the Chinese Political Culture* (Berkeley: University of California Press, 1971).

Mexican Immigrants in Courts

1. California Department of Finance, *California Demographics,* Summer 1995, 1996.

2. Jeffrey Passell, The Urban Institute, cited in Patrick J. McDonnell, "Immigrants Not Lured by Aid, Study Says," *Los Angeles Times,* January 29, 1997, p. 3.

3. Reported by Patrick J. McDonnell, "Illegal Immigrant Population in U.S. Now Tops 5 Million," *Los Angeles Times,* February 8, 1997, p. 1.

4. Rodolfo de la Garza, Louis De Sipio, F. Chris Garcia, John Garcia, and Angelo Falcon, *Latino Voices: Mexican, Puerto Rican, and Cuban Perspectives on American Politics* (Boulder, Co.: Westview Press, 1992), pp. 22-26.

5. See the classic work of two prominent observers of Mexico: Eric R. Wolf, *Sons of the Shaking Earth* (Chicago: University of Chicago Press, 1959); and Leslie Simpson, *Many Mexicos* (Berkeley: University of California Press, 1966).

6. Wolf, *Sons of the Shaking Earth,* p. 21.

7. Mestizaje, or racial mixture, has throughout Mexico's history comprised a major cultural theme. Criollos are Mexicans of European descent.

8. Wolf, *Sons of the Shaking Earth,* p. 21.

9. In Spanish, *La Raza Cósmica,* a term coined in the 1920s by Mexican education minister and academic José Vasconcelos, describes the objective of incorporating Indians into the mainstream of Mexico's mestizo society through education. Michael C. Meyer and William L. Sherman, *The Course of Mexican History,* 4th ed. (New York: Oxford University Press, 1991), pp. 572-73.

10. For an excellent and highly readable discussion of the merging of the two great cultural traditions of Mesoamerica and Europe, see Colin M. MacLachlan and Jaime E. Rodríguez O., *The Forging of the Cosmic Race: A Reinterpretation of Colonial Mexico* (Berkeley: University of California Press, 1980).

11. Two useful volumes providing more detailed information about the Mexican legal system are Francisco A. Avalos, *The Mexican Legal System* (New York: Greenwood Press, 1992); and James E. Herget and Jorge Camil, *An Introduction to the Mexican Legal System* (Buffalo, N.Y.: William S. Hein and Co., 1978).

12. Andres Oppenheimer, citing a personal interview with a minister of the Interior Ministry, in *Bordering on Chaos: Guerillas, Stockbrokers, Politicians and Mexico's Road to Prosperity* (Boston: Little, Brown and Co., 1996), p. 301.

13. Oppenheimer, *Bordering on Chaos,* p. 305.

14. As cited in James F. Smith, "Report on Common Human Rights Abuses in Mexican Criminal Defendants in Mexico and Mexican Immigrants in the United

States," unpublished manuscript, April 21, 1995.

15. The position of *notario público* in Mexico is a legitimate and official function, quite different from those who advertise themselves as notarios in some areas of the United States, where their purpose is to provide unofficial legal advice and forms, especially in immigration matters. Mexican immigrants are frequently victimized by U.S. paralegals or completely untrained individuals who use the term *notario* to gain respect among Mexican immigrants. They may provide illegal and inaccurate advice upon which their clients rely, thus exacerbating their legal problems.

16. Juan-Vicente Palerm, "Latino Settlements in California," in Kathryn Roberts (ed.), *The Challenge: Latinos in a Changing California* (Riverside: The University of California Consortium for Mexico and the United States, 1989), pp. 127-71.

17. Manuel Gamio, *Mexican Immigration to the United States: A Study of Human Migration and Adjustment* (Chicago: University of Chicago Press, 1930); Douglas Massey, Rafael Alarcon, Jorge Durand, and Humberto Gonzalez, *Return to Aztlan: The Social Process of International Migration from Western Mexico* (Berkeley: University of California Press, 1987).

18. Douglas Massey et al., *Return to Aztlan;* and Juan-Vicente Palerm and José Ignacio Urquiola, "A Binational System of Agricultural Production: The Case of the Mexican Bajío and California," in Daniel G. Aldrich, Jr., and Lorenzo Meyer (eds.), *Mexico and the United States: Neighbors in Crisis* (San Bernardino, Calif.: The Borgo Press, 1993).

19. David Runsten and Michael Kearney, *A Survey of Oaxacan Village Networks in California Agriculture* (Davis: California Institute for Rural Studies, 1994).

20. Wayne Cornelius, "Mexican Immigrants in California Today," in Ivan Light and Parminder Bhachu (eds.), *Immigration and Entrepreneurship: Culture, Capital, and Ethnic Networks* (New Brunswick, N.J.: Transaction Publishers, 1993).

21. Lawrence A. Herzog, *Where North Meets South: Cities, Space and Politics on the U.S.-Mexico Border* (Austin: University of Texas Press, 1990).

22. The study, cited in Patrick J. McDonnell, "Immigrants Not Lured by Aid," *Los Angeles Times* on January 29, 1997, p. 3, was written by economist Belinda I. Reyes, a research fellow at the Public Policy Institute of California.

23. Juan-Vicente Palerm, *Immigrant and Migrant Farm Workers in the Santa Maria Valley, California,* Center for Chicano Studies Working Paper Series (Santa Barbara, Calif.: Center for Chicano Studies, 1997).

24. Jorge A. Bustamante, "Undocumented Migration from Mexico to the United States: A Legal or Labor Issue?" in Jaime E. Rodríguez O. and Kathryn Vincent (eds.), *Myths, Misdeeds, and Misunderstandings: The Roots of Conflict in United States–Mexican Relations* (Wilmington, Del.: Scholarly Resources, 1997); de la Garza et al.

(eds.), *Latino Voices,* pp. 27-29.

25. In Roberts (ed.), *The Challenge,* p. 76.

The Shari'a: Islamic Law

1. Mecca is the holiest shrine of Islam. All Muslims, no matter where they are, turn toward Mecca for their daily prayers. Jerusalem is the second holiest place because the Prophet ascended to the heavens from what is called "The Rock," which is where the Dome of the Rock Mosque is located in East Jerusalem.

2. The Islamic calendar year one is equivalent to 622 A.D. Muslims follow the lunar calendar instead of the solar calendar, which is followed in almost all countries of the world. The lunar calendar is 10 or 11 days shorter than the solar one.

3. There are other differences involving the structure of Islam. One example is the existence of an organized Shi'a clergy that does not exist in the Sunni tradition. Another example is the amount of governmental latitude the Shi'a allow the *imam* as compared to the restrictions the Sunni place on the *imam* due to the principles of consensus and equality.

4. In Arabic the distinction is referred to as *al dhaher* (the apparent) versus *al-baten* (the hidden) meaning of the Qu'ran. Thus, the Shi'a religious hierarchy plays a determining role in interpreting the Qu'ran. This role reinforces their spiritual and temporal influence in the Shi'a society.

5. See Maulana Muhammed Ali, *A Manual of Hadith* (London: Curzon Press, 1977). The various *Hadith* referred to hereafter are from the compilations of Al-Bukhri's Sahih and are translated by the author. See generally Gamal M. Badr, "A Survey of Islamic International Law," 76 *American Journal of International Law and Procedure* 55 (1982); Saad El-Fishawy, "Contracts and Litigation in Islamic Law," 76 *American Journal of International Law and Procedure* 55 (1982); Farooq A. Hassan, "The Sources of Islamic Law," 76 *American Journal of International Law and Procedure* 65 (1982) (the last three presentations were made in the Panel on Islamic Law); and Salah-Eldin Abdel-Wahab, "Meaning and Structure of Law in Islam," 16 *Vand. L. Rev.* 116 (1962) (discussing Islamic law).

6. For a brief history of these khalifa and their personalities, see Abu-Bakr Fazl Ahmad, *The First Caliph of Islam* (Lahore, Pakistan: Ashraf Publishers, 1960); Omar Fazl Ahmad, *The Second Caliph of Islam* (Lahore, Pakistan: Ashraf Publishers, 1966); Othman Fazl Ahmad, *The Third Caliph of Islam* (Lahore, Pakistan: Ashraf Publishers, 1966); Ali Fazl Ahmad, *The Fourth Caliph of Islam* (Lahore, Pakistan: Ashraf Publishers, 1965).

7. By analogy, it would be like examining the common law of crimes as it applied in England in the 1300s and then tracing its evolution and application in various

states that have followed this tradition throughout the past 700 years. Indeed, the present-day common law of crimes is different in England, the United States, Canada, Australia, South Africa, India, and Kenya, to name only a few countries that use this system. Yet, all these legal systems consider themselves part of the family of common law systems. One recent controversial case was the condemnation by Iranian Mullas for apostasy of a Muslim author, a U.K. citizen of Indian origin, Salman Rushdie, because his book *Satanic Verses* was thought to contain blasphemous statements. Some secular Muslims disagreed, as did some traditionalist *alama* (religious scholars). See M. Cherif Bassiouni, *Remarks,* 1989 Proceedings of the American Society of International Law, p. 432. C. Alaa-El-Din Kharoofa, *H Al-Islam Fi Jara'ini Salman Rushdie* (The Judgment of Islam on the Crimes of Salman Rushdie) (Jeddah, Saudi Arabia: Al-Asfahani Publishers, 1410 H., 1987).

8. Though the judge may consider it for other purposes.

9. Syed abul Ala Maudoodi, *Human Rights in Islam* (Leicester, UK: Islamic Foundation, 1976), p. 19.

10. The legal capacity of a witness varies according to the different jurisprudential schools as does their required number for the different crimes.

11. There are different evidentiary requirements for different crimes in *hudud.* See J. N. D. Anderson, *The Malki Law of Homicide* (n.d.).

12. In contrast, one questions religious holidays practiced on an official or unofficial basis, such as the dates of the birth and resurrection of Christ (Christmas and Easter), and the Jewish Yom Kippur and Roshashana.

The Russian Federation

1. Law on the Procedure Concerning Exit from the USSR and Entrance into the USSR by Citizens of the USSR, 1991.

2. The Office of Procurator-General, a state organ, prosecutes cases and supervises compliance with the law by state agencies, including the courts.

3. "On the Urgent Measures to Protect the Population from Banditism and Other Displays of Organized Crime," 1994.

4. Article 50, Constitution of the Russian Federation.

5. For example, 11 prisoners of the Novokuznetsk city jail died of oxygen starvation due to summer heat in June 1995.

Vietnamese Immigrants in American Courts

1 . The most influential was the Code of the Tang Dynasty, c. 618-907.

2. Articles 83 and 79, The 1967 Constitution.

3. Article 81, The 1967 Constitution.

4. In practice, however, extreme anti-Communism led to some police abuses against suspected agitators.

5. Article 83, Constitution.

6. Article 84, Constitution.

7. These include heading the armed forces; nominating candidates for Prime Minister, Chief Justice, and Chief Procurator; signing treaties; and declaring war with the Assembly's consent.

8. Articles 115 and 116, Constitution.

9. For example, in the 1997 elections, restricted contests were held involving only four or five candidates, from which three Assembly members were elected.

10. While the practice of bypassing the required procedure for the adoption of laws has been criticized, the World Bank has commented that this flexibility of promulgation may have some economic advantages, as it permits Vietnam to promptly adapt its laws to reality. World Bank, *Vietnam: Economic Policy for Transition to an Open Economy,* May 1993, p. 161.

11. Article 130, Constitution; Article 5, Law on Court Organization.

12. Professor Jerome Cohen of New York University Law School aptly termed the reform a "virtual blizzard" of new laws.

13. Article 62, Criminal Procedure Code.

14. Articles 63 and 64, Criminal Procedure Code.

15. Articles 68 and 69, Criminal Procedure Code.

16. Article 197, torture is punishable under Articles 234 and 235 of the Criminal Code.

17. Articles 70, 71, and 72, Criminal Procedure Code.

18. Articles 75 and 76, Criminal Procedure Code.

19. Articles 10, 11, 12, 14, and 17, Criminal Procedure Code.

20. Article 36, Criminal Procedure Code.

21. The financial situation of attorneys is generally bad, according to Attorney Nguyen Trong Ty, vice president of the Hanoi Bar Association. Fee payments to each attorney depend on the number of cases he or she handles. Some do not have even one case in a month, so most of them, especially young attorneys, must have second or even third jobs to make ends meet. Domestic and international social organizations have offered to provide help to the Hanoi Bar Association members, but the government refuses to let them accept it, probably for fear of "jeopardizing or distorting the legal system." "Interview with Nguyen Trong Ty," *Ngay Nay* (Houston), September 1, 1997.

22. Report on Vietnam, *Human Rights Watch/Asia,* 1993 and 1994.

23. Vietnamese Attorney Nguyen Trong Ty reports that in a 1997 trial of a group

of international drug dealers, as well as in ordinary criminal cases, the Hanoi Bar Association has provided defense counsel for a number of defendants. *Ngay Nay,* September 1, 1997.

24. For example, parental responsibility laws are being adopted in some localities and states, placing civil fines and in some cases confinement on parents whose children violate the law.

Appendix 4: Resources for Teaching Immigrants About the Law

1. For more information about the Speakers Bureau, call (206) 296-3637.

2. Judge James Cayce is the Presiding Judge of the King County District Court. Chris Zhao is the court's Interpreter Coordinator.

Appendix 5: Immigration Status and Battered Immigrants

1. S. Schechter, *Guidelines for Mental Health Practitioners in Domestic Violence Cases,* National Coalition Against Domestic Violence 4 (1987), cited in Leni Marin's update of Debbie Lee's article, "Identifying Battered Immigrant Women," *Domestic Violence in Immigrant and Refugee Communities: Asserting the Rights of Battered Women* (San Francisco, CA: Family Violence Prevention Fund, 1997), p. 8.

2. Because research reveals that 95 percent of battered individuals are women, this essay refers specifically to battered women.

3. Adapted from *WorkFirst Training Family Violence Manual,* prepared by Grace Huang, Columbia Legal Services, West/Southwest Office, 1006 5th Avenue, SW, Olympia, WA 98502-5412, and from *Working with Battered Immigrant Women: A Handbook to Make Services Accessible,* produced by the Family Violence Prevention Fund; written by Leti Volpp and edited by Leni Marin.

4. Leni Marin's update of Debbie Lee article, "Identifying Battered Immigrant Women," *Domestic Violence in Immigrant and Refugee Communities: Asserting the Rights of Battered Women,* (San Francisco: Family Violence Prevention Fund, 1997), p. 5.

5. Robert C. Davis and E. Erez, "Immigrant Populations as Victims: Toward a Multicultural Criminal Justice System," The National Institute of Justice, Research in Brief, May 1998.

Appendix: 6: Summary of Consequences of Criminal Cases

The discussion of the immigration consequences of adult convictions that follows is largely drawn from K. Brady and N. Tooby, "Protecting Defendants from Immigration Consequences," in 24 *California Attorneys for Criminal Justice FORUM,* p. 42, No. 3 (August 1997), © 1997 California Attorneys for Criminal Justice, all rights reserved, reprinted by permission.

1. *Matter of Ozkok,* 19 I & N (BIA 1988). This has not changed under IIRIRA § 322, which amends INA § 101(a)(48)(A) to create a statutory definition of conviction that is more encompassing than the definition set out by the BIA in *Matter of Ozkok,* 19 I & N 546 (BIA 1988).

2. *In re Batista-Hernandez,* Int. Dec. 3321 (BIA 1997), but defendant must not be ordered to serve one year or more in custody—either as a condition of probation or state prison sentence (even if execution is suspended)—or the conviction may trigger deportation as an obstruction of justice aggravated felony under 8 USC § 1101(a)(43)(S).

3. This is cited as the INA. The Act appears in Title 8 of the United States Code. To make things interesting, the same statute has a different section number in the INA from that in Title 8. For example, the aggravated felony definition appears in INA § 101(a)(43) and in 8 USC § 1101(a)(43).

4. See 8 USC § 1101(a)(43), and discussion below, for definition of aggravated felony offenses.

5. See 8 USC § 1227(a), INA § 237(a).

6. See 8 USC § 1182(a), INA § 212(a) (grounds of inadmissibility); 8 USC § 1101(f), INA § 101(f) (bars to establishing good moral character).

7. 8 USC § 1101(a)(48)(B), as amended by IIRIRA § 322(a)(1).

8. *Matter of Fernandez,* 14 I & N 24 (BIA 1972).

9. See 8 USC § 1326(b)(2).

10. Before the passage of IIRIRA in 1996, certain older convictions were not aggravated felonies depending upon the effective date of the statute that included the offense in the list of aggravated felonies. IIRIRA § 321(c) purports to remove all previous statutory effective dates and makes every offense listed in INA § 101(a)(43) an aggravated felony, regardless of the date of conviction. An exception is for federal prosecution of illegal reentry after conviction of an aggravated felony and deportation. There the offense had to have been classed as an aggravated felony as of the date that the person made the illegal reentry. See IIRIRA § 321(d) discussing INA § 276(a), (b), and 8 USC 1326(a), (b). For more information, see D. Kesselbrenner and L. Rosenberg, *Immigration Law and Crimes,* 7.4 (a)(1), pp. 7-45 (1997); K. Brady et al., *California Criminal Law and Immigration.*

11. 18 USC § 16 defines a "crime of violence" for this purpose to include any offense that (a) requires as an essential element "the use, attempted use, or threatened use of physical force against the person or property of another ..." or (b) "by its nature, involves a substantial risk that physical force against the person or property of another may be used in the course of committing the offense." This determination is made on the basis of the elements in the abstract, without consideration of the

actual conduct of the accused, which is held to be not relevant to the decision. (*United States v. Gonzalez-Lopez,* 911 F.2d 542 (11th Cir. 1990); *Matter of Alcantar,* Int. Dec. No. 3220 (BIA 1994); *In re Magallanes-Garcia,* Int. Dec. 3341 (BIA 1998) (DUI is a "crime of violence").

12. See INA § 101(a)(43); 8 USC § 1101(a)(43)(F), (G), (J), (R), (S).

13. 8 USC § 1101(a)(43)(B); *United States v. Garcia-Olmedo,* 112 F.3d 399 (9th Cir. 1997); *United States v. Zarate-Martinez,* 133 F.3d 1194 (9th Cir. 1998).

14. 8 USC § 1101(a)(43)(C).

15. 8 USC § 1101(a)(43)(A).

16. 8 USC § 1101(a)(43)(D), (M).

17. 8 USC § 1101(a)(43)(K). This includes an offense that "relates to the owning, controlling, managing, or supervising of a prostitution business" or that is described in 18 USC §§ 2421-2423 and 1581-1585, 1588, relating to peonage, slavery and involuntary servitude.

18. 8 USC § 1101(a)(43)(L).

19. 8 USC § 1101(a)(43)(Q), (T).

20. 8 USC § 1101(a)(43)(N).

21. 8 USC § 1101(a)(43)(J).

22. See 8 USC § 1182(a)(2)(A)(i)(I)(II) (ground of inadmissibility) and 8 USC § 1227(a)(2)(B) (ground of deportability).

23. *Garberding v. INS,* 30 F.3d 1187 (9th Cir. 1994). The Board of Immigration Appeals held in accord. *In re Manrique,* Int. Dec. 3250 (BIA 1995).

24. 8 USC § 1182(a)(2)(C).

25. 8 USC § 1182(a)(2)(A)(i)(II).

26. 8 USC § 1182(a)(1)(A)(iii) (inadmissible if currently a drug abuser or addict); 8 USC § 1227(a)(2)(B)(ii) (deportable if addict or abuser since entering the United States).

27. See discussion in *California Criminal Law and Immigration,* § 3.4.

28. 8 USC § 1182(a)(2)(A).

29. See an immigration text, such as *Immigration Law and Crimes,* Appendix E (similar discussion for federal and various state offenses); or *California Criminal Law and Immigration* (chart following Chapter 12, discussing over 70 California offenses).

30. See INA § 212(a)(2)(A)(ii); 8 USC § 1182(a)(2)(A)(ii).

31. INA § 101(a)(48)(B); 8 USC § 1101(a)(48)(B).

32. See, e.g., administrative decisions by the Board of Immigration Appeals (BIA): *Matter of M.,* 6 I & N 346 (BIA 1954); *Matter of Castro,* Int. Dec. 3073 (BIA 1988).

33. An example of a destructive device is a bomb or grenade; see 18 USC § 921(a)(4)(A).

34. 8 USC § 1101(a)(43)(C), (E).

35. Conviction under any law of "purchasing, selling, offering for sale, exchanging, using, owning, possession or carrying in violation of any law, any weapon, part, or accessory which is a firearm or destructive device," or of conspiracy or attempt to do this, is a basis for deportation. 8 USC 1227 § (a)(2)(C).

36. See *Matter of Rodriguez-Cortez,* Int. Dec. 3189 (BIA 1992).

37. *Matter of Perez-Contreras,* Int. Dec. 3194 (BIA 1992).

38. See *In re Madrigal-Calvo,* Int. Dec. 3274 (BIA 1996); *In re Teixeira,* Int. Dec. 3273 (BIA 1996); *In re Pichardo-Sufren,* Int. Dec. 3275 (BIA 1996) (where the record of conviction failed to identify the subdivision under which the alien was convicted or the weapon he was convicted of possessing, deportability is not proved even where the alien testified in immigration proceedings that the weapon he possessed was a gun).

39. A person married to a U.S. citizen, for example, might be able to immigrate or "re-immigrate" through the spouse. *Matter of Rainford,* Int. Dec. 3191 (BIA 1992). The new INA § 240A(a) cancellation of removal for long-term permanent residents can now—in deportation proceedings filed after April 1, 1997—waive a firearms conviction.

40. See INA § 237(a)(2)(E); 8 USC § 1227 (a)(2)(E).

41. 18 USC § 16.

42. INA § 237(a)(2)(E)(i); 8 USC § 1227 (a)(2)(E)(i).

43. The time necessary for this relief stops accruing at the time of service on the noncitizen of a Notice to Appear in immigration court or *commission* of a criminal act rendering the respondent inadmissible or deportable. INA § 240A(d)(1).

44. IIRIRA § 304(a)(3), creating INA § 240A(c).

45. *Matter of Ramirez-Rivero,* 18 I & N 135 (BIA 1981); *Matter of C.M.,* 5 I & N 327 (BIA 1953) (juvenile finding of commission of crime involving moral turpitude does not constitute a "conviction" or trigger inadmissibility).

46. K. Brady et al., *California Criminal Law & Immigration* (Immigrant Legal Resource Center, 1997), § 2.1, p. 2-1, and Chap. 5.

47. See *Matter of C.M.,* 5 I & N 327 (BIA 1953); *Morasch v. INS,* 363 F.2d 30 (9th Cir. 1966).

48. IIRIRA § 383 amending the Immigration Act of 1990 § 301(e)(3).

49. See INA § 237(a)(2)(E); 8 USC § 1227 (a)(2)(E).

50. Immigration Act of 1990 §153, amending INA § 101(a)(27)(J), 8 USC § 1101(a)(27)(J).

51. Immigrant Legal Resource Center, *Special Immigrant Status for Children in Foster Care* (IRC, 1997).

52. See Gail Pendleton, "Relief for Women and Children Suffering Abuse," II 1997-98, *Immigration & Nationality Law Handbook* 482 (American Immigration Lawyers Ass'n, 1997).

53. 194 Cal. App.3d 1470, 240 Cal.Rptr 328 (1987).

54. *Morales v. State,* 910 S.W.2d 642 (Tex. App. 1995); *Lotero v. People,* 203 Ill. App.3d 160, 560 N.E. 2d 1104 (1990); *People v. Maranovic,* 201 Ill. App. 3d 492, 559 N.E.2d 126 (1990); *People v. Miranda,* 184 Ill. App.3d 718, 540 N.E. 2d 1008(1989); *People v. Pozo,* 746 P.2d 523, 527-529 (Colo. 1987) and authorities cited therein; *People v. Padilla,* 151 Ill. App.3d 297, 502 N.E. 2d 1182 (1986), appeal den. 508 N.E. 2d 734 (1987); *Lyons v. Pearce,* 298 Or. 554, 694 P.2d 969 (1985); see *Daley v. State,* 61 Md. App 486, 487 A.2d 320 (1985).

55. See *People v. Kadudu,* 169 Mich. App. 278, 425 N.W. 2d 784 (1988) (arraying split of authority), recons. den. 523 N.W. 2d 629 (1994). See Annot., *Ineffective Assistance of Counsel: Misrepresentation, or Failure to Advise, of Immigration Consequences of Waiver of Jury Trial,* 103 A.L.R. Fed 867; Annot., *Ineffective Assistance of Counsel: Failure to Seek Judicial Recommendation Against Deportation Under § 241(b) of Immigration and Nationality Act of 1952,* 94 A.L.R. Fed 868.

56. The discussion of counsel's duties that follows is largely drawn from K. Brady and N. Tooby, "Protecting Defendants from Immigration Consequences," in 24 *California Attorneys for Criminal Justice FORUM,* p.42, No. 3 (August 1997), reprinted with permission.

57. For a national directory of such agencies, write the National Center for Immigrants' Rights, 1636 W. 8th Street, Suite 215, Los Angeles, CA 90017 (*Directory of Nonprofit Immigration Agencies*).

58. The best secondary sources of information in this area are D. Kesselbrenner and L. Rosenberg, *Immigration Law and Crimes,* West Group, 610 Opperman Drive, Eagan, MN 55123, (focusing on federal offenses and the laws of several states); and K. Brady et al., *California Criminal Law and Immigration,* ILRC, 1663 Mission St., Suite 602, San Francisco, CA, 94103, (including federal immigration law and California criminal law and practice).

59. *People v. Soriano,* 194 Cal. App.3d 1470, 240 Cal. Rptr. 328 (1987) (general warning given; conviction reversed for ineffective assistance of counsel in failing to research, advise, and defend client against immigration consequences).

Contributors

M. CHERIF BASSIOUNI is professor of law, DePaul University, Chicago, and president of the International Human Rights Law Institute; the International Institute of Higher Studies in Criminal Sciences; and the International Association of Penal Law.

JANET BAUER is associate professor of anthropology, Trinity College, Hartford, Connecticut. Refugees and immigrants are among her areas of emphasis.

PAUL J. DEMUNIZ is an associate judge of the Oregon Court of Appeals. Before his appointment to the appellate bench in 1990, Judge DeMuniz was a criminal trial and appellate lawyer in Oregon.

MARGARET E. FISHER is a Seattle attorney who works with the Office of the Administrator for the Courts on education projects.

MOSABI HAMED is a legal services attorney in Detroit, who specializes in immigration and litigation.

ANTTI KORKEAKIVI, who was legal advisor on the Russian Federation for the Lawyers Committee for Human Rights while co-authoring these chapters, holds Finnish and New York law degrees.

RON A. MAMIYA, Seattle Municipal Court judge, has served continuously on court interpreter advisory committees for the state of Washington from 1985 to the present.

JOANNE I. MOORE directs the Office of Public Defense in Washington State and formerly directed the Court Interpreter Certification Program at the Washington State Office of the Administrator for the Courts.

JUAN-VICENTE PALERM is director of the University of California Institute for Mexico and the United States, and professor of anthropology, University of California, Riverside.

PITMAN B. POTTER is professor of law and director of Chinese Legal Studies at the University of British Columbia.

TAI VAN TA is with the Asian Law Center, Harvard Law School. He formerly taught at Saigon Law School.

NORTON TOOBY, of Oakland, California, is an attorney specializing in criminal defense of immigrants, both before and after conviction.

BOBBY R. VINCENT is commissioner of the Superior Court, San Bernardino, California.

KATHRYN VINCENT is assistant director, University of California Institute for Mexico and the United States, University of California, Riverside.

MARIA ZOLOTUKHINA, a Russian attorney and member of the Moscow City Bar, has worked with the Lawyers Committee for Human Rights and various New York law offices.

Index